W9-CBA-111

the Unofficial Guide™ to Picking Stocks

Paul Mladjenovic

IDG Books Worldwide, Inc.
An International Data Group Company
Foster City, CA • Chicago, IL • Indianapolis, IN
• New York, NY

IDG Books Worldwide, Inc.
An International Data Group Company
919 E. Hillsdale Blvd.
Suite 400
Foster City, CA 94404

Copyright © 2001 by IDG Books Worldwide, Inc.

All rights reserved, including the right of reproduction in whole or in part in any form.

This publication contains the opinions and ideas of its author and is designed to provide useful advice to the reader on the subject matter covered. Any references to any products or services do not constitute or imply an endorsement or recommendation. The publisher and the author specifically disclaim any responsibility for any liability, loss, or risk (financial, personal, or otherwise) that may be claimed or incurred as a consequence, directly or indirectly, of the use and/or application of any of the contents of this publication.

Certain terms mentioned in this book that are known or claimed to be trademarks or service marks have been capitalized.

IDG Books Worldwide, Inc., does not attest to the validity, accuracy, or completeness of this information. Use of a term in this book should not be regarded as affecting the validity of any trademark or service mark.

Unofficial Guides are a trademark of IDG Books Worldwide, Inc.

For general information on IDG Books Worldwide's books in the United States, please call our Consumer Customer Service department at 1-800-762-2974. For reseller information, including discounts and previous sales, please call our Reseller Customer Service department at 1-800-434-3422.

ISBN: 0-7645-6202-9

Manufactured in the United States of America

10 9 8 7 6 5 4 3 2 1

First edition

To Fran and our growing family,
I thank God that you are in my life.
And to all good people concerned with building their
prosperity for themselves and their loved ones.

Acknowledgments

Most importantly, I acknowledge my wife Fran for her boundless love and support. Without her in my life, I doubt that I would have undertaken projects as challenging as this book. *Te amo, Lipa Zyenska, con todo mi corazón.*

A very special thanks to Karen Doran at IDG Books for being a magnificent acquisitions editor. Her patience, professionalism, and caring nature have boosted my spirit throughout this process. I can only hope that every author will have the type of guidance she provided.

My deep gratitude to my development editor, Pam Sourelis. There are not enough superlatives to describe her editing and writing abilities. Considering the type of writer I was, I also give her my deepest thanks for her patience. If anyone ever needs the best at the craft of writing and editing, Pam should be your first choice.

I am very grateful to all the people at IDG Books who do such a phenomenal job of producing and marketing books such as this one and so many great works that have helped millions increase their knowledge and build better lives.

A special thank-you to Sheree Bykofsky, a remarkable book publishing agent and an excellent writer in her own right. Authors would be very fortunate to work with you.

It is also my pleasure to thank another great writer, Rob Schlieffer. Your involvement and encouragement are greatly appreciated.

These acknowledgements would not be complete without expressing my tremendous appreciation to Dr. Milo Sobel. During my tough moments, his encouraging words helped me maintain focus and perspective.

Most of all, I thank God for bringing into my life the people, resources, and energy that have guided me in my personal and professional life. I sincerely hope that books such as this can help as many people as possible with their prosperity.

Contents

The *Unofficial Guide* Reader's Bill of Rights

We Give You More Than the Official Line

Welcome to the *Unofficial Guide* series of business titles—books that deliver critical, unbiased information that other books can't or won't reveal—*the inside scoop.* Our goal is to provide you with the *most accessible, useful* information and advice possible. The recommendations we offer in these pages are not influenced by the corporate line of any organization or industry; we give you the hard facts, whether those institutions like them or not. If something is ill-advised or will cause a loss of time and/or money, we'll give you ample warning. And if it a worthwhile option, we'll let you know that, too.

Armed and Ready

Our hand-picked authors confidently and critically report on a wide range of topics that matter to smart readers like you. Our authors are passionate about their subjects but have distanced themselves enough from them to help you be armed and protected, and to help make you educated decisions as you go through the process. It is our intent that, after having read this book, you will avoid the pitfalls everyone else falls into and will get it right the first time.

Don't be fooled by cheap imitations; this is the genuine *Unofficial Guide* series from IDG Books Worldwide, Inc. You may be familiar with our proven track record of the travel *Unofficial Guides*, which have more than three million copies in print. Each year thousands of travelers—new and old—are armed with a brand new, fully updated edition of the flagship *Unofficial Guide to Walt Disney World*, by Bob Sehlinger. It is our intention here to provide you with the same level of objective authority that Mr. Sehlinger does in his brainchild.

The Unofficial Panel of Experts

Every work in the business *Unofficial Guides* is intensively inspected by a team of three top professionals in their fields. These experts review the manuscript for factual accuracy, comprehensiveness, and an insider's determination as to whether the manuscript fulfills the credo in this Reader's Bill of Rights. In other words, our panel ensures that you are, in fact, getting "the inside scoop."

Our Pledge

The authors, the editorial staff, and the Unofficial Panel of Experts assembled for *Unofficial Guides* are determined to lay out the most valuable alternatives available for our readers. This dictum means that our writers must be explicit, prescriptive, and, above all, direct. We strive to be thorough and complete, but our goal is not necessarily to have the "most" or "all" of the information on a topic; this is not, after all, an encyclopedia. Our objective is to help you narrow down your options to the best of what is available, unbiased by affiliation with any industry or organization.

In each *Unofficial Guide*, we give you:

- Comprehensive coverage of necessary and vital information
- Authoritative, rigidly fact-checked data
- The most up-to-date insights into trends
- Savvy, sophisticated writing that's also readable
- Sensible, applicable facts and secrets that only an insider knows

Special Features

Every book in our series offers the following six special sidebars in the margins that are devised to help you get things done cheaply, efficiently, and smartly.

1. **Timesaver**—Tips and shortcuts that save you time.

2. **Moneysaver**—Tips and shortcuts that save you money.

3. **Watch Out!**—More serious cautions and warnings.

4. **Bright Idea**—General tips and shortcuts to help you find an easier or smarter way to do something.

5. **Quote**—Statements from real people that are intended to be prescriptive and valuable to you.

6. **Unofficially...**—An insider's fact or anecdote.

We also recognize your need to have quick information at your fingertips and have thus provided the following comprehensive sections at the back of the book:

1. **Stock Exchanges**—Lists of all of the stock exchanges and their Web sites.

2. **Resource Directory**—Lists of relevant Web sites, newsletters, and other resources.

3. **Index**

Letters, Comments, and Questions from Readers

We strive to continually improve the *Unofficial Guide* series, and input from our readers is a valuable way for us to do that.

Many of those who have used the *Unofficial Guide* travel books write to the authors to ask questions, make comments, or share their own discoveries and lessons. For business *Unofficial Guides*, we would also appreciate all such correspondence—both positive and critical—and we will make our best efforts to incorporate appropriate readers' feedback and comments in revised editions of this work.

How to write to us:

Unofficial Guides
Business Guides
IDG Books Worldwide, Inc.
645 N. Michigan Ave.
Suite 800
Chicago, IL 60611
Attention: Reader's Comments

Paul J. Mladjenovic is a certified financial planner practitioner and an investing adviser and instructor with 19 years experience writing and teaching about common stocks and related investments. He has also covered the topic of online investing in recent classes and publications. Currently the owner of PM Financial Services, he has spoken and written extensively on national and international investment strategies and has been featured on television and radio stations throughout the country. He conducts more than 150 seminars and workshops annually, teaching beginners and professionals how to invest in common stocks, bonds, options, figures, and global securities.

Mr. Mladjenovic has published numerous articles on investing fundamentals and advanced techniques, and has been quoted in such business and consumer publications as *Nation's Business*, the *Boston Globe, New York Newsday*, and the *Daily News*. He has been a featured speaker at many major events, including the Toastmasters International Regional Conference in New York; the Learning Exchange of Sacramento, California; the Learning Annex in New York; and the Boston Center for Adult Education.

In 1989, he conducted the first conference in the United States on management and investing opportunities for the home-based business, setting a precedent for seminars in this area that have since blossomed throughout the country. And to further help his students, he has written three publications: *Zero Cost Marketing*, *How to Make Any Expense Tax-Deductible*, and, more recently, *Internet Wealth Building Tools for Investors*, which is available on software. To simplify a complex subject, Mr. Mladjenovic is currently the author and publisher of *Prosperity Alert*, a newsletter that focuses on the stock market, options, futures, and global investing. His Web site, www.supermoneylinks.com, gives investors extensive links and information on stock investing and other personal finance topics. The Web site also includes all the resources mentioned in this book.

The *Unofficial Guide* Panel of Experts

The *Unofficial Guide* editorial team recognizes that you've purchased this book with the expectation of getting the most authoritative, carefully inspected information currently available. Toward that end, on each and every title in this series, we have selected a minimum of two "official" experts comprising the Unofficial Panel who painstakingly review the manuscripts to ensure the following: factual accuracy of all data; inclusion of the most up-to-date and relevant information; and that, from an insider's perspective, the authors have armed you with all the necessary facts you need—but that the institutions don't want you to know.

For *The Unofficial Guide to Picking Stocks*, we are proud to introduce the following panel of experts:

> **Michael Molinski** is Mutual Funds Editor at CBS MarketWatch, the world's largest financial news Web site. He is also founder of InvestinginLatAm.com, a personal finance Web site dedicated to Latin America, and is author of the book *Investing in Latin America:*

Best Stocks, Best Funds (Bloomberg Press, 1999). Prior to MarketWatch, he spent seven years at Bloomberg News, most recently as Emerging Markets Correspondent, based in New York, and prior to that he was Senior Latin America Correspondent, Brazil Bureau Chief, and Seattle Bureau Chief.

Mr. Molinski holds a bachelor's degree in journalism and international relations from the University of Southern California and an MBA in business economics and finance from Columbia University in New York. He was a recipient of the prestigious Knight-Bagehot Fellowship for business journalists at the Columbia School of Journalism and the Wiegers Fellowship at Columbia Business School. He lives in Novato, California, with his wife and two sons.

Hotstocks.com is an investment supersite, owned by Billingtons Publications, Inc. (www.billingtons.com) since 1994. Hotstocks' format is advertorial, featuring in-depth investor information on various companies. Hotstocks.com also provides stock research and resources, such as a tech chart server, online stock consultants, a financial link directory, stock quotes, real time quote access, a discount broker list, and investor packages on all featured companies. Hotstocks has access to all the leads and resources of Billington Publications, an 11-year-old stock market newsletter specializing in penny stocks. These resources include investment advisors, money managers, hedge fund managers, analysts, stock brokerage house owners, and stock brokers.

Whed is a successful stock? The answer is easy. It's any stock that is rising rapidly, especially when compared to the market as a whole. But, while recognizing a successful stock after it has made its ascent is easy, picking one beforehand is much more difficult. Easily a hundred or more factors affect a stock's price. This book is about identifying the most important factors and choosing the next winning stock.

Keep in mind that experts may differ in their approach to selecting stocks. Legendary investor Warren Buffett's approach to stock selection is different from some of today's hot analysts, such as Goldman Sach's Abbey Cohen.

Sometimes you get contradictory opinions on the same stock from renowned pundits. Frequently, a stock that's sizzling this month or this year is a total loser next year. How does a cautious investor make sense of this?

Being a good stock picker is not luck, and it's not rocket science. It's work. It requires discipline and knowledge. This book will guide you through this exciting and profitable process.

Picking a hot stock requires patience. It also requires awareness of the world around you. Sound stock selection does not happen in a vacuum. The general environment—the stock market, the economy, society-at-large, politics, cultural megatrends—all make a major difference in the success or failure of a company and its stock. You need to be attuned to this environment to maximize your success.

Are we in a new golden era of prosperity, or have we entered possibly the most treacherous economic period in our history since the 1920s? The evidence suggests that caution is necessary for all investors. Successful stock picking in the coming months and years will require more research and care than most investors in today's environment are accustomed to. Because the general stock market rose 20 to 25 percent per year during 1995–1999, it didn't require much work to find a winning stock, so investors didn't do the necessary research. But when the market takes a downturn, careless investors lose their wealth very quickly (as past markets have clearly shown).

If this book had been written in 1982, it would have been quite brief. It would have simply said, "Buy stock in any company that has steady earnings and hold it. Be patient and watch yourself get rich." In 1982, the greatest bull market in American history began. For the uninitiated, a bull market is a period of rising prices for a given investment, such as stocks. A bear market is a period of decreasing prices for that investment. In the long run, markets generally experience both.

In the 1980s and 1990s, the stock market experienced a virtually unbroken climb to heights never seen before, at speeds previously unimaginable. The Dow Jones Industrial Average ended 1982 at 1,046.54. In 1999, a mere 17 years later, it finished at 11,497.12.

It took 86 years for the Dow to reach (and permanently stay above) the 1,000-point plateau. Yet it skyrocketed to the breath-taking level of 10,000 points in about a fifth of that time. (The Dow closed above that plateau on March 29, 1999.) The market's meteoric rise during the late 20th century has made millionaires of common folks. In the 1990s, millions of people (and their money) have been drawn to the stock market. What is now a mature bull market has lulled many investors into believing that picking stocks is as easy as buying groceries. This thinking is financially dangerous.

Many economists hail current economic conditions as a new paradigm: "Business cycles are a thing of the past;" "Prosperity will extend indefinitely." The financial TV and radio pundits are downright giddy at the pace of change: "The Old Economy is giving way to the New Economy;" " Old companies are tired and must yield to high-tech upstarts and the Internet;" "The stock market will continue its spectacular ascent indefinitely;" "If you're not in the stock market, you're missing out on easy riches." Or so it goes. When "everybody" thinks you should be in stocks, that's precisely the time you should be wary.

In 1999, millions of investors believed that the stock market was a no-lose proposition. Stock-watching became America's favorite pastime. Picking hot stocks seemed easier than shooting fish in a barrel, as the cliché goes. If this is so, why bother writing a book on stock investing? Why analyze anything or research any company when it seems that nothing could go wrong in this hot economy? Why not take a chance on that great new Internet company that your co-worker told you about the other day in the cafeteria? If everybody's buying those "wave-of-the-future" stocks, why not you? The fortunes are awaiting you, right?

Not necessarily. This is a difficult and very strange market. The stock market today looks nothing like it did 18 years ago. The current market has many of the characteristics of a speculative boom fueled by easy credit and excessive debt. Investors who are not careful will risk great loss. What many people don't realize is that throughout history, every major credit-induced boom has been followed by a massive decline. Every single one! More and more investment analysts are seeing disturbing similarities today with past booms and many question the possibility (inevitability?) of a bear market.

When a bull market reaches staggering levels that have crossed the line from growth to being overpriced, it is considered a "mania" or "bubble." Bear markets have followed without fail in these conditions.

Does this mean that it is a bad time to buy stocks? Is a book on stock investing actually discouraging stock investing? No, far from it. No matter how good or bad an economy might be, there are always opportunities for investing in stocks. The emphasis is that investing done correctly and profitably takes great care. A successful investor does research and this book will give you the tools and resources to do it well.

Successful investing is about more than what to invest in. It's also about how to invest. It is possible to invest in the stock of a fundamentally troubled company yet still make money (or avoid loss) by learning how to go about doing it. The "how" means being disciplined and using a variety of techniques covered in this book that minimize the risks and maximize the return on your money.

All too often, people invest in a stock without understanding the "how" and "why" of investing. It's happening right now in a pervasive and disturbing manner. Stocks such as Amazon.com, Yahoo.com, and similar "dot-com" stocks and related high-tech companies have received tremendous attention from stock pickers despite the fact that most of these stocks have dubious financial prowess (little or no profit and too much debt). Investors are ignoring the risks while they reach for the promise of future success. These stocks have risen to high levels because millions of investors bid up their shares without logic or rationality. However, at some point, economic reality will set in. A company can not go on indefinitely overloaded with debt and with little or no profit generated. When the company's financial difficulties start becoming evident, stockholders bail out. Excessive selling sets in, and the stock price plummets.

The lesson is clear: No matter how hot a company's concept, how beautiful its Web site, or how breath-taking its technology, the company must be able to generate a profit!

Investors must take note of history. We must understand that the age of the Internet is not the first time our economy has seen revolutionary changes in the way business is conducted. Ignore the lessons of history and basic economics at your own financial peril. Gain this knowledge and you will do better than most in both bull and bear markets.

The information and resources in this book will help you navigate these interesting, invigorating, yet uncertain times. Don't fall prey to guesswork when you make your stock selections. The most successful investors in history don't invest by rumors, fads, or speculation. Investors like billionaire Warren Buffett achieve their wealth through diligent research and thorough analysis of the relevant data available to them.

We will look at both the internal and external factors of investments. Internal factors refer to how the company is doing according to financial criteria and the "fundamentals," specifically the company's earnings, sales, assets and liabilities, and so on. Internal factors also refer to any new products and services the company is creating.

External factors refer to the influence the outside world has, or will have, on the company's prospects. This includes analyzing competition, politics, culture, investor sentiments, and other factors generally outside the realm of company control.

Be aware of the ultimate factor on the value of your stock: supply and demand. This means that no matter how well you select a stock, its value will only rise if the demand for the stock rises. You may have chosen a fantastic stock with all the earmarks of greatness, but the stock won't go anywhere unless the market starts buying it too. Since stocks are in finite supply, the price goes up as a greater number of investors bid it up.

It has become a cliché that you make money by "buying low and selling high." Be alert to mass psychology and behavior. If the market's selling pressures have forced the share price of a sound company down, that is a signal to investigate that company. Buying a strong company at a cheap price is a powerful strategy that has been practiced successfully by many savvy investors. The reverse is also important to note. If a company's share prices have been bid up to astronomical levels, that is a signal to investigate the possibility of selling. If everybody's buying the stock, its share price is probably over-valued and may be ripe for a fall. We will cover strategies for buying, selling, and even holding stock investments.

The last, and possibly the most important, point that you must understand as a successful investor is that the market is really just a collection of human beings. No more, no less. We refer to "the market" as if it were a monolithic entity with a single mind or mood. The financial analysts on TV talk about what "the market is doing" and "how the market reacted." It is impossible to read the mind of the market since the market is really a collection of millions of people with individual goals, problems, dreams, aspirations, objectives, and strategies.

Trying to outguess this or any market for the short term is a losing proposition. Picking a stock based on how and what the market is thinking and planning is gambling. This is why your best strategy is to pick stocks on rational and measurable criteria. Once you choose a stock that is a solid company and hold it for the long-term, the market will discover your choice, too. When others get excited over a stock that you own, you have taken a giant step towards building true wealth as a successful stock market investor.

Laying the Groundwork

PART I

GET THE SCOOP ON...
What are stocks? ▪ What is the stock market?
▪ Why invest in stocks? ▪ Risks to be aware of

Stock Investing Defined

Chapter 1

These are heady times for the world of stock investing. From late 1999 through early 2000, the main market indexes hit record levels. While it may seem that accumulating wealth in stock investing is so simple that you'd be a fool to not be in the market, the truth is that successful long-term stock investing is good old-fashioned work. You work to find and analyze your prospective investment. You monitor its progress regularly. You watch the news and read the papers for changes with the company, its industry, the economy, and the world-at-large.

To achieve long-term success, an investor must understand how stocks and markets work. Sound investing means diligent research. Anything less is guesswork and a danger to your financial well-being. Even in a market where general prices are rising, some stocks can fall dramatically.

This chapter is about increasing your chances for success. Before you start picking stocks, it is extremely important to build a solid foundation of knowledge. Understanding basic economics is essential. Taking the time to learn to use financial tools such as balance sheets and income statements will be very useful. Reading an annual statement and the financial pages (such as the stock tables) also will be important. The groundwork to do this will be covered throughout this book.

What are stocks?

Simply put, stock represents ownership of a corporation. When you own a share of stock, you own a small portion of a company. If the company has one million shares and you own one share, you own one millionth of everything that the company owns—buildings, chairs, computers, trademarks and so on.

The physical evidence of ownership is a stock certificate that shows what stock you own and how many shares you have. These days, though, people rarely get the certificates; they simply trade through brokerage accounts and shareholder service departments that hold the stock.

When you own a stock, you're called a shareholder or a stockholder. The benefit of stock ownership is whenever the corporation profits, you profit as well. For example, if you buy stock in General Electric and they come out with an exciting new consumer electronics product that everyone buys in massive quantities, you reap great profits along with GE, depending on how much stock you own. A stock also gives you the right to make influential decisions. Each stock you own entails a little bit of voting power, so the more you own, the more decision-making power you have.

Timesaver
You can find excellent stock investing tutorials for beginners on the Internet. Some of the better ones are found at the following Web sites:
New York Stock Exchange
www.nyse.com
National Association of Securities Dealers
www.nasdaq.com
Investor FAQs
www.
invest-faq.com

To vote, you must either attend a corporate meeting or fill out a proxy ballot. The ballot contains a series of proposals that you may vote for or against. Common questions are who should be on the board of directors, whether to issue additional stock, and whether the stock should split (I discuss splitting in the next section).

You can profit more by making good decisions, such as voting for a better board of directors. Or, if you think that issuing additional stock could increase your stock's value, you would vote for that.

What is a stock split?

When a company wants to make its shares more affordable to more investors, it may split its stock. To do so, the company simply distributes more shares and decreases the price per stock. If you own stock in a company that splits *two for one*, you'll get twice the number of stocks that you had before, but each stock decreases in value by 50 percent. Stocks can split into any number, but they can also reverse split—this means that the stocks double in value, but you get to keep only half the stocks you had before. In either split, you don't lose any money.

For example, consider this scenario: XYZ Corporation has one million shares outstanding valued by the market at $50 per share. XYZ decides to do a two for one stock split. Now XYZ has two million shares outstanding at $25 per share. The total market value is still the same, but the number of shares has doubled. This makes it less expensive for investors to buy the stock. If you owned 100 shares of XYZ Corporation before the stock split, your total value was $5,000 (100 shares × $50 per share). After the stock split, you would then own 200 shares at $25 per share. The market value is still $5,000.

Watch Out!
A balance sheet gives you insight into the value of a company at a specific point in time. It can answer the question, "What is the company worth if it ceases operations and converts everything to cash?" If the company's total assets doesn't equal or surpass its total liabilities, invest your money elsewhere.

What is the value of a company?

A company's worth can be measured in two basic ways: book value and market value (or market capitalization).

With book value, the company's value is based on its balance sheet (assets and liabilities). Assets minus liabilities equals the net equity or net worth of the company.

For example, if XYZ Corporation has $1 million in assets (cash, property, equipment, and so on) and $700,000 in liabilities, then the net book value of the company is $300,000 ($1 million minus $700,000).

Frequently, a company's book value may in fact understate the true worth of the company. Let's continue the previous example and say that XYZ Corporation owns an office building it bought 20 years ago. On the books, the building might have been purchased for $100,000. Assume the property depreciated in value by $80,000 during that time span. In this case, the book value of that property would show up as $20,000 (the purchase price of $100,000 minus depreciation of $80,000). This is not the true value: That building is worth far more than $20,000 today. In fact, it's probably worth significantly more than the original purchase price. Be aware that book value may not present a realistic picture.

The market value (capitalization) is calculated differently. If XYZ Corporation's stock is a total of 10,000 outstanding shares at $40 per share, then its market value is $400,000 (10,000 shares × $40 = market capitalization of $400,000). In this case, market value is greater than book value.

Historically, the stock of a company is considered fairly valued if the market value is equal or up to double the book value. Keep in mind that a company's value takes into account other major factors as well, such as earnings

If the book value of a company is equal to or greater than its market capitalization, this is a positive indicator—the company is considered "undervalued" by the market. Conversely, if a company's market value exceeds book value, the company's stock might be "overvalued."

Again, take XYZ Corporation for example. If it has a market cap of $3 million, its market value is 10 times greater than its book value (which, as previously stated, is $300,000). All things being equal, most analysts would probably see this as a major warning that the company is overvalued, which may be the precursor to a declining share price. When investors put their money in a company, the expectation is that the company will grow in value. Ultimately, growth is generated by the company's earning capability. The more profits it generates, the more value it gains. If the market drives up the stock's price and the company's profits don't rise, investors will see that the company won't grow. If the company doesn't grow, investors will sell their stock. The perception is that the stock is therefore overvalued, and investors subsequently will sell. This, in turn, drives the stock price down.

Beginning investors should note the size of the company they're considering investing in because size can be a factor in the safety of that investment. All things being equal, large-cap stock is considered safer than small-cap stock. A company with greater financial strength can weather a poor economy, whereas a smaller company may be at greater risk.

Bright Idea
Earnings are critical in the market valuation of a company. Companies with strong, rising earnings can justify higher market valuations. Companies with flat or falling earnings ultimately will see their stocks fall in value.

Unofficially ...
Everyone's defin-
ition differs, but
here's a general
breakdown
of market
capitalization
categories:
Micro-cap =
Less than
$250 million
Small-cap =
$250 million to
$1 billion
Mid-cap =
$1 billion to
$5 billion
Large-cap =
$5 billion to
$25 billion
Ultra-cap = More
than $25 billion.

However, when the economy is doing well, small-cap stocks have an opportunity to grow faster than larger, more mature companies.

Why does a company issue stock?

A company issues stock when it needs to raise capital for expansion, to finance product development, to pay off debt, among other reasons.

Issuing a stock is usually done by two types of companies:

- A company "going public." This is either a private company that will use stock investors' money to finance expansion, or a brand new start-up company needing "seed capital."

- An existing public company that issues secondary stock to gain the capital it needs for expansion or other purposes.

The first time a company sells stock to the public is known as an initial public offering (IPO), sometimes referred to as "going public." A list of some of the most prominent new offerings can be found each day in financial publications such as *The Wall Street Journal* and *Investors Business Daily*.

Why should you own stock?

You should evaluate your individual situation to see whether stocks are suitable. Refer to Chapter 3, "Preparing to Invest in Great Stocks," for help in analyzing your current financial picture.

The best argument for owning stock is they've proven to be the best-performing investment over time. But there are other advantages to owning stock:

- The stockholder shares in the profits and success of a corporation through dividend payments and changes in stock prices.

- As part owner, you participate in determining a corporation's major policy decisions by voting your shares at stockholders' meetings.

- Your liability as a stockholder is limited to your original dollar investment. You cannot lose more than your initial investment.

Types of stock

The two basic types of stock are common stock and preferred stock. Both types have their pros and cons, so before buying a corporation's stock, you need to decide which type suits your objective.

A common stock is the basic stock that a corporation issues, and shows you own a fraction of the company. Common stocks are directly influenced by failures and successes of the company and are considered riskier than preferred stock. However, common stock has the greatest opportunity for growth when the company is doing well. The bottom line is common stockholders take on the greatest risk in the enterprise, but in exchange they have the greatest opportunity to profit.

When the company is failing or declining, the least desirable investment is its common stock—in the worst-case scenario of a bankruptcy, the common stockholder is last in line in the liquidation of company assets.

Preferred stock is a second legal class of stock. Its name is derived from the fact that preferred stockholders receive preferential treatment over common stockholders in certain instances. In the case of a company bankruptcy, preferred stockholders get paid first. Also, if and when dividends get paid, preferred stockholders get theirs before common stockholders. Preferred stock is a more conservative investment.

Timesaver
For purposes of picking the best-performing stocks in terms of appreciation and capital gains, stick to common stocks. Preferred stocks are for risk-adverse investors who are more concerned with income.

Because preferred stock typically pays a higher dividend than common stock and has a more stable share price, it's a more desirable selection for investors seeking current income. Many view it as a hybrid between common stock and a bond. The main drawback of preferred stocks is that they cannot benefit as much from company profits because the dividend is usually a fixed payment.

Preferred stock has classes, often labeled A, B, C, and so on. The classes usually have different market prices, restrictions, and dividend payments.

"Common stock" and "preferred stock" are legal titles and do not necessarily describe the characteristics of stocks. To invest properly in stocks, you must look closely at what stage of development the stocks are in and what category they fall into. Keep in mind that over many years, a company may evolve. Cisco Systems, for example, was a small-cap stock that was barely noticed by investors when it first went public in 1990, but became a stock market powerhouse during the late 1990s. By March 2000, it had become the largest publicly traded stock in the United States, with a market capitalization of nearly $500 billion! In only 10 years, the company went from a speculative IPO to an ultra-cap.

The life cycle of a successful stock

A company's stock goes through various stages in its development. If you want excitement and a sense of investing in an obscure company that may become tomorrow's General Motors or Intel, then you'll want to check out a company in its beginning phase. If you want proven growth, you'll want to investigate companies that are in their growth phase. If you want greater safety, you should seek mature companies that are a dominant presence in their industry.

Phase I: The speculative phase of a public stock

When companies are in the beginning stages of their existence and development, investors should understand that there are more unknown factors than known factors about the company's ability to succeed. Stocks at this point are speculative.

The initial public offering (IPO)

A company issuing an IPO can be an existing private company that has gone public or can be a new start-up venture that is going immediately public. Most new companies start out as "penny stocks," so called because their share prices are generally cheap, from $5 to under $1 per share. Additionally, these companies have a low market capitalization of typically less than $100 million.

A safer way to speculate

Frequently, the IPO is of a private company that is already operating and has decided to expand by going public.

These IPOs are of companies that already have a track record and are generally a safer bet for investors. A good example is United Parcel Service, which had been operating profitably for decades as a private package delivery service company when it went public in 1999.

Phase II: The growth phase

After a company has established itself in the market, it must continue to sell its products and services and expand its share of the market. As a relatively new entrant, this company has plenty of room to grow and test itself against competition. Companies in the growth phase generally do not issue dividends because the money is better used to finance expansion. Growth companies have a high need for

Moneysaver
Risk-adverse or beginning investors should stay away from penny stocks. The companies that sell them are usually untested, and far more people have lost money with penny stocks than have gained. If you are intent on investing in penny stocks, make sure that the company selling them has already succeeded as a private company.

capital to finance matters such as research and development for new products, to expand operating capacity, or to fund innovative processes. This may lead to new inventions or technologies. The company may engender profitable new ways of doing business or open new markets for existing products and services.

Phase III: Maturity

The highest level of stocks that you can buy are *blue-chip stocks*. These tend to be large capitalization stocks that are major players in their respective industries.

Of course, even blue-chip companies need to continue to innovate and grow to prevent stagnation and decline. A good example is General Electric. In 1896, it was one of the original stocks on the Dow Jones Industrial Average (DJIA). More than 100 years later, it is the only original company still in the DJIA. General Electric is a still a solid, innovative company.

For stock investors who are adverse to risk, blue-chip companies are the best place to start your investment program. Blue-chip stocks are the safest category of stock investments. But because blue-chip stocks are well established, they obviously do usually not grow as fast as companies in one of the first two phases.

What is the stock market?

The focal point of the United States economy is Wall Street. Almost every large company in the United States and around the world is traded on a stock exchange, from Allied Chemical to Yahoo!.

To learn more about how the stock market can earn money—and even keep the economy healthy—we have to look at how it works. You will learn how the stock market was created and about the inner workings of the stock exchange, brokerage firms, buying and selling, mutual funds, and much more.

Some of you might be wondering why should you care about the stock market. Maybe you're too young to be investing or can't see how the market relates to your everyday life. The fact is, even if you have no money in the stock market, or even if you are in school, the stock market still affects you. You may work for a publicly traded company, or maybe your retirement fund invests in stocks. As of March 2000, more than 55 percent of Americans own stock directly or indirectly through mutual funds and pensions. Companies touch virtually every aspect of our economic lives. We buy their products and services every day.

The term *stock market* generally refers to the physical locations or computerized networks where organized trading of securities takes place. The majority of trading occurs in the three major markets: The New York Stock Exchange (NYSE), the American Stock Exchange (Amex), and Nasdaq. Nasdaq is frequently referred to as the over-the-counter (OTC) market, although the terms are not synonymous.

We'll take an in-depth look at the stock market and the major indexes in Chapter 2, "The Stock Market Environment: Where Stocks Are Bought and Sold."

Why invest in stocks?

Common stocks are versatile investments. They can be aggressive or conservative. They can offer income or capital appreciation. Some stocks are safe

Unofficially ... Nasdaq was formally created in 1971. Originally, the name was an acronym for National Association of Securities Dealers Automated Quotations system. Since then, the market has ceased to look at Nasdaq as an acronym.

and boring. Others are speculative. You'll find out more in the sections that follow.

Income or growth ... or both?

What is your primary objective in stock investing? Is it income or growth? Many investors may be looking for supplemental income. Perhaps they are retired and need those stock dividends for their daily living expenses. Most stock investors are primarily concerned with growth. You will make this choice based on your particular situation.

Capital appreciation

The number one reason that people invest in stocks is capital appreciation, or growth. A diversified selection of solid stocks does better than virtually any other financial asset when measured over an extended period of time such as 10 years, 15 years, or more.

Over the past seven decades, stocks have appreciated at the annual rate of 11 percent. This return has easily beat out investments such as bonds or bank accounts in the same time period.

The two basic categories of growth stocks are aggressive growth and established growth. These can be generally recognized by the size of the company or its market capitalization. Established growth companies offer steady appreciation, while aggressive growth stocks offer the potential for rapid appreciation.

"Steady appreciation" versus "rapid appreciation"

Owning stock that increases in share price over time is indeed the primary goal. However, even appreciation can be further categorized. Do you want steady, established growth over the long haul, or do you want rapid growth in a relatively short period of

Watch Out!
A growth stock without a track record is speculative, no matter how many analysts give it a favorable review. When a stock is labeled a growth stock based on its future potential without a reference to a track record, investors will take on greater risk.

time? Is getting 15 percent per year, year after year, better than getting 50 percent in one year? No one would want to pass up the opportunity to quickly increase wealth by 50 percent. Why accept less than maximum appreciation, especially since that is the primary purpose of buying stock? Isn't a hot stock supposed to experience rapid appreciation in its share price?

Yes, rapid appreciation is preferable. But at what risk? History tells us that stocks that experience meteoric rises can just as easily plummet. We have many reminders of this, in bull as well as bear markets. In recent years, Internet stocks rose dramatically, but many of the same stocks experienced their own private market crashes. Rapid appreciation stocks require extra attention by the investor in the selection process—and steel nerves for when the market reverses itself.

Keep in mind that the rapid appreciation you're looking for may not appear at all. Analysts and investment newsletter gurus may give the "thumbs up" to a particular stock, but the final judge is the market itself. You could wait for years for your stock to make that big move; you could even see it drop. Rapid appreciation happens when a stock garners the attention of interested stock buyers because it was well-positioned at that moment for a variety of reasons, often outside the control of the company.

When you choose a company that has strong fundamentals highlighted by steady growth in sales and earnings, analysts and investors eventually notice its stock. Holding the stock for the long term increases the chances that it will appreciate as the market starts buying the stock as well.

Bright Idea
Make sure that
the stock you're
considering has
a proven track
record of at least
three to five
years of earnings
growth that
exceeds the mar-
ket average and
especially its
industry average.

Dividend income from income stocks

Stock investors need to carefully consider income potential. This is typically the secondary reason for stock selection. The majority of stocks either have no dividends or a small dividend. Anyone interested in gaining greater income from dividends should consider stocks called *income stocks*. Income stocks are usually large companies that have enough cash flow to provide their shareholders with a higher-than-average dividend.

Don't confuse income from dividends with income from interest. A dividend is a payout made to owners (shareholders). Interest is a payment made to creditors (such as bondholders); it is evidence of a debt being repaid. Investors purely seeking stable and safer income should consider bonds as an alternative to stocks. Stocks are best suited for growth but also can be a source of income because of dividends.

Historically, the average dividend-paying stock had a yield of 2 to 3 percent. Bonds have historically paid 7 percent.

Investment categories of common stocks

We've touched on the two general categories of stocks based on what they give you: growth and income. However, it is useful to further break the mix into subcategories of stocks to recognize what kind of stocks they are and how they fit the criteria and objectives of serious investors.

Diversifying your stock portfolio is important, especially in a volatile market, as has been the case since 1998. Stock selection must take into account the various subcategories of stocks because, at any given time, one group of stocks could do better (or worse) than the general market.

You may have five stocks in your portfolio. But what if they are all in the technology sector? If the technology sector does well, you will do well. But if the industry is having problems, your portfolio will suffer.

Having all of your stocks in one category or industry is not necessarily a bad strategy, but you need to monitor your portfolio carefully and be ready to sell if that particular sector or industry is heading into a bear market. It's better to have a diversified mix especially if you are investing for the long term. We will touch further on diversification in Chapter 12, "Monitoring Your Investments."

As you read the following sections, keep in mind that a particular stock could easily fall into one or more categories. This categorization is based on the characteristics of a given group of stocks, but different groups of stocks have different strengths and weaknesses depending on how the general economy is performing. For example, you could have an income stock that is also a defensive stock, and so on.

Defensive stocks

Different categories of stocks perform differently in various economic environments. When the economy is slowing down or is in a recession (or even a depression), some companies will retain (or even grow) share value because their products or services are necessary regardless of how poorly the general economy is performing. Defensive stocks fit this criteria.

For example, no matter how good or bad the economy is, people still need the essentials, such as food, water, utilities, and other necessities of day-to-day living. Companies that provide these essentials at a profit will survive a market or economic downturn. For this reason, defensive stocks can be a great consideration for stock investors during bear markets or tough economic times.

How does a defensive stock grow?

A defensive stock can grow based on a variety of factors not necessarily tied to an expanding market. If the population is steadily increasing, that alone is a catalyst for growth. Additionally, defensive stocks can increase their income by introducing new products or expanding into new markets. For example, when Proctor & Gamble wanted to sell more of its products, the company was able to expand into new markets overseas, such as China.

A defensive stock usually doesn't do as well as other categories of stock in a market upswing. When the market and the general economy are doing well, that doesn't mean that people will be eating more, using more electricity, or brushing their teeth twice as often. Investors concentrating on growth during a market upswing will probably obtain bigger and faster gains elsewhere.

Cyclical stocks

The fortunes of some stocks rise and fall with the ebb and flow of the economy. As the name suggests, cyclical stocks are companies whose success follows the economic cycle. When the economy is down, these companies sell fewer goods and services. When the economy is up, these companies sell more. Good examples of cyclical industries are the automobile, industrial equipment, and construction industries. Other cyclicals include capital goods-makers (who supply manufacturing equipment) and manufacturers of tractors and other heavy vehicles.

When the economy is doing well, most individuals and companies are more optimistic. For example, individuals spend more on bigger-ticket items, such as a new car or a fancier vacation. When the economy is doing well, the greater affluence spurs greater interest in the sale of new homes or second homes. People who are doing well are more apt to take on greater financial commitments, such as that new auto loan or mortgage.

Much can be said about the "psychological" economy. The bottom line is that people are more confident about their economic condition (and near-term prospects), and this is reflected in greater sales and brighter economic statistics.

Cyclical stocks also have a ripple effect on the economy. When the automobile industry is doing well, this affects other industries that sell goods and services to automobile-makers. When real estate is doing well, as reflected in housing starts and new construction permits, this has a positive economic effect on a wide spectrum of smaller industries that cater to the real estate market.

Being a long-term investor and a patient contrarian is necessary when you invest in cyclicals because economic cycles can take years to pan out. Also, cyclicals are a leading economic indicator, which makes timing them tricky. In other words, they run up before an economic upturn, so you have to monitor them skillfully to catch them before they rise.

When the headlines in the financial press are shouting "Auto Sales Hit New Record High," this is probably not the best time to invest in auto-makers. Invariably, production will have peaked and probably will start to decrease. Record car sales serve as a

Unofficially ...
A contrarian is one who goes counter to the group mentality on Wall Street. A contrarian seeks to acquire out-of-favor stocks or may sell when others buy.

catalyst for the industry's labor union to push for greater benefits, which in turn exerts a downward pressure on the company's earning power. When sales and earnings start to sag, market analysts invariably issue cautious advisories to the investing public. This then dampens excitement for the stock and the near-term prospects for the company and its industry.

A contrarian would consider investing in a cyclical stock during a pessimistic period. When a market batters a stock, it frequently offers adventurous investors the opportunity to buy a stock at a great price. To a contrarian, general market pessimism is a buying tool.

When the economic cycle is up and the public is flocking to a stock, contrarian investors see this as a sign to be cautious. If they were considering a stock purchase, they might have second thoughts or would do more research to see if the opportunity still has growth potential. If they already own the stock, they might consider selling. Additionally, they might use trailing stops. (See Chapter 10, "Going It Alone or Using a Broker," regarding the use of trailing stops.) to protect profits from vanishing in a downturn.

Blue-chip stocks

Blue-chip stocks are considered the most prestigious stocks on Wall Street. Companies that fall into this category are companies such as Dupont, General Electric, IBM, and Proctor & Gamble. These companies are well-established, high-grade, investment-quality stocks. They have usually paid dividends for a long time, during both good years and bad.

Industry stocks

In any given economic period, some industries gain special prominence as new megatrends unfold. In recent years, some industries have leaped to prominence, such as biotechnology stocks and Internet stocks.

Frequently, it's easier to judge the direction of an industry than the direction of an individual company. If a particular industry looks poised for gains, investors would do well to invest in the industry leaders. When the price of oil went from $10 a barrel in early 1999 to $30 a barrel in early 2000, the oil service and exploration industry did well. The stock of leading oil services companies such as Schlumberger rose rapidly.

Speculative stocks

These are stocks whose current fundamentals are very poor or whose prospects are uncertain. The allure is based on the potential prospects for the company. Two types of companies could fit this description:

1. **New companies with untested methods, products, or markets.**

   New companies can be speculative if the market doesn't immediately see the benefits of their products or services. Maybe they have a new product or invention, or an innovative process. Perhaps the company is revolutionary or is attempting new methods or approaches. It may sustain losses until the market catches on. Investors are faced with the prospect of getting in immediately and possibly yielding great fortunes, or waiting it out. Waiting it out is safer but may mean missing out on rapid growth.

Moneysaver
If you are investing for income, stay away from speculative or growth stocks. Instead, go for large-cap stocks with dividends that yield 4 percent or higher. A dividend yield is a stock's dividend expressed as a percentage of the share price. At the end of 1996, the average S&P dividend yield was 2.2 percent, versus an average of 4.3 percent from 1950 to 1995.

In this stage, risking your money is more a gamble than an investment. This category requires much research, disposable funds (not rent money), and a strong stomach for risk. Keep in mind that for every speculative stock that becomes an IBM or a Microsoft, hundreds barely survive or just go out of business.

Low-priced speculative stocks are also called "penny stocks." These don't trade on any of the major exchanges, and the share price typically is less than $1. Because penny stocks are prone to all sort of speculative bubbles, trading inefficiencies, and other difficulties, they are quite risky.

To track them, investors turn to the pink sheets. These are daily listings of price quotations for thousands of over-the-counter securities not traded on Nasdaq. Published on pink paper by the National Quotation Bureau (a unit of Commerce Clearing House), the pink sheets list stocks that are smaller, newer, and generally riskier and less actively traded than those listed on Nasdaq and the other traditional exchanges. Also listed are the dealers who make a market in those securities. Due to the nature of pink sheet quotations—the need for printing, distribution and so on—the market for pink sheet stocks is less efficient than for stocks traded on major exchanges. An electronic version of the pink sheets is known as the OTC Bulletin Board.

2. **Established companies that have experienced a downturn.**

This could be a company that was doing well for many years but recently has fallen on hard times. Perhaps its sales fell dramatically because the company lost a major customer. Maybe the company is faced with a significant lawsuit. For any one of a variety of reasons, the company has declined sharply. Reasons for the decline could be internal or external.

These companies are also known as "special-situation" or "turn-around" stocks. Contrarian investors see fundamental value as the company falls out of favor with the general market. The thinking is that if the company remedies its situation, it has the potential to regain its status. Sometimes the stock market punishes a company to the point that its shares are considered a bargain with a minimum of downside risk.

Investing in these categories also requires a great deal of research and a strong stomach for risk.

Example A:

In the mid-1980s, Cincinnati Gas & Electric was a solid electric utility trading on the NYSE. Investors bought the stock at $25 per share in 1985. It generated a good dividend ($2.16), equating to an 8.5 percent dividend yield (an annual dividend of $2.16 divided by the share price of $25), and had sound fundamentals.

However, the company experienced a major problem with its nuclear facility. Within a matter of weeks, the share price plummeted to $14 as panicked investors dumped their stock holdings. Contrarian investors saw this as a buying opportunity, feeling that the situation was overblown and could be remedied. The company eventually resolved the problem, and the stock price recovered within a year to $28. Adventurous investors that bought when the stock hit rock bottom were rewarded handsomely. Cincinnati G&E had a total annualized return of 115 percent in just 12 months. The stodgy utility's gain was a combination of 100 percent capital appreciation (the share price went from $14 to $28) and 15 percent yield (the dividend of $2.16 divided by the purchase price of $14).

Example B:

For many years, Philip Morris was a defensive stock. It was a premier blue-chip stock and a market leader, with a diversified portfolio of food, tobacco, and other consumer goods. However, the political and social mood changed during the 1990s. Tobacco became a controversial issue as more critics cited the negative aspects of smoking. As lawsuit after lawsuit was announced, the market turned on Philip Morris. Shareholders sold their holdings, and the stock fell to record lows. Here was a profitable company with strong fundamentals and steady sales, yet the share price steadily shrank from the $50-plus range to less than $19 in 1999. Could this be a contrarian opportunity? Possibly. However, risk-adverse investors might be better off waiting on the sidelines until either the lawsuits are resolved or a more benign political environment emerges.

International stocks

The U.S. stock market is only part of the picture. A world of opportunities lies beyond our borders.

International stocks could range from huge multi-national corporations that span the globe or small-cap stocks that keep to a certain region or country. Investing in international stocks has many of the same characteristics as U.S. stock investing, such as earnings, sales, assets, and debt. However, investors must analyze or understand other factors as well, such as the nation or region's culture, history, politics, and trade rules.

Individual investors are usually better off investing in foreign stocks and markets through mutual funds that specialize in these markets.

Special-purpose stocks

This is the catch-all category for stocks that are not readily placed into another category but that have a special focus to their activities. At first glance, they may be considered industry stocks with a twist. Stocks that fall into this category are those of companies involved in precious metals or real estate.

If you believe that the real estate market will experience its own bull market, you should consider stocks known as real estate investment trusts (REIT). REITs are a hybrid between a mutual fund and a common stock. In spite of their tax-favored status as investment trusts, they have all the hallmarks of a common stock. REITs are bought and sold on stock exchanges, issue dividends, and so on. However, they are similar to mutual funds in that they buy, sell, and manage a portfolio of real estate and real estate-related investments (such as mortgages).

A REIT will invest in real estate based on considerations such as location, cash flow, and type of property. The management team analyzes property in the same manner that any serious investor in real estate would. A REIT resembles income stocks in that it offers better-than-average income potential and the opportunity for long-term appreciation.

For passive investors interested in real estate investing, REITs offer many advantages. For starters, buying and selling REITs is as easy as buying and selling any other stock. You purchase them through brokers either by phone or the Internet. You don't have the same management headaches that you normally have when you invest directly in real estate. And no one calls you at 2 A.M. complaining about a broken toilet.

By law, REITs must pay out 95 percent of their income to shareholders, so they tend to have higher-than-average dividends. During 1999, typical yields were in the range of 8 to 11 percent.

Concept stocks

These are really speculative stocks, but we've broken them out here to address their presence in the marketplace. With the advent of the Internet and advances in technology in the "new economy," concept stocks have returned to the public eye.

A concept stock is just that: stock in a company with a new, interesting, and usually untested idea or an intriguing process or technology. Typically, this company has little or no earnings. If the concept takes off, it could be a lucrative investment. If it doesn't, you could lose your investment. Losers vastly outnumber winners here, but people will continue to seek out concept stocks to find the next Microsoft.

Microsoft was considered a speculative concept stock when it first emerged in the marketplace in the early 1980s. Today it is a huge company with a powerful presence in our economy. Early investors were handsomely rewarded as the company grew into an established market leader.

Still, beginning investors should stay away from concept stocks until they have a track record and a proven market acceptance.

Alternatives for stock investors

Many alternatives to stock investing exist. You can invest your money in bank certificates of deposit, money market funds, government bonds, corporate bonds, and tax-free municipal bonds, most of which are considered safer and less volatile than stocks. Some investments are considered riskier than stocks, such as options and futures. Where do you begin? Reviewing each investment category is beyond the scope of this book. You may wish to consider *The Unofficial Guide to Investing* for an expansive treatment of investments available today.

Stocks can carry risks greater than you may want to undertake. If the different choices in stock categories seem overwhelming, then perhaps your best stock investment is not a stock at all.

Mutual funds can offer people the benefits of stock investing without some of the inherent risks. Because mutual funds offer the benefits of professional management by investment advisers, diversification, and services such as individual retirement accounts (IRAs), they are excellent for risk-adverse stock investors. Over the long term, however, the average stock investor has achieved a greater return on investment than the average mutual fund investor—this is an example of the risk versus return equation. Mutual funds offer greater safety, while investing directly in common stocks offers greater investment returns.

Over the long term, the average returns of the stock market have achieved a greater return on investment than the average mutual fund. This is an example of the risk versus return equation. Mutual funds offer greater safety, while investing directly in common stocks offers the potential for greater investment returns. However, keep in mind that the average small investor in the stock market has also significantly underperformed the stock market averages over time.

A common stock mutual fund will invest in a diversified portfolio of common stocks. The fund will do only as well as the stocks that it has selected for its portfolio (minus transaction costs, management fees, and sales charges).

Most investors should consider allocating a portion of their investment funds to a well-managed mutual fund or to an index fund, which passively tracks the overall market or a portion of it, such as the stocks that make up the S&P 500 index. Although it makes sense to invest directly in stocks to maximize your return, mutual funds diversify your holdings and minimize overall risk in your investment strategy.

Consider the following mutual funds as an alternate (or adjunct) to your stock investing program:

If you are considering ...

- **Aggressive growth stocks**—Consider aggressive growth mutual funds that have a solid track record. Is the mutual fund of your choice in the top 20 percent of its category for at least the most recent three to five years?

- **Established growth stocks (or blue chips)**— Consider a conservative growth mutual fund. When you see the fund's most recent portfolio, do you see companies that are recognizable market leaders?

▪ **Stock investing in a particular industry—**
Consider a mutual fund that is a sector fund.
For instance, if you feel that utility stocks are a
strong consideration, then look into a mutual
fund that specializes in the utilities industry.

▪ **Speculative stocks or penny stocks—**Consider
a mutual fund that specializes in these high-
risk investments. Make sure that the fund has a
solid track record that spans at least three to
five years.

For more information on mutual fund investing,
check the following resources:

> ***The Unofficial Guide to Mutual Fund
> Investing,*** published by IDG Books
> Worldwide, Inc.

> **The Investment Company Institute
> trade group**
> Washington, D.C.
> www.ici.org

> **Mutual Fund Education Alliance**
> Kansas City, MO
> www.mfea.com

Understanding risk

Investors face many risks. However, risk is not something to fear, but something to understand and
plan for.

First, you need to get familiar with the concept
of risk. You must understand the oldest equation in
the world of investing: risk versus return.

One of my students told me that he had most of
his money in a bank certificate of deposit. He com-
plained to me that the rate of return on his money
wasn't great. He wanted to have his money make

> **"**
> I'm not worried
> about a return
> on my money
> as much as
> I am worried
> about a return
> of my money.
> —Will Rogers
> **"**

more money. I asked him, "How about investing in common stocks? They're a proven growth investment." He responded "Stocks? I don't want to put my money there—it's too risky!" Okay then. If you don't want to tolerate more risk, don't complain about earning less on your money.

Here's the premise behind risk versus return: If you want a greater return on your money, you need to tolerate more risk. If you don't want to tolerate more risk, you must tolerate a lower rate of return.

Risk is present even in the safest investment. How can this be? There are different kinds of risk. The risk that most people are familiar with is financial risk. This is the idea that if you put your money in XYZ, you can see it partially or totally lost. We can all understand that type of risk. The image of the troubled stock investor standing on a ledge getting ready to jump after a market crash wipes out his nest egg is evocative. The thought makes us pause and encourages us to tread cautiously with our money.

In the next sections, we discuss individual types of risk.

Financial risk

Financial risk is the outright loss in value, partially or totally, of your investment because the investment has lost intrinsic value. If it is a stock, the danger is that the company could go bankrupt. You can greatly reduce your financial risk if you do your research before you select your investment. Making sure that the stock is financially strong is your first priority. As of March 2000, the stock of plenty of companies has gained the attention of a delighted stock-buying public despite the companies' very poor financial status.

A good example is Amazon.com. This company has lost money three years in a row and has amassed

nearly $1.5 billion in debt. If it doesn't start gener-
ating significant profits soon, the company's future
will be in jeopardy. If losses continue, shareholders
will have to decide whether to seek greener pastures
elsewhere. Amazon's stock plummeted from a high
of $113 during the summer of 1999 to under $45 in
June 2000. Serious investors avoided this stock altogether because of its dubious profit and loss statement and highly leveraged balance sheet.
Unfortunately, many investors flocked to the stock
because of the promise of Internet fortunes and the
company's high-profile reputation.

Interest rate risk

Let's say that we invest in a bank certificate of
deposit at 5 percent. The money is safe, and we have
locked in a return. But what happens if the day after
you commit your money, the rate increases to 6 percent? You've lost that incremental gain, and the only
way to get out of your 5 percent rate is to absorb
penalties for early withdrawal.

That's a generic example of how interest rate
risk can affect you. However, interest rates offer a
special risk to stock investors. Historically, rising
interest rates have had an adverse effect on stock
prices. There are several reasons for this:

1. **Company internal operations**—When interest
   rates rise, this increases the borrowing costs for
   companies that carry a significant debt load.
   This ultimately reduces the company's earnings and its ability to grow. When earnings
   shrink, the stock becomes less attractive.

2. **Industry sales**—If the company sells products
   or services to an industry that is susceptible
   to increased interest rates, the fate of the

company is affected. Perhaps a company's products sell well to the housing industry when housing sales are up. Rising interest rates typically dampen the prospects for home sales. This in turn dampens the sales and prospective earnings for that company.

3. **Investor considerations**—When interest rates rise, investors start to change their investment strategies. This can manifest itself in two ways:

   ▪ They may sell any shares in interest-sensitive stocks that they are holding. Interest rate changes affect some industries more than others. Some examples are utilities and financial service companies such as banks.

   ▪ Investors seeking a higher current income would find the interest too attractive to ignore. Higher rates could entice investors to exit stocks and get into money market funds or bonds.

4. **Indirect effects**—High or rising interest rates will have an impact on the investor's total financial picture. What happens when an investor is burdened with excessive debt such as a second mortgage, credit card debt, or margin debt? Higher interest rates may inadvertently force the sale of a stock to service debt.

Interest rates versus stocks: A historical perspective

The following example gives you a good idea of the power of interest rates when looking through the eyes of an investor. Look at the period from 1964 through 1981. Here's the long-term performance of the Dow Jones Industrial Average:

As of December 31, 1964, it was 874.12.

As of December 31, 1981, it was 875.00.

It barely moved in nearly 17 years! However, during that same period, the gross domestic product (GDP) of the United States—that is, the goods and services produced in the United States—went up nearly fivefold, rising by approximately 370 percent. The sales of the Fortune 500 (the 500 largest public companies) went up sixfold. The DJIA barely moved.

During that same period, interest rates rose significantly. Government bond rates went from 4 percent in 1964 to more than 15 percent in 1981. The lesson here is that even though the economy grew significantly, investors put their money elsewhere. The increasing interest rates made debt instruments such as cash equivalents and bonds attractive investments that were hard to pass up.

Rising interest rates ultimately have a downward effect on stock prices that stock investors should not ignore. Although stocks have proven to be a superior long-term investment over extended periods of time, stock investors are urged to maintain a balanced portfolio that includes other investment vehicles such as money market funds and bank investments.

Market risk

The risk is that the investment we put our money in has gone down in value not because of the investment itself, but because the market for it changes or lowers the value. For instance, let's say that you buy

> **❝**
> The first rule is not to lose. The second rule is not to forget the first rule.
> —Warren Buffett
> **❞**

eggs for $1.00, hoping to resell at a higher price. If eggs become plentiful, the price of eggs will probably drop. If the price drops to 90 cents, you would lose 10 percent on your money. The eggs were the same before and after the price change, but the market incurred the price change.

Inflation risk

Say that you have money in a bank savings account currently earning 4 percent. This account has flexibility in that if the market interest rate goes up, the rate you earn in your account goes up. It is safe from both financial risk and interest rate risk. But what if inflation is running at 5 percent? Inflation is the artificial expansion of the quantity of money so that too much money is used in exchange for goods and services. To consumers, inflation shows up in the form of higher prices for goods and services. In an inflationary economy, 5 percent inflation means that if your money is earning 4 percent, you're actually losing money. The purchasing power of your money decreases, so you end up buying less instead of more.

Tax risk

Because the tax laws change so frequently, tax risk is part of the equation as well. Many investors set up their wealth in tax-advantaged instruments such as municipal bonds and tax shelters only to have their plans thwarted by changes in the tax laws. In the mid-1980s, real estate was a booming investment market. However, the Tax Reform Act of 1986 significantly changed the rules of real estate investing. Subsequently, it played an important role in the decline of the real estate market in 1987.

Political and regulatory risks

What if your money is in oil futures and you find out that Saudi Arabia's policy toward oil exports has changed drastically because of a political revolution? What if you invest in gold options and the federal government passes new laws restricting gold transactions? These risks would have a significant impact on your investment. What if you invest in companies or industries that become political targets? Tobacco companies were the targets of political firestorms that battered their stock prices. Whether you agree or disagree with the political machinations of our day is not the issue. For investors, the question that must be asked is, "How do politics affect the market value and prospects of my chosen investment?"

Personal risks

Other risks are not relevant to the investment but relate to the investor. Say that Bob puts $10,000 into a selection of common stocks. Imagine that the market experiences a drop in prices that week, and Bob's stocks drop to a market value of $9,000. Because stocks are good for the long term, this type of decrease is usually temporary, especially if Bob chose high-quality companies. (Incidentally, if a portfolio of high-quality stocks does experience a temporary drop in price, it can be a great buying opportunity.)

In the long run, Bob would probably see his investment grow in value substantially. But what if during the period his stocks declined, he was in a financial bind and needed the money? This happens all too frequently for investors who don't have an emergency fund to handle large expenses that happen suddenly. Maybe Bob had a car accident or a medical emergency. Maybe his basement flooded and the repair bill was very high. If Bob had put money aside for large "rainy day" expenses, he wouldn't be faced with the task of prematurely liquidating his investment. Because Bob didn't have an emergency fund set apart from his investment portfolio, he would be forced to liquidate his portfolio and sustain a $1,000 loss.

Don't let these different kinds of risk frighten you. Just make sure that you understand them before you start navigating the investment world. It's especially important as you enter the speculative world of options and futures. Be mindful of risk, and learn about the effects of risk on your investments and personal financial goals.

Just the facts

- Stocks are a versatile and powerful component of almost any portfolio.

- Good stock picking is not luck; it is diligent work.

- Make sure that you take a comprehensive look at your total financial picture to determine to what extent stocks will benefit you.

- Stocks have a great potential for gain, but they also carry significant risk.

- If stock picking is too difficult or risky a task for you, consider alternatives such as mutual funds.

GET THE SCOOP ON...
The New York Stock Exchange ▪ NASDAQ and
The American Stock Exchange ▪ The Dow Jones
Industrial Average ▪ Other major indexes
▪ A special look: investing in the Internet

The Stock Market Environment: Where Stocks Are Bought and Sold

Chapter 2

Becoming a successful investor means understanding the investing environment—the marketplace where stocks are bought and sold. The best place to start is with the established exchanges. These stock exchanges offer a well-organized way to buy and sell stocks, bonds, and other securities with rules and regulations to ensure orderly transactions. In addition, the major exchanges work with organizations such as the Securities and Exchange Commission (SEC) and the National Association of Securities Dealers (NASD) to safeguard investors in cases such as investor fraud and abuse by securities brokers and agents. In this chapter, we'll take a look at this stock market environment and learn how a stock transaction is made.

It is also important to understand the major stock indexes such as the Dow Jones Industrial Average (DJIA). The DJIA and many other indexes are used as barometers of how well the stock market is progressing. Frequently, when people ask, "How is the market doing?" the answer has to do with the progress of an index, such as, "Well, the Dow just passed 10,000." If you own a stock, you obviously need to understand how well it is doing compared to such an index. After all, when we say our stock is doing well, the retort may be, "Compared to what?" Understanding and tracking the major market indexes will be important because the general market performance will affect your stock as well. You'll learn about the major indexes in this chapter.

For novice and beginning-to-intermediate investors, investing on the established exchanges is a good place to start. The nation's main exchange is the New York Stock Exchange.

The New York Stock Exchange

Wall Street became a major financial center in 1792 when a small group of investors and brokers signed an agreement that started the New York Stock Exchange (NYSE). They agreed to sell shares or parts of companies among themselves and to charge people commissions, or fees, to buy and sell for them. The organization became headquartered at 40 Wall Street in New York City. When the NYSE outgrew the space, it moved into what is currently the New York Stock Exchange Building.

The 1900s brought the Industrial Revolution and, along with it, a boom in Wall Street. Everyone wanted a piece of the action, and Wall Street grew. The New York Stock Exchange was not the only way to buy stocks at that time, however. Many stocks that were deemed not good enough for the NYSE were traded outside on the curbs. This so called "curb trading" eventually became the American Stock Exchange (Amex).

The New York Stock Exchange (also known as the Big Board) is the largest equities marketplace in the world and is home to 3,025 companies worth more than $16 trillion in global market capitalization. As of year-end 1999, the NYSE had 280.9 billion shares listed and available for trading worth approximately $12.3 trillion.

More than two-thirds of the rosters of NYSE companies have listed here within the last 12 years. These companies include a cross-section of leading U.S. companies, midsize companies, and small-capitalization companies. Non-U.S. issuers play an increasingly important role on the NYSE. As of July 1999, 382 non-U.S. companies were listed here—more than triple the number listed in 1994.

Investors who want to buy or sell stock can do so only with brokers who are members of the stock exchange where that particular stock is traded. This usually does not pose a problem, because the vast majority of stock brokerage firms are members of the major stock exchanges. An exception to this rule is the growing number of companies that offer direct-purchase plans.

In the late twentieth century, the New York and the American Stock Exchanges were joined by Nasdaq. Now hundreds of local and international stock exchanges all play a part in the national and global economy.

Watching the development of the New York Stock Exchange is important because the changes that have happened and that will happen affect all

Bright Idea
To learn about the history of the New York Stock Exchange and see the current information available on the exchange, company listings, stock quotes, and stock market data, go to the NYSE's extensive Web site at www.nyse.com.

investors. There is speculation that the NYSE's trading floor will eventually disappear and become an entirely Internet-based trading system. This would revolutionize the way that we buy and sell stocks.

How a stock is bought and sold

The following is a detailed explanation of how a stock is traded on the New York Stock Exchange. The New York and American Stock Exchanges conduct stock transactions in a centralized marketplace (the "Trading Floor"). This illustrates how one transaction looks from three different perspectives: that of the buyer, the seller, and the stock market professionals who execute the trade. You'll also see a description of the language used during a stock transaction in the next section.

1. Ed Jones of Bakersfield, California, decides to invest in the stock market.

2. Jane Smith of Detroit, Michigan, decides to sell 100 shares of General Motors Corp. (GM) to pay for a home improvement project.

3. After discussing his investment objectives, Ed instructs his broker (a member of the NYSE) to buy 100 shares of GM at the current market price.

4. Jane instructs her broker to sell 100 shares of GM at the current market price.

5. The two brokers send their orders to the Trading Floor via the NYSE's sophisticated electronic trading system.

6. At a trading post on the centralized trading floor, the NYSE has a professional trader known as a specialist who handles GM to make sure that the transactions are executed fairly and in an orderly manner.

7. The specialist implements the order as the representatives of the two brokers compete with other brokers on the Trading Floor to get the best price for their customers. The brokers representing Ed and Jane agree on a price.

8. After the trades are executed, the specialist's workstation electronically sends notices to the brokerage firms and to the NYSE's consolidated trading ticker tape. This is the famous tape that is a running record of trading activity in each stock. Although today's advanced computer system has replaced the scrolling paper tape of the past, it is still referred to as the ticker or ticker tape. This is then seen across the nation and the world on brokers' screens and public media such as TV financial shows.

9. Ed and Jane are sent confirmations of their trades from their brokerage firms.

10. Within three business days, Ed's brokerage firm receives payment to cover the purchase of stock plus commission.

11. Jane's trade is also settled in three business days. Her account will be credited with the proceeds of the sale of stock, minus commission.

What does a stock transaction actually sound like?

What do the participants (investors and brokers) say during the stock transaction itself? The following example is somewhat simplified, but you'll understand the typical exchange of information behind a stock transaction. Although the Internet is quickly gaining prominence as a medium for trading stock, the same elements apply.

Mary is in her preretirement years and wants to choose a blue-chip stock to achieve steady growth for her portfolio. Michael is a computer consultant living in Chicago. They don't know each other. But, at nearly the same time, they've reached opposite decisions on the common stock of Giant Blue Corporation, a fictitious company whose shares are traded on the NYSE. The stock symbol will be GBCORP.

Mary has decided to buy stock in GBCORP. By doing so, she believes that she'll enhance her wealth for a more secure retirement. Michael, on the other hand, has decided to sell his GBCORP shares. He needs some cash to purchase a new car. Michael and Mary telephone their brokers.

"I think your recommendation of the stock GBCORP is on target," Mary tells Ralph, her broker. "Please order 100 shares for my account."

"Will this be a market order or a limit?" Ralph asks.

Investors must give their brokers specific instructions on how to handle their transactions. Here are some of the more common types of orders:

- A *market order* tells the broker to buy or sell at the best price currently available on the market. The broker initiates the order immediately. The majority of trades are market orders.

- A *limit order,* also called a limited order or limited price order, tells the broker to buy or sell at a specific price or better. For example, if you place a limit order to buy a certain stock at $42 a share when its current market price is $45, the broker will not buy the stock until it hits the price of $42 or better.

- A *day order* instructs the broker to buy or sell at a specified price before the end of the trading day. This type of order expires if it is not filled.

▪ A *good-til-canceled (GTC) order* operates similarly to the day order except that, in this case, the order does not expire until the investor gets the specified price or cancels it. Although a GTC is in effect indefinitely, some brokers do impose a time limit (such as 60 days).

When the order tells the broker to buy or sell 100 shares or more of a particular stock, that is called a *round lot*. An order for shares of stock from 1 to 99 shares is referred to as an *odd lot*.

"What's GBCORP stock priced at?" Mary asks her broker.

"The last sale in GBCORP was 52," Ralph says, "and the current bid and offer are 51³/₄ to 52." This information tells Mary that, at the moment, buyers are willing to pay $51³/₄ ($51.75) per share, but sellers are asking $52.

"Buy it at the market," Mary says.

Ralph implements the order immediately.

As the order is confirmed, Mary says, "I'll be on an extended business trip next month. What can I do to protect myself against a sudden drop in GBCORP's stock price?"

"You can check regularly by calling our office or visiting our Web site on the Internet," says Ralph. "A sale can easily be done. But you can also place a limit order now that will automatically trigger a sale if GBCORP's stock reaches any price you specify."

Mary decides on a limit order price, and Ralph sends it to the firm's order room for immediate transmission—together with her buy order—to the NYSE Trading Floor. At about the same time, Michael tells his broker in Chicago to sell his 100 shares of XYZ "at the market."

Mary's buy order and Michael's sell order are implemented almost immediately on the Trading Floor. As the floor broker representing Mary's order enters the crowd gathered at the GBCORP trading post, he observes that GBCORP has been trading quite actively. He also discovers that GBCORP'S market price has been rising steadily.

"How's GBCORP?" he asks the specialist. "It's 52 to 52½ ten by ten. The last sale was at 52¼," responds the specialist.

This market shorthand tells Mary's floor broker that, at any moment, the highest price anyone is willing to pay for XYZ shares is $52½, and the lowest price at which anyone is willing to sell is $52. The phrase "ten by ten" tells him that buyers want a total of 1,000 shares and sellers are offering a total of 1,000 shares.

The broker evaluates this information in light of the specialist's statement that the market price of GBCORP has been rising steadily and that the last sale occurred at 52¼. Michael's floor broker arrives at the trading post and hears the specialist's quote. Computer screens at each post display current quotes for each stock traded there, but floor brokers generally ask the specialist for the quote anyway—a question that traditionally begins the auction process. Any broker in the crowd can participate in the trading.

"100 at 52¼," Michael's broker says, offering to sell 100 shares at that price—¼ point below the lowest quoted offer.

"Take it!" Mary's broker replies, accepting the offer. In the auction process, brokers must act quickly or risk missing the market. For example, if Mary's broker had hesitated, another broker in the crowd could have bought 100 shares from Michael's broker at 52¼. And that trade might have triggered another, pushing the price higher.

Within seconds the trade is entered into the NYSE's Market Data System, which flashes it onto electronic displays and market information inquiry systems around the world. Ralph, Mary's broker in Pittsburgh, phones her and says, "You just bought 100 shares of GBCORP at 52¼." At almost the same moment, Michael's broker in Chicago says. "We've sold your 100 shares at 52¼."

The same electronic system that reports the transaction to the ticker tape also creates the electronic bookkeeping entries that will update the records of the two brokerage firms. These entries enable the NYSE to reconstruct details of the trade if any question about it should arise in the future. Within three business days, Mary's account will be adjusted to show that she now owns 100 shares of GBCORP. The transfer of shares is almost completely automated. For the most part, about the only papers involved in the transaction are order tickets, which are filled out by the brokers in the branch office, and a trade confirmation, which is mailed to both the buyer and the seller immediately after the trade is executed. The confirmation slip includes details of the trade, such as price, number of shares, and terms and conditions.

The only other paper that may be involved in this process is a stock certificate, and then only if Mary decides that she wants the securities to be registered in her name and mailed to her. When investors decide to keep the securities in their brokerage account, the securities are kept in "street name"—that is, in the name of the brokerage firm.

Securities held in street name can be sold more quickly than securities registered in the name of the owner. Although the securities are in street name, the investor that bought the securities is the legal and beneficial owner and has the right to sell or transfer these securities.

Nasdaq and The American Stock Exchange

The Nasdaq Stock Market

Created in 1971, The Nasdaq Stock Market was the world's first electronic-based stock market and has become the model for developing markets world-wide. Today about 5,000 companies trade their securities on this electronic market. These include small, growing companies, as well as many large corporations that have become household names, such as Microsoft and Yahoo!.

Nasdaq operates using today's information technologies and a system under which market makers compete with each other for the best buying and selling prices. Approximately 450 broker/dealer firms—market makers representing many of the world's largest securities firms—took 60,018 positions in the first half of 1999, adding liquidity to the market.

Nasdaq's market makers use their own capital to buy and sell Nasdaq securities. The combined competitive activity and capital provide active, continuous trading; orderly markets; and immediacy of execution for large and small investors alike. Nasdaq has augmented the best elements of a dealer market with recent enhancements to its trading systems. For example, these improvements now enable Nasdaq to route investor orders to electronic communications networks (ECNs, electronic systems that disseminate orders to third parties) in a manner similar to an auction market.

Nasdaq's use of the latest communications and information technology and its system of competing market makers distinguishes it from a traditional exchange. Investors and brokers no longer must meet on a centralized trading location to buy and sell securities. The competition among market makers benefits investors because it forces an efficient pricing system.

Nasdaq is actually made up of two markets: the Nasdaq National Market and the Nasdaq Small-Cap Market. The Nasdaq National Market is the more prominent and well-known of the two. Stocks traded on this market must meet specific criteria, such as market capitalization and company size, before being listed. The Nasdaq Small-Cap Market lists the stock of smaller, emerging companies.

Over-the-Counter Bulletin Board stocks and pink sheet stocks

The majority of stocks in the United States are traded over the counter (OTC). There is no actual "counter" anymore, of course—this is just a reference to stocks that are not traded on formal, organized, and centralized exchanges such as NYSE or Amex. OTC encompasses the stocks on Nasdaq as well as many other stocks that couldn't qualify for listing on the NYSE or Amex. It is officially called the OTC Bulletin Board (OTCBB) and is regulated by the NASD. To find out more, visit the OTCBB Web site at www.otcbb.com.

Stocks that are not traded on the NYSE, Amex, or the Nasdaq National Market are found on the OTCBB, or the pink sheets. Before computerization, dealer quotes on OTC securities were printed

Unofficially...
Nasdaq, originally an acronym for the National Association of Securities Dealers Automated Quotation (or NASDAQ) System, is the commonly used term for The Nasdaq Stock Market, the world's first electronic-based trading market. (Note: Nasdaq should not be written in all capital letters, as the acronym is obsolete.)

Watch Out!
The investment
quality of stocks
on the OTCBB
and the "pink
sheets" is
questionable.
Although many
good companies
are traded in
this unregulated
environment,
many companies
have dubious
value. Beginning
investors should
avoid small-cap
or "penny"
stocks because
much expertise
and research is
necessary to find
true value and
potential.

on pink-colored paper, hence the designation of OTC securities as "pink sheet" stocks. The "pink sheets" are still published by the National Quotation Bureau (NQB). In addition, an electronic version of the pink sheets is updated once a day and disseminated over market data vendor terminals. NQB's stock data is also available by subscription at the Web site www.nqb.com.

The American Stock Exchange

The American Stock Exchange is the second-largest floor-based securities exchange in the United States. It has a significant presence in both listed equities and derivative securities.

Amex's history began more than 100 years ago. Until 1953, it was known as the Curb Exchange, a name inspired by the hundreds of brokers and traders who literally practiced their trade in the streets of New York City. The institution moved indoors in 1921 and remains in the same Trinity Street location in downtown New York today.

Amex is an auction market in which securities prices are determined by public bids to buy and offers to sell. Auction-market procedures ensure public buyers and sellers the best available price by centralizing order flow and requiring professionals to yield priority to public investors.

Amex trades more than 700 equity issues and more than 1,100 stock options. Options are offered on 26 broad-based international and sector indexes, along with about 50 structured products and index shares.

The American Stock Exchange is an innovative creator of derivative products. Amex-derivative products include index-based equities such as

Standard & Poor's Depositary Receipts (SPDRs), MidCap SPDRs, Select Sector SPDRs, DIAMONDS (based on the Dow Jones Industrial Average), and World Equity Benchmark Shares (WEBS).

SPDRs (pronounced "spiders") are a way for small investors to invest in the Standard & Poor's 500 Index without having to allocate funds for each of the 500 stocks represented by the index. When you buy SPDRs, you are buying shares in a unit investment trust (UIT) that owns a portfolio of stocks that reflects the S&P 500 stock index. A share is priced at approximately $1/10$ the value of the S&P 500. You participate in the ups and downs of the index, so this simulates a mutual fund. In addition, when dividends are issued by the underlying stocks, holders of SPDRs are eligible to receive these as distributions. You can receive them as a cash payment, or you can exercise the option to reinvest the distributions to buy additional shares.

A new product, Stock Return Income Debt Securities (STRIDES), which is linked to the value of the Nasdaq-100 Index, began trading in February 1999. On March 10, 1999, the Nasdaq-Amex Market Group introduced a new innovative product based on the Nasdaq-100 Index, enabling investors to make a single investment in the Nasdaq-100 companies as a whole: Nasdaq-100 Index Tracking Stock. This product is similar to SPDRs and DIAMONDS in that it acts like an index fund, but it trades like a stock on the floor of the American Stock Exchange under the ticker symbol QQQ. This proved to be the most successful product launch in Amex history, trading 2.6 million shares in its first day. It now trades more than five million shares a day and has assets of more than $2 billion.

More types of exchange-traded index funds are surfacing all the time. Barclays Plc, for example, launched in May 2000 the first of more than 40 such funds, called "iShares," which will track everything from the S&P 500 to sector and international indexes. Increasingly, these funds are giving investors a low-cost alternative to mutual funds that have the added advantage of being priced and traded intraday, as opposed to only at daily closing values, as is the case for mutual funds.

The merger of Nasdaq and Amex

On November 2, 1998, the National Association of Securities Dealers, Inc. (NASD), and the American Stock Exchange LLC (Amex) announced the completion of their merger. That date also marked the formation of The Nasdaq-Amex Market Group, Inc., a newly created subsidiary of the NASD. This holding company oversees the operation of The Nasdaq Stock Market and Amex, and explores technological efficiencies and international opportunities for the combined operation. This combination created the world's first major financial market that brings together a central auction specialist system (Amex) and a multiple market maker system (Nasdaq).

The Nasdaq-Amex Market Group was created in part to produce more efficient pricing, faster trade execution, and reduced transaction costs. Cost efficiencies for members have been realized as a result of the increased economies of scale and reduced order-handling charges. In spite of the merger, Nasdaq and Amex operate as separate markets.

The Nasdaq-Amex Market Group today

The first half of 1999 was a period of records for the Nasdaq-Amex Market Group. Among its many accomplishments, Nasdaq became the world's largest stock market in dollar volume terms, trading an average of $40 billion shares each day, with a record high of 1.4 billion shares traded on April 14, 1999. Since then, Nasdaq has had many trading days exceeding 2 billion shares.

Amex index shares continue to show steady growth. Total assets for index shares have increased by $5 billion since the beginning of the year 2000 to $19.6 billion. Additionally, average daily trading volume was up by an average of 5 million shares compared to the same period last year.

In 1999, 270.1 billion shares were traded on Nasdaq. The dollar volume rose 88% to $10.8 trillion—up from $5.8 trillion in 1998. In 1999, Nasdaq captured 51% of the total dollar volume traded on the three primary U.S. markets.

Amex is currently developing an investor relations support service for companies that list on the Exchange. Each company will have its own Web page on an Amex Web site specifically designed to be an investor relations page.

The combining of Nasdaq and the American Stock Exchange is important for investors to watch. This development has implications for investors as the markets continue to improve their efficiency. This will usher in new and better ways for investors to trade. The Internet will have a revolutionary impact, which will most likely result in new investment products and lower transaction costs for investors.

Stock indexes: measuring stock market performance

Activity on the stock market is reported every business day in averages and indexes that are designed to

Bright Idea
The Web site for the Nasdaq-Amex Market Group (www.nasdaq-amex.com) offers a comprehensive array of current market data. Quotations for individual stocks are offered on a 15-minute delay. Indexes are offered on a 1-minute delay. Market news and portfolio tracking are among the most popular functions.

assess the health of the general economy. The Dow Jones Industrial Average (DJIA), or simply "the Dow," is the most widely reported market indicator. We watch the Dow and other indexes to measure the stock market's general performance, and we draw conclusions about how well the investment world is doing. If the major indexes are rising, then the market is bullish. A bullish market bodes well for millions of investors, along with thousands of mutual funds and pension managers. Frequently the performance of a single stock or a portfolio is compared with a major index to see how well it is doing. As investors, we need to see that our investments are appreciating in comparison to an acceptable standard.

Dow Jones Industrial Average

The Dow Jones Industrial Average, when first published on May 26, 1896, by publisher Charles Dow, the co-founder of Dow Jones & Company, consisted of 12 stocks. Only one of the original 12, General Electric, is in the DJIA as of 2000. And even GE dropped out for a while—it was deleted in 1898 but came back nine years later as a replacement for Tennessee Coal & Iron.

Several companies in the 1896 average are ancestors of firms active today. American Tobacco was broken up in 1911 but was the forerunner of such companies as Fortune Brands and R.J. Reynolds Tobacco. Distilling & Cattle Feeding Co., became Distilling Co., of America, and later Millennium Chemical.

The 30 stocks in the average today were added gradually over the decades. General Motors joined in 1915, Sears Roebuck joined in 1924, and International Business Machines joined in 1979. Walt Disney entered the Dow in 1991.

March 1997, however, saw a significant shift in the dynamics of the DJIA, as Hewlett-Packard Co., Johnson & Johnson, Travelers Group Inc., and Wal-Mart replaced Bethlehem Steel Corp., Texaco, Westinghouse Electric, and Woolworth. That was the largest change in the composition of the DJIA in recent history, and except for Travelers' merger with Citicorp to form Citigroup, the average has not changed since.

In November 1999, the DJIA added Microsoft, Home Depot, Intel, and SBC Communications while dropping Chevron, Goodyear Tire & Rubber, Sears, and Union Carbide. This change was made to make the DJIA more representative of the changes in our economy, such as the growth of the computer and telecommunications sectors.

Dow Jones Transportation Average

The Dow Jones Industrial Average is the best-known U.S. stock index, but it's not the oldest. The Dow Jones Transportation Average (DJTA) has that honor. Assembled in 1884, it was composed of nine railroads, including the New York Central and Union Pacific, and two nonrails, Pacific Mail Steamship and Western Union.

Dow Jones Utility Average

Created in 1929, the Dow Jones Utility Average (DJUA) tracks 15 major utilities. This index is watched by analysts concerned with the effects of interest rates. It is acknowledged that the DJUA usually acts conversely to interest rate movements. In other words, when the interest rates decline, utilities' stock tends to rise, and vice versa.

Utilities are big borrowers whose financial conditions are sensitive to interest rates. Rising interest

Timesaver
To get full details on the Dow Jones Industrial Average, go to www.indexes. dowjones.com. The site gives plenty of useful information on the market's most popular index that normally can't be found as easily elsewhere.

rates have a negative effect on utilities' earnings. Additionally, when interest rates rise, investors in utilities tend to sell their stock in favor of alternatives that take advantage of increased levels of interest. Because utilities get hit first by increased interest rates, the DJUA is seen as a advance warning for the market in general—rising interest rates are seen as generally negative for stock investments.

Calculating the Dow Industrials

When Charles Dow invented the Dow Jones Industrial Average in 1896, calculating it was easy as pie. You added the prices of 12 stocks—including such now-forgotten outfits as U.S. Leather and Tennessee Coal & Iron—and divided by 12.

Simple. And a good thing it was, since Mr. Dow was working before the invention of electronic calculators, let alone computers.

Today the principles of the calculation are the same as 100 years ago, but a few things have changed. There are 30 stocks in the index instead of 12. And the divisor has undergone a series of adjustments to preserve continuity.

Some of the adjustments reflect switches in the stocks that compose the average. Suppose, hypothetically, that Dow Jones & Co., had decided to remove Boeing from the index and substitute Microsoft on January 1, 1998. With Boeing trading at $48.9375 a share on December 31, 1997, and Microsoft trading at $129.25, then without a compensating adjustment, the switch would have made the DJIA rise by 202 points. (Incidentally, Microsoft was added to the Dow in late 1999.)

Adjustments in the divisor also are made whenever a company splits its stock. In a 2-for-1 split, for example, each shareholder gets one additional share for every share held. Normally, this cuts the price per share in half. The divisor must be adjusted downward to compensate.

As a result, the divisor nowadays is a fraction—0.24275214 in October 1998—which means that it has become, in effect, a multiplier. A 1-point move in any component stock pushes the average up or down about 4.12 points. (Current divisors for each of the Dow Jones averages appear on page C3 of *The Wall Street Journal* every day.)

The DJIA is old-fashioned in that it is price-weighted. In other words, if a Dow stock valued at $100 changed 5 percent, that would have more impact on the DJIA than would a 5 percent move in a stock that was valued at $35.

Critics say that means that the DJIA is a crude index. Maybe so. But the industrial average is useful for several reasons. It is a barometer of blue chips, the cream of American industry. For the most part, it tracks with broader, more sophisticated indexes. And it has one thing that no other index can claim: more than a century of market history and experience attached to it.

Other indexes

THE S&P 500

Standard & Poor's is an investment services and publishing company that is among the most influential information sources in the financial industry. It publishes a large range of reports and guidebooks on securities, industries, and the general market. It also has an independent financial rating service that rates the financial strength and creditworthiness of stocks, bonds, and other securities. Standard & Poor's is also known for compiling stock market indexes such as its famed S&P 500 stock index.

The S&P 500 tracks the performance of 500 large-capitalization stocks. It is the most widely used benchmark by money managers and mutual funds to gauge how well they are doing. Like the Dow, it is revised from time to time to reflect changes in the economy and has recently added such companies as Cisco Systems, Qualcomm, and Yahoo!.

The Nasdaq Composite Index

The Nasdaq Composite Index measures the market value of all the domestic and foreign common stocks listed on the Nasdaq Stock Market. Price changes in each security affect either a rise or fall in the index, in proportion to the security's market value. The market value, the last sale price multiplied by total shares outstanding, is calculated continually throughout the trading day.

The Nasdaq Composite is a valuable market barometer representing a wide variety of industries. It includes the securities of 4,894 companies, more than nearly any other single stock market index. These companies represent a wide array of industries, from computers to toys to medical devices. As a result of this broad base, the Nasdaq Composite is a more comprehensive index than the S&P 500 or the Dow Jones Industrial Average (DJIA), which contains just 30 large companies. Created on February 8, 1971, and set at 100, the Nasdaq Composite has soared more than 21 times its original value during Nasdaq's first 28 years.

The Nasdaq-100 Index

The Nasdaq-100 Index includes 100 of the largest nonfinancial companies listed on the Nasdaq National Market. The Nasdaq-100 reflects Nasdaq's largest growth companies across major industry groups, although it is heavily weighted toward technology and other "new economy" companies. All index components have a market capitalization of at least $500 million and an average daily trading volume of at least 100,000 shares. On January 31, 1985, the Nasdaq-100 Index began with a base of 250.

Industry-Specific Indexes

The Nasdaq Composite Index comprises eight industry-specific subindexes: Bank, Biotechnology, Computer, Finance, Industrial, Insurance, Telecommunications, and Transportation. Each of the subindexes was created on February 8, 1971, except for the Biotechnology and Computer indexes, which were created on November 1, 1993. Also on that date, the Utilities Index became the Telecommunications Index and now contains only telecommunications firms; all other utility companies were added to the Industrial Index.

Nasdaq Bank Index

More than 750 financial institutions make up this index—that includes trust companies not engaged in deposit banking; firms performing functions related to banking, such as check-cashing agencies, currency exchanges, and safe deposit companies; and banking corporations overseas. On December 14, 1998, savings institutions and holding companies for banks and savings institutions were added to the Bank Index.

Nasdaq Biotechnology Index

This index includes 136 companies engaged in biomedical research to develop new treatments and cures for a wide range of human diseases.

Nasdaq Computer Index

One of Nasdaq's premier indexes, it represents the securities of 661 companies manufacturing hardware, software, data processing, office equipment, and electronic components/accessories.

Nasdaq-Financial Index

This index includes 172 credit agencies (except banks), savings and loan associations, security and commodity brokers, exchanges and dealers, and real estate and holding and investment companies, excluding those regulated under the Investment Company Act of 1940.

Nasdaq Industrial Index

The largest industry-specific index, this index includes 2,923 agricultural, mining, construction, manufacturing (except electronic components), services, and public administration enterprises.

Insurance Index

This index includes 93 life, health, property, and casualty insurance companies and agents/brokers.

Nasdaq Telecommunications Index

A key twenty-first century industry sector, this index includes 172 communications companies.

Transportation Index

This index covers 115 railroads, trucking companies, airlines, pipeline companies (except natural gas), and services such as warehousing and travel arrangements.

Nasdaq Financial-100 Index

The Nasdaq Financial-100 Index consists of 100 of the largest financial organizations listed on the Nasdaq National Market. It was introduced on January 31, 1985, with a base of 250.

Nasdaq National Market Composite Index

The Nasdaq National Market Composite SM Index is a subset of the Nasdaq Composite Index and consists of all companies included in the Nasdaq Composite Index that are listed on the Nasdaq National Market. On July 10, 1984, the Nasdaq National Market Composite Index began with a base of 100.

New York Stock Exchange Index

This index tracks the market value of all the common stocks on the NYSE. The index is market capitalization-weighted, which means that companies with the greatest market value have a greater impact on the index than companies with fewer shares or lower prices.

Amex Composite Index

The Amex Composite Index is a market capitalization-weighted price appreciation index that replaced the Amex Market Value Index on January 2, 1997. The new index is more comparable to other major indexes.

The level of the Amex Composite Index is not altered by stock splits, stock dividends, or trading halts, nor is it affected by new listings, additional issuances, delistings, or suspensions. In addition, at the same time, the Amex introduced five subindexes that track the performance of companies in major industry sectors: Information Technologies, Financial, Healthcare, Natural Resources, and Industrials.

Industry-Specific Indexes

Like Nasdaq, Amex has its subsets of market indexes. Securities listed in the Amex Composite Index are included in one of the following subindexes. The subindexes have been calculated with a base of

100 as of December 29, 1995, and are disseminated at approximately 4:20 P.M. and 5:00 P.M. every business day.

Financial Subindex

Included here are commercial banks, thrift institutions, broker/dealers, closed-end funds, finance companies, insurance underwriters and agents, trusts, REITs, and diversified financial firms.

Healthcare Subindex

This subindex comprises pharmaceutical companies; medical, surgical, and dental equipment manufacturers; clinics, hospitals, nursing, and personal care facilities; home healthcare services; and medical laboratories. It excludes distributors of pharmaceuticals and medical equipment (which are included in the industrial subindex).

Information Technology Subindex

This subindex is comprised of manufacturers of computer hardware and peripherals, telecommunications equipment, semiconductors and electronic components; software programmers; computer systems integrators; data processing services; telecommunications carriers, radio and television broadcasters; cable television companies; and motion picture producers/distributors. It excludes distributors of computer hardware and software (which are included in the industrial subindex).

Natural Resources Subindex

Companies in this subindex are engaged in mining (metals, minerals, and coal), oil and gas exploration and extraction, petroleum refining, and the transmission and distribution of oil and natural gas.

Industrial Subindex

This subindex includes all companies not listed in any of previous subindexes, including companies engaged in manufacturing, commercial services, construction, utilities, and wholesale and retail trade.

Russell 2000 Index

This index is considered a benchmark index for small-capitalization stocks. Developed by the Frank Russell Company of Tacoma, Washington, the Russell 2000 tracks the stocks of 2,000 small public companies.

Wilshire 5000 Index

Despite the name, the Wilshire 5000 Index actually tracks more than 7,000 stocks. Developed by Wilshire Associates, Inc., of Santa Monica, California, it keeps adding stocks as the market expands. It is considered the broadest market index of American stocks. It tracks all the stocks on the NYSE, Amex, and the Nasdaq market.

The Internet: a special look

The most profound change in the stock market in recent years has been the emergence and dramatic ascent of the Internet. It is a development that will have far-reaching effects on our investment portfolios, our economy, our businesses, and our lives. Investors are right to eye the incredible opportunities that the Internet provides. As of this writing, the Internet has already created numerous millionaires in a very short period of time. If this is the wave of the future, why not jump in and buy up shares of famous companies such as Amazon.com, Yahoo!, America Online, and other big names helping us navigate the future?

The problem is that investing in new technologies or new industries can be a treacherous process. Today's investors have predominantly ignored the hard lessons of the past as they rush in seeking easy wealth. As new technologies emerge, we must realize that history has shown us, time after time, that most investors lose money in the first stages of innovation. When looked at through the prism of a century of stock investing, the Internet is actually not that novel after all.

In the late 1800s, the railroad industry was heralded as a major advance for society. Investors rushed in to invest in railroad stocks. The first major stock index created was the Dow Jones Transportation Index in 1884 to track the progress of the major transportation companies. The railroad was definitely a fantastic boon to our society and economy at that time. It enabled us to move people and goods across the national landscape inexpensively. So how did investors fare?

The vast majority of investors lost money during the initial stages of the railroad revolution. Railroads required tremendous human and financial capital to establish the network of tracks, locomotive vehicles, and so on. How, then, did investors make money in the railroad industry?

The real money for investors happened in the second stage as the railroad industry matured. The second wave of companies profited from the infrastructure that had previously been created. The second wave of companies learned from the lessons of the trailblazers and set up business models to become profitable entities.

The dawn of the automotive industry is also an important lesson for Internet investors. Automobile manufacturing was in its innovative heyday from 1919 to 1949. Investors became enamored of this technology that was set to dominate the paths and byways of America. At that time, more than 200 major auto-makers in the country were producing more than 2,000 different makes of cars. Any public company that had the word *motors* in its name saw its stock skyrocket. Sound familiar?

The majority of auto-makers subsequently went out of business. Competition forced weak or unprofitable companies to go bankrupt or be bought out by stronger companies.

Today there are only three domestic auto-makers, and one of them, Chrysler, was recently acquired by a foreign competitor. The largest auto-maker today, General Motors Corporation, was nowhere to be found during the first stage of the automobile revolution. Investors didn't profit with GM until years later.

History abounds with examples of exciting new developments that hurt the majority of investors in the beginning. The investors who were patient and sought value (that is, stocks of enduring companies that made consistent profits) were rewarded with the lion's share of capital gains. The second wave of companies almost invariably capitalized on both the mistakes and the triumphs of the earlier companies that laid the groundwork for growth.

Recall other developments in American economic history:

- **Radio in the 1920s**—Investors bought up RCA, the biggest radio company at the time, and sent the stock soaring to $498 per share by the end of the decade. The stock plummeted to less than $10 as the general market fell. RCA didn't regain its pre-1929 crash price until nearly 30 years later.

■ **Airline stocks 1919–1939 (and again in the 1960s)**—The airplane was another great invention. It transformed business and society, but investors who rushed in got burned. Approximately 300 aircraft manufacturers were around in the 1919–1939 period, but only a handful exist today. Investors were again enamored of airline stocks during the 1960s, yet many of these stocks subsequently declined. From 1970–1999, nearly 130 airlines went bankrupt.

■ **Computer manufacturers 1980–1985**—Dozens of personal computer-makers competed in a booming PC industry. Most went bankrupt or were bought out by stronger companies.

The current Internet stock-buying boom is acknowledged by most observers to have started unofficially in 1995. On August 9, 1995, Netscape Communications became the first Internet stock to capture the market's attention. Netscape's stock price more than doubled in less than two days. As more Internet companies went public, the market overwhelmingly responded. Internet stocks doubled, tripled, and quadrupled during the opening days of trading.

The Internet gold rush had begun. Stocks of companies such as Amazon.com, eBay, ETrade, priceline.com, and others went through the roof. Companies with no significant products, profits, or prospects scrambled to position themselves as they seized the public's imagination. In some cases, the results were stunning. When the financial information Web site MarketWatch.com went public on

January 15, 1999 (despite large net losses), its shares escalated 475 percent in its first day of trading! From November 1998 to November 1999, 10 companies had first-day price increases of more than 300 percent, despite the fact that they had either miniscule profit or had losses. Along with related technology companies such as Cisco Systems and Qualcomm, these companies have been dubbed the "New Economy" stocks, ready to leap-frog over the "Old Economy" stocks such as General Motors and Proctor & Gamble.

The measure of success in high technology and "new economy" stocks came to be embodied by the Nasdaq Composite Index. This particular stock index is heavily represented with "New Economy" stocks such as Yahoo! and Microsoft. During the first quarter of 2000, The Nasdaq Composite index briefly surpassed the 5,000 level for the first time in the index's history. As of early April 2000, the Nasdaq Composite Index had fallen below 4,000, a drop in value of 20 percent as investors sold their holdings, which, in turn, pushed prices down. This type of volatility has resulted in losses for inexperienced stock buyers.

Even as this book is being written, the shakeout in Internet stocks has begun. Many "dotcom" companies that soared because of investor enthusiasm have fallen dramatically because investors have started to see that companies in the New Economy need something from the Old Economy: profits. No matter how fancy or interesting a Web site or technology is, a company still has to generate profits if it's going to not only survive but also thrive. Profitability is the primary measure by which we can measure how well a company and its products and services are being accepted. Value investors need to be patient and invest in the Internet companies that have solidified their position in the New Economy.

Some examples of Internet companies plunging to grievous levels are breathtaking to behold. In early 1999, the Web site drkoop.com started trading publicly. Its stock skyrocketed to a high of $45^3/_4$ per share.

Unfortunately for investors, the company could not generate profits. Its financial difficulties drove investors away, and the stock fell to 1 per share in May 2000. Amazon.com's stock hit 112 in the summer of 1999. The stock made a steady descent to below 50 in May 2000.

Look at history for answers. In the mid-1800s, the famed California Gold Rush captured America's imagination. People headed west seeking fortunes after hearing stories of how common folks became rich prospecting for gold. Yes, there were success stories of people getting rich panning for gold on the riverbeds of California. However, the vast majority sought riches but never saw their fortunes materialize. Those who made the most secure profits were companies that sold the pans, shovels, and tools to the wealth-seekers. The greater wealth was generated not by the participants in the Gold Rush, but by the companies that offered products and services to the Gold Rush. Is there a lesson here for Internet investors?

Aggregately, thousands of Web sites sold tons of products and generated millions of dollars in revenues. Despite the impressive sales, most of these Web sites lost money because their expenses exceeded income. Companies such as UPS and Federal Express made big money from Internet transactions because, after all, these products had to be shipped.

Yes, the Internet is here to stay and will offer magnificent growth opportunities for our economy. However, investors must still do the research to separate the few companies that will succeed from the many that will be mediocre or worse. Keep these general points in mind when considering Internet investments:

■ The Internet will have a major impact on investing for the foreseeable future. Most stock investments will be affected directly or indirectly by the evolution of the Internet. Companies that take advantage of the Internet are a good consideration for your portfolio.

■ Remember the lesson of the California Gold Rush: What companies sell products and services most profitably either to or with the Internet?

■ Understand the risks. Many dotcom stocks are losing money; many will go bankrupt. Make sure that you choose companies that show consistent and growing earnings.

■ Consider "commercial" before ".com." As a general rule of thumb, companies that have already succeeded in the marketplace and that are expanding into the Internet are a safer bet than companies that began as a Web site. Many Internet companies will go bankrupt because of intense competition and high marketing costs.

As of June 2000, many Internet companies have experienced cash flow problems and growing losses that will put many of them out of business. This underscores the point that business success starts and ends with products and services that the public

Watch Out!
When a company goes public, company insiders often sell off their stock holdings. Insiders, such as the president of the company or any investor who owns 5 percent or more of the company, must file the public document #13D with the Securities and Exchange Commission (SEC). (Find out more about insider trading in Chapter 9, "Succeeding in Both Bull and Bear Markets.")

wants and needs regardless of how "flashy" the technology involved. Investors should follow the lead of consumers and company management that continues to satisfy them.

Just the facts

- The best stock investing environment for beginning and intermediate investors is the NYSE, Amex, and the Nasdaq National Market.

- Understanding the elements of a stock purchase or sale will increase your investing ability and knowledge.

- The Dow Jones Industrial Average and other indexes are important barometers of general market performance.

- You can judge the performance of an individual stock by comparing it against accepted standards of market performance, such as the S&P 500 Index.

- History tells us that unwary investors lose money with new technologies. However, sound research and analysis can help you pick the companies that can survive and prosper.

GET THE SCOOP ON...
Your starting point before you invest
▪ Investing versus saving ▪ Your personal balance
sheet ▪ The personal cash flow statement ▪ Your
short-term and long-term financial goals
▪ Determining your risk tolerance

Preparing to Invest in Great Stocks

Chapter 3

In Chapter 1, "Stock Investing Defined," we discussed the various types of risk. In this chapter, the emphasis is on reducing risk and maximizing your potential for gain by taking control of your finances.

Long before you invest your first dollar in a share of stock, you should understand your personal financial picture. Do you know how much you have in assets? How much do you have in liabilities? What interest are you paying to maintain your debt? Are you aware of your spending habits? What is your level of knowledge about investing? What do you want to accomplish with your money? Why do you want to invest in stocks when there are so many other choices? Getting answers to these vital questions is your first step to taking control of your finances.

Frequently, people invest in stocks because they are drawn in by the excitement. Perhaps they see the TV shows and hear the pundits talk about the

benefits of stock investing. Maybe they hear investment success stories from friends, relatives, and
neighbors involved in the stock market, and they
feel left out. They believe that everyone but themselves is getting rich.

Maybe you have a sense of falling behind in
reaching financial goals. The mutual fund that you
invested in might be performing reasonably well,
but it's not skyrocketing like your neighbor's investment. Or maybe investments are falling short of
your retirement target amount. Do you owe it to
yourself and your family to give a boost to your
investments by adding some high-octane growth
stocks?

These situations are common in a mature bull
market, as we've had in 1999–2000. When your
investments are plodding along and other people's
investments are rocketing forward, it's easy to let
emotions and fear take over money management
concerns. But it's important for your financial well-
being to look at your investment concerns and
goals. A well-reasoned, rational approach to investing will push you farther and faster over the long-
term than you currently believe is possible.

The neighbor who made a killing on XYZ.com
stock isn't going to brag about the money he lost
investing on that "hot tech stock" he heard about at
the company cafeteria. You can't always judge how
well you are doing financially with others because
you don't have complete information on their successes or failures. Then again, you should be more
concerned about measuring your success against
your own standard: How well are you doing now versus how well you did last year? Is your net worth
greater than it was 12 months ago? What are you

doing now to increase your net worth a year from now?

Your starting point

Gather your financial documents, and tally your assets and liabilities. What are you invested in now? Do you have money in savings? Before you invest in stocks, you need to know your starting point and decide on your investment approach.

Why invest?

You invest to grow your wealth so that you can achieve your financial goals, either short-term or long-term. When you're just starting out, deciding where to put your money can be daunting. You must decide which investment vehicles suit your needs and temperament. Your choices include stocks, bonds, mutual funds, treasury securities, cash, futures, options, currencies, and commodities—a combination of several is usually wise.

Although people invest for different reasons at different times in their lives, they generally have the same objective: achieving and retaining financial security for themselves and their families. Whether you're interested in purchasing your first home, saving for your children's education, or beginning to think about funding your retirement, you need to develop a solid investment foundation.

Why invest in stocks? When all investments are analyzed for how well they have performed, stocks have consistently outperformed other investment categories, such as bonds and bank certificates of deposit. Although in any given year, any particular investment does better or worse than any other given investment, stocks have been proven winners when measured over long periods of time such as

10 years or longer. Stocks are excellent for long-term growth, but they have shown that they can be good income vehicles as well. The research has shown that dividend-paying stocks have kept pace with inflation. This is important as the cost of living continues to increase.

Inflationary pressures on our pocketbooks are relentless. In many cities, home prices are well into six figures. These days a college education can set you back almost $100,000. Even a car is a major purchase that must be considered carefully. A good investment strategy can help finance your needs for today and tomorrow.

Estimates indicate that middle-class Baby Boomers will need between $1 million and $2 million at retirement to maintain their lifestyles. You should not completely rely on social security or Medicare for assistance because their futures remain uncertain. A secure and comfortable future is in your own hands. Will you have enough money to retire?

Home ownership no longer guarantees a generous nest egg, either. Today many real estate professionals are telling clients to buy a home primarily for shelter. You can't count on a huge gain from the sale of your personal residence to fund your retirement or your children's education.

Consequently, more Americans are becoming active investors. About 55 percent of American households invest in the stock market, either through direct stock investment or through intermediaries such as mutual fund companies and insurance companies.

Smart investors know firsthand how profitable, exciting, and fun investing can be. But smart investing requires solid information and good advice. True, some people do "play" the market— they gamble and occasionally make money from "hot tips" and hunches. But you don't want to trust your future to a roll of the dice!

Risks and potential returns vary greatly from investment to investment. Stocks offer investors growth, but they can be volatile. Bonds provide investors with income but are also subject to volatility in the value of the underlying principle. Treasury bills, certificates of deposit (CDs), and money market funds are insured but offer low returns. But whatever investments you choose, remember this: Impulsive decisions are usually decisions that you may regret. Take your time, do your homework, and don't ever let someone pressure you into an investment that you're not sure of.

In the long run, the difference between a winning investment strategy and a losing one isn't luck—it's knowledge and discipline. In this book you will find the necessary tools and information to make safe, smart, and rewarding stock investments.

Investing versus saving

In the current investing environment, investors have lost track of the critical difference between investing and saving. Millions of investors do not have money set aside for savings to protect against unforeseen situations and problems. These same investors have instead opted to use their stock portfolio as a savings vehicle, which is wrong. Investors should opt to have both investments and savings. This simple method of diversification is very important to guard against potential losses in an uncertain economy.

Bright Idea
For free pamphlets on budgeting, investing, and money management, order the free Consumer Information Catalog from the federal government: Consumer Information Center, Box 100, Pueblo, CO 81009. Or, download the publications free from the Web site www. pueblo.gsa.gov.

Saving

The classical economic definition of *savings* is the portion of your income remaining after paying your expenses. If at the end of the month you paid all your expenses and immediate debts and had $20 left, that constitutes your savings.

For most people, savings today means money set aside in safekeeping. It would typically earn interest if it's kept in a financial institution. Your "savings" are usually put into the safest places, or products, that allow you access to your money at any time.

Savings products include saving accounts, checking accounts, and certificates of deposit. At some banks and savings and loan associations, your deposits may be insured by the Federal Deposit Insurance Corporation (FDIC). But there's a trade-off for security and ready availability: You earn a relatively low rate of return on your money. A lower rate of return is acceptable, however, because you also have lower risk.

Most smart investors put enough money in a savings product to cover an emergency, such as sudden unemployment. Some make sure that they have three to six months of gross living expenses in savings so that they know it will absolutely be there for them when they need it.

But how "safe" is a savings account if you leave all of your money there for a long time, and the interest it earns doesn't keep up with inflation? What if you save a dollar when it can buy a loaf of bread, but years later when you withdraw that dollar plus the interest you earned on it, it can buy only half a loaf? This is the reason many people put only a portion of their money in savings. They hope to invest for growth so that they can earn more over long periods of time—say, three years or longer.

Investing

Investing is the act of purchasing securities and tangible assets for the purpose of gaining current income, future gain (capital appreciation), or both.

When you invest, you have a greater chance of losing your money than when you save. Unlike FDIC-insured deposits, the money you invest in securities, mutual funds, and other similar investments is not federally insured. You could lose your principal, or the initial amount you've invested. But you also have the opportunity to earn a greater return on your money.

Your personal balance sheet

The first step in analyzing your picture is to create a personal balance sheet. Treat your finances as if you are a company. Keeping track of your assets, liabilities, income, and expenses is the prerequisite to your investing.

Sit down and take an honest look at your entire financial situation. You can never take a journey without knowing where you're starting from, and a journey to financial independence is no different. On paper or using a computer spreadsheet program, figure out your current situation. What do you own and what you owe?

This personal balance sheet is also called a net worth statement. Use Table 3.1 on page 77, or create your own. First list your assets (in order of liquidity) in column A, and then list their current, realistic market value in column B. What do you own? How much is it worth? Is it growing in value?

In column C, write in the growth rate for that asset. For example, for a savings account, put in the annualized interest rate, such as 3 percent. For mutual funds and stocks, put in the total return. For

> 66
> Budgets are not merely affairs of arithmetic, but in a thousand ways go to the root of prosperity of individuals, the relation of classes, and the strength of kingdoms
> —William E. Gladstone
> 99

example, for a stock that appreciated by 10 percent and also issued dividends that equated to a 3 percent yield, your total return would be 13 percent. For assets that neither appreciated nor lost value, enter 0. For depreciating assets (such as autos) put the number as a negative. If your car was worth $10,000 last year but this year it's worth $9,000, then column B would show $9,000 and column C would show −10 percent to show decreasing value.

Then list your liabilities. What are your debts? List all your liabilities, including credit cards, auto loans, margin debt, and your mortgage(s). How much do you owe?

When you are done, subtract your total liabilities from your total assets to arrive at your financial net worth. If your assets are larger than your liabilities, you have a positive net worth. If your liabilities are greater than your assets, you have a negative net worth.

You should regularly review and update your net worth statement. Do it at least annually, and preferably more frequently.

Analyze your balance sheet

When you do your balance sheet, analyze it for financial opportunities. For many people, simply shifting around assets will increase their wealth.

For example, if you have $5,000 in a savings account earning 5 percent, and you also have credit card debt of $4,000 on which you are paying 15 percent, then your finances would improve significantly by paying off the credit card debt with $4,000 from your savings account. After all, the 5 percent interest income you're earning is taxable, while the 15 percent you're paying is not even tax-deductible.

TABLE 3.1   PERSONAL BALANCE SHEET

COLUMN A	COLUMN B	COLUMN C
Current Growth	**Assets Market Value**	**Rate %**
Cash on-hand	$_____	___%
Checking account	$_____	___%
Savings accounts	$_____	___%
Cash value of life insurance	$_____	___%
Mutual fund #1 _____	$_____	___%
Mutual fund #2 _____	$_____	___%
Stock #1 _____	$_____	___%
Stock #2 _____	$_____	___%
Stock #3 _____	$_____	___%
Other financial investments	$_____	___%
Retirement accounts (401(k), etc.)	$_____	___%
Real estate investments	$_____	___%
Business investments	$_____	___%
Personal residence	$_____	___%
Automobile(s)	$_____	___%
Other assets	$_____	___%
Personal property	$_____	___%
Other_____	$_____	___%
Total Assets	$_____	___% *

* Put the average for the total assets. At what rate are your total assets growing?

COLUMN A	COLUMN B	COLUMN C
Liabilities	**Current Interest Balance $**	**What % Are You Paying?**
Credit card balance(s)	$_____	___%
Auto loan	$_____	___%
Other personal loans	$_____	___%
Mortgage balance	$_____	___%
Other debt	$_____	___%
Total Liabilities	$_____	___% **

NET WORTH
(Assets minus liabilities) $_____

** Put the average for total liabilities. What are you paying to maintain this total debt?

If you have $10,000 sitting in an interest-bearing checking account earning 2 percent interest while you have $2,000 in a mutual fund growing at 14 percent, then you should consider reallocating your funds. Perhaps all you need in that checking account is $6,000 because it is used as a safe, interest-bearing emergency fund. The $4,000 ought to be shifted to the mutual fund to maximize your potential for capital appreciation.

Perhaps you have $3,000 in an auto loan, and the rate you are paying is 11 percent on that outstanding balance. But you also have the ability to borrow against your residence using a home equity line of credit. If this rate is lower than 11 percent and the monthly payment is equal to or less than the auto loan payment, then consider paying off the $3,000 auto loan by writing a check from your home equity line account. Besides paying less in interest, you also gain a tax benefit. Interest paid on a home equity account is usually mortgage interest and is generally 100 percent tax-deductible as an itemized expense; auto loan interest, on the other hand, is considered consumer interest and is not deductible.

It's important to remember that building wealth is not one big thing you do with your money; it's a hundred little things that you do month-in and month-out, all year round. If you increase your investment return by only 1 percent here and also reduce the interest you're paying by 1 percent over there, your total financial picture improves significantly. The wealth builds much faster.

Review all the line items on your balance sheet. What other ways can you increase your net worth by reallocating assets and liabilities? If your total assets are increasing in value at a greater rate than you are paying to maintain your debt, then you are heading in the right direction.

Personal cash flow statement

Doing a personal cash flow statement means looking at money flowing in and flowing out in your finances. This is different from an income and expense statement, although they have similarities. For most investors, the cash flow statement is a more useful tool. Refer to the cash flow statement example that follows.

Assessing your cash flow

The next step in evaluating your present financial status is to look at your monthly cash flow. Begin by looking at your monthly net income, the money you take home every month after taxes. Your monthly income includes your salary and other steady and reliable sources of income, such as income from a second job or business venture, interest on a bank account, child support or alimony, or social security. If you already own some stock, you may be receiving dividend payments. Factor that amount into your income, too.

Next, calculate what your average monthly living expenses are. These include legal obligations and average expenses. Your obligations are payments that you are legally or contractually obligated to make, such as your rent or mortgage payment, a car lease or loan, credit card payments, and child support or alimony. Legal obligations are generally paid in fixed amounts over a long period of time.

Your expenses are those things that you must purchase or that you need to spend money on regularly. They're not as binding as legal obligations and can vary in amount, but these are generally

Moneysaver
If you get into
credit card
trouble, contact
the Consumer
Credit Counseling
Service, a
nonprofit
organization:
The National
Foundation for
Consumer Credit
8611 2nd Avenue,
Suite 100
Silver Spring, MD
20910
Phone:
301-589-5600
Toll-free:
1-800-388-2227

necessary expenses—for example, what you typically spend on groceries, utilities, childcare, and insurance. Transportation is an expense that virtually everyone has, and it takes on many different forms: public transportation, car maintenance and registration, gasoline, and parking. Come up with a monthly estimate for the total of your expenses.

The rest of your monthly expenditures cover the range of products and services that you choose to spend money on each month. These are generally discretionary items that you can probably do without, but to get a sense of what you're spending each month, you should identify them as expenses. For example, do you subscribe to cable television or any other monthly services? What is your average long-distance phone bill? What is your Internet bill? Do you pay dues to a club or organization or pay for education? How much do you spend at the dry cleaner or when getting your hair cut? Do you have a pet? Estimate the total for your monthly expenditures.

Add your monthly obligations, average expenses, and discretionary expenditures. Subtract this figure from your monthly net income to see what your leftover cash supply is.

If you come up with a negative cash flow—that is, if you are spending more each month than you earn—you may be heading for serious trouble. Take a good hard look at what your expenses are and what you could reduce or eliminate. You might want to seek help from a professional financial adviser. Before you can start investing, you'll need to be spending less than you earn with some to spare.

If you have a positive cash flow but you're spending nearly everything you make, you're probably not ready to start investing right now. Most people have more control over their expenses than their income, so taking a look at which of your expenses could be eliminated or reduced is a good first step. Maybe some of your discretionary expenses are luxuries you could live without. Perhaps you could refinance or consolidate some of your debts to reduce your monthly payments. A financial professional may be able to help you see options that you hadn't considered before. Even if you're not ready to start investing today, it's still a perfect time to start learning about your investment options.

If you have a positive cash flow and plenty of money to cover your entertainment (restaurants, movies, video rental) and incidental expenses, you are well on your way to embarking on an investment plan. But there are still a few more things to consider.

If you have any credit card debts, you may want to pay them off before embarking on an investment plan. Ideally, the money you invest should be free of other obligations. If you want to pay off your credit card debt but can't do it immediately, work out a structured plan to pay off the bill as quickly as possible. When you come up with a monthly payment figure, though, remember to include it in your monthly expenses, and recalculate your leftover cash supply.

Some investments tie up your money for a relatively long period of time. Before you invest, it's probably a good idea to set aside some money about the equivalent of a few months of living expenses in a liquid (easily accessible) form. A regular savings account at your bank or credit union gives you some return on your deposit, but you can still withdraw it at any time without penalty. Having a living expense

Watch Out!
1999 became the third year in a row that the United States personal bankruptcy rate exceeded one million filings. In the year 2000, personal bankruptcies will exceed one and a half million, according to the Federal Reserve.

cushion ensures that you have something to rely on in the event of an illness, unemployment, or some other unexpected situation without disrupting your investment plan.

When you're comfortable that you have an adequate emergency fund and a positive cash flow with money to spare, you're ready to explore investment options. Knowing how much you can safely and reasonably invest is the first step to investing wisely. Because your income and monthly expenses change over time, you'll want to re-evaluate your finances on a regular basis.

Finally, figure out the annualized amount available for investment. Using the cash flow statement in Table 3.2, get a picture of your situation. Fill out columns A, B, and C, and calculate the totals for the month and year.

Analyze your cash flow statement to see where you can make improvements.

Other financial considerations

Decreasing your debt and your monthly expenses are two major ways to increase your wealth. Even decreasing the utility or telephone bills will have a large impact. However, keep in mind other factors that will affect your wealth, such as taxes, insurance, and estate planning.

Taxes

The single greatest expense in your lifetime is taxes that you pay directly and indirectly. There are federal, state, and local taxes. There are income taxes, capital gains taxes, and sales tax. There are payroll taxes, business taxes, excise taxes, and a wide array of nuisance taxes that you pay in some way, shape, or form. The Tax Foundation calculates that the average family's tax bill is greater than food, clothing, and shelter expenses combined.

TABLE 3.2   CASH FLOW STATEMENT

Name:_____

For period __/__/__ to __/__/__

COLUMN A ITEM$	COLUMN B Monthly Amount$	COLUMN C* Annual Amount
Income:		
Source #1 _____	$_____	$_____
Source #2 _____	$_____	$_____
Source #3 _____	$_____	$_____
Total Income:	$_____	$_____
Out-going:		
Rent or mortgage	$_____	$_____
Utilities	$_____	$_____
Food	$_____	$_____
Clothing	$_____	$_____
Telephone	$_____	$_____
Property tax	$_____	$_____
Auto expenses	$_____	$_____
Auto insurance	$_____	$_____
Life insurance	$_____	$
Other insurance	$_____	$_____
Charity	$_____	$_____
Recreation	$_____	$_____
Vacation	$_____	$_____
Auto loan payments	$_____	$_____
Credit card payments	$_____	$_____
Other loan payments	$_____	$_____
Other_____	$_____	$_____
Other_____	$_____	$_____
Other_____	$_____	$_____
Other_____	$_____	$_____
Other_____	$_____	$_____
Other_____	$_____	$_____
Total Expenses:	$_____	$_____
NET INFLOW/ (OUTFLOW)	$_____	$_____ **

* In this column, multiply the amount in the monthly column by 12 to derive the annual amount.

** This is the annual amount available in your cash flow for investing.

Moneysaver
If the average
taxpayer reduces
her tax burden
by only a few
percentage
points per year
during a typical
40-year career,
she can increase
her nest egg
by more than
$100,000.
Learn more at
the Web site
www.ntu.org.

Therefore, any tax strategies that you use and deductions that you take will be extremely beneficial for you. Whenever you are making a major financial move in your life, check with a tax adviser regarding the potential tax pitfalls that you may face.

Frequently, investors don't look at all their options when they are faced with a major financial decision. For example, say that you need $10,000 for an emergency and the only asset you have is $15,000 in a 401(k) pension plan. Do you take out $10,000 and incur the tax penalties? Maybe the plan gives you the ability to borrow against your 401(k) plan. Borrowing the money would be a less expensive option than liquidating a portion of your 401(k).

What if you chose to remove that $10,000 from the plan? According to tax laws for the year 2000, the entire $10,000 would be included in taxable income, plus you would pay a 10 percent penalty. If you were in the 28 percent tax bracket, your tax liability from this single transaction would be $3,800 (28 percent of $10,000 = $2,800 plus $1,000, which is the 10 percent tax penalty = total amount of $3,800)! This amount doesn't include other tax penalties and interest potentially triggered because of underwithholding.

Insurance

Insurance is an important component of your finances. Having too little or too much can have an adverse impact on your financial situation. Whether it is life insurance or disability insurance, you should review your insurance needs with a professional adviser.

Too much insurance means that you're paying for coverage you don't need. This is money that you could put to much better use in your investment program. Not enough insurance means that you are lacking coverage in the event of potential problems. What happens when a catastrophe or a medical emergency occurs and you don't have enough insurance to cover the big expenses? What happens when the main earner in your family dies and you have no life insurance? In those cases when there is not enough insurance coverage, you must pay for costs yourself. Frequently, that means liquidating your investments prematurely.

Say that you don't have disability insurance. If you become disabled, you're going to need money for your daily expenses because you won't be able to work. Where will the money come from? If the money is not available from an account such as a savings account or another emergency fund, your disability may mean liquidating investments to cover your living expenses. What if it means selling stock that you purchased as a long-term investment? The disability may force a premature sale of stock, which would mean either a capital loss or a taxable capital gain.

Either scenario isn't good. A capital loss could have been avoided if the stock had been held for long-term growth. If the sale incurred a capital gain, it would then be subject to capital gains tax.

Estate planning

Your estate is the financial assets and liabilities that you leave behind when you die. To calculate your estate, you add up all your assets and determine their value to arrive at the gross estate. From this amount, you calculate what the estate owes, such as loans outstanding, income taxes, and estate settlement costs.

Timesaver
To find informa-
tion on estate
planning and
other legal issues,
visit the following
comprehensive law
library Web sites:
**Internet Legal
Resource Guide**
www.ilrg.com
**Lectric Law
Library**
www.lectlaw.com
LawCrawler
www.lawcrawler.
com

Depending on the size of the estate and what state is the legal authority, you may face estate taxes. Federal estate taxes can be as high as 55 percent.

Estate planning takes into effect strategies for minimizing estate taxes while helping you decide who gets what property you'll leave behind. Among the things you need to consider is a will. This can be a complicated matter, so seek the services of an estate-planning specialist.

Your financial goals

Setting financial goals is something that far too few people do. It has become a cliché that "those that fail to plan, plan to fail." Make goals an integral part of your financial activities.

Set financial goals

What are your financial goals? I realize that you're out to make money by choosing stock investments, but choosing stocks is not enough. Stock investing is not always the right vehicle. You need to ask yourself some hard questions about your financial goals.

Are your goals long-term or short-term? Stock investing is not appropriate for short periods of time such as three, six, or nine months. Even a year is not suggested. Because stocks fluctuate and can be subject to volatility, you could easily lose a chunk of your investment. Stocks are not a place to "park your cash" until you need it for something such as down payment on investment property.

For short-term purposes or emergency needs, consider a vehicle that proves stability and liquidity, such as these:

1. An interest-bearing bank checking account

2. A bank savings account

3. A money market fund

4. A short-term bond fund

5. A Certificate of Deposit

Stocks are not appropriate for an emergency fund. What happens the day you desperately need your money but your funds suddenly shrunk because the market had a bad day?

"Don't use rent money to invest in stocks or other volatile investments." How many times have you heard this admonition? Tempted with the allure of easy riches, people can get careless with their money. People can get desperate to increase their wealth to the point of buying stocks with money allocated to day-to-day living expenses. In recent years, people have lost fortunes in day trading. Many investors have lost 80 percent of their money in Internet stocks. Frequently, this was money that was originally meant to be saved for some other purpose. Please use only money set aside for investment purposes.

Before investing, ask yourself, "Why do I need my money to grow, and when do I want to use it?" In other words, do you want to save for a major purchase, such as a car or a house, in the near future? Or are you saving for a child's college education? Maybe you are setting up a retirement fund. It's important to know the why and when of your investment goal because investing for the short term involves different goals than investing for the long term.

If you've decided to save for a car or a down payment on a house, you'll need to have access to your money in a relatively brief period of time. On the other hand, if you are in your 20s and are saving for retirement, your money does not need to be as readily available; you can afford to take more risk and

Watch Out!
The short term is generally considered one or two years. Because stocks are better for long-term purposes (generally five or more years) they are not suitable for short-term goals. Investors are more apt to lose money in stocks when they try to gain in the short term.

Unofficially ...
Are you bullish
or bearish? Your
view of the mar-
ket will have a
bearing on how
you invest. If
you feel that the
general market
for a particular
entity will see
rising prices,
then you are
"bullish on the
market." If you
feel that the
general market
for a particular
investment will
see declining
prices, you are
"bearish."

invest your money in ways that will allow it to multiply over the long term. When you know your time
frame, keep in mind the following points:

1. How important is growth in your equation?
   Growth is the rate at which your money appreciates during the time it is invested. If you'll
   need access to funds sooner rather than later,
   you might look for an opportunity that provides a fairly safe, steady growth rate.

If your money is being invested over a long
term, you may be comfortable placing your
money in securities that could offer a high
growth rate over a period of time. For example, you might choose to invest in stocks or
bonds. Although the return on these may fluctuate over the course of the investment, this
won't affect your daily needs; what you're concerned about is how the investment performs
over time. Long-term investments that are
influenced by factors such as the inflation rate
may lose money in the short term, but they still
can grow over an extended time frame. What
will matter is not whether your growth rate
slows during a particular period, but whether
you achieve a high growth rate over time.

When thinking about growth over the long
term, keep in mind the role of taxes in that
growth. With long-term investments, your
investment can grow tax-deferred if it is in
an individual retirement account (IRA), a
401(k) plan, a Keogh plan, or another retirement plan. Until you withdraw funds from
these plans, your money is not taxed. Your
plan administrator can provide you with the
details on this.

2. Like growth, yield, which is the interest or dividends paid to you for your investment, can vary in importance depending on your needs. Savings accounts tend to yield small percentages; bonds, on the other hand, can yield higher percentages, but their yield rate is affected by inflation.

   If you are saving for retirement, you may also seek investments that will generate enough yield to let you live off the interest when you do retire. After retirement, you may reinvest some funds into CDs so that you can receive a steady and reliable yield.

3. The third factor to consider is income. If you are investing for a short-term goal, such as a down payment or a car, you need an investment that is safe and can easily be converted into cash. Short-term certificates of deposit are an example of this kind of investment. The regular, periodic income that they generate is of secondary importance.

   However, if you are saving for retirement, your investments will ultimately serve as your source of income once you are retired. Retirement professionals can use strategies and formulas to help you gauge what income you will need to maintain your present lifestyle after retirement. A general rule of practice is that you should plan on needing an income equivalent to 80 to 100 percent of your current gross salary. However, factors such as inflation and how many years you plan to be retired can influence this figure.

Short-term goals

Although we could span the panorama of investments and discuss the pros and cons of each, we will limit our discussion to stocks and cash investments. When we think of the short term, the time frame is usually anywhere from a day to a year. Some consider two years the short term. If you are considering a major purchase or financial move within 12 to 24 months, the best choice for you is investments geared for safety and the highest interest rate available. The selection should be limited to the following:

- **Savings accounts**—Available at your local bank, this traditional vehicle for savings is an acceptable alternative given the limited time frame. This could be either a passbook account or a statement savings account. It is insured by the Federal Deposit Insurance Corporation (FDIC), and the interest rate is generally low. This type of account is best suited as a place to park your cash until you deploy more productive venues such as stocks, real estate, or mutual funds. The minimum amount needed to open a savings account varies depending on the individual bank. The amount can range from $100 to $500.

- **Money market funds**—These are mutual funds that invest in short-term debt securities such as certificates of deposit, short-term money market instruments such as commercial paper and jumbo CDs. Most money market funds offer check-writing privileges. This is the safest category of mutual funds available on the market. When money market interest rates are low, money in these accounts should be there only until a better alternative is found. However, when money market interest rates are high in the marketplace or are rising, money market funds are great places for your money. Those in a high tax bracket also can take advantage of tax-free money market municipal funds. These are money market funds that invest in a portfolio of short-term municipal securities. Money market funds do not guarantee FDIC insurance.

However, because they invest in high-quality debt instruments, coverage by FDIC is usually not needed. Most money market funds require a minimum investment of $1,000 to $2,500.

▪ **Money market accounts**—Many banks have bank savings accounts that pay interest rates comparable to money market funds. These accounts are covered by the FDIC, and the rates fluctuate with market rates. These accounts usually pay a slightly lower rate than money market funds, and service charges may apply if your balance falls below specified levels. A money market account at a local bank is a good consideration for risk-adverse investors.

Long-term goals

The main focus of this book is stocks, and they are the premier investment for long-term investors. However, as discussed in Chapter 1, "Stock Investing Defined," stocks can fall into different categories. Different investors can choose stocks that fit their individual investor profile. This profile can be split into two categories: risk-tolerant and risk-adverse.

Timesaver
Use the "Rule of 72" to judge how long it will take for an investment to double given a fixed rate of return. For example, if you have an investment that grows at 7 percent per year, your investment would double in a little more than 10 years. We get that time frame by dividing the number that represents the rate into 72. In our example, 72 ÷ 7 = 10.3 years.

Bright Idea
Learn more
about mutual
funds by visiting
the top Web
sites for mutual
fund investors.
The main organi-
zation with
information on
mutual funds is
the Investment
Company
Institute, at
www.ici.org. The
Web site www.
morningstar.com
has free profiles
on more than
10,000 mutual
funds.

Risk-adverse investors

Long-term investors that are risk-adverse should consider one of the following two investments:

- **Blue-chip stocks**—Invest in large-capitalization stocks of companies that are industry leaders with a long track record of established growth. Choose 5 to 10 stocks in a cross-section of industries that are integral to our economy, such as food and beverage, utilities, and energy.

- **Common stock mutual funds**—A mutual fund that specializes in established growth stocks is a good consideration for investors who may not have the time or the inclination to manage a portfolio of stocks. Mutual funds offer services such as IRAs, reinvestment options, and the ability to do automatic payments from your checking account to increase your investment for as little as $50 per month.

Risk-tolerant investors

Long-term investors don't mind tolerating extra risk because the greater attraction is the potential for growth. These investors should consider one of the following:

- **Growth stocks**—Invest in stock of companies that exhibit a growth rate that regularly exceeds the rest of the market. Choose 5 to 10 stocks in a cross-section of industries that are on the cutting edge of economic innovation, such as high technology.

- **Growth stock mutual funds**—A mutual fund that specializes in aggressive growth stocks is a good consideration for investors who may not have the time or the inclination to manage a portfolio of stocks. Mutual funds offer services such as IRAs, reinvestment options, and the ability to do automatic payments from your checking account to increase your investment for as little as $50 per month.

Your investing personality

Obviously, everyone is different. Every personality is complex. Your investing personality refers to what type of stock investor you will emulate. For the sake of simplicity, I will break down investors into two personality types: successful and unsuccessful. All of us exhibit behaviors of both, but we need to recognize the basic differences; we can gravitate to being a stock investor that has personality traits that increases the opportunities for wealth-building.

The most successful investors (MSIs) of our time use a rational, well-researched approach that rarely looked exciting to anyone at any given point. MSIs didn't hop in and out of the stock market. They didn't seek out a stock that would double in a week, although occasionally that would happen. They also realized that if they did try to find a stock that would double in a week, they could just as easily see their investment lose 50 percent or more. MSIs looked at a company's value and invested for the long haul. They didn't gamble or speculate. They saw patience as a financial virtue. They also made sure that their financial house was in order. Stock investing was considered a commitment to a financial goal, usually a long-term goal. In this way, the stock portfolio was segregated from other financial concerns. In other words, stocks were not used as a "savings account" to be accessed for a few spare bucks to cover last-minute expenses.

Because I coined the term *MSI* to represent most successful investors, I will use the phrase *USI* for unsuccessful investors. The following clearly delineates the two:

Most successful investors (MSI):

- Choose stocks carefully. They consider many sources for a variety of views and facts regarding the same stock selection.

- Use common sense. Does the company I am considering have products and services that the public wants and needs?

- Use a budget. MSIs look at their total financial picture and allocate their resources accordingly. Money is set aside to pay regular bills, pay off debts, and so on. This prevents the need to cash in stocks prematurely to cover expenses.

- Invest with a long-term approach. MSIs see the long term as beneficial to financial success. Investments need time to grow.

- Reduce or limit transaction costs. MSIs realize that transaction costs cut into financial success. Frequent trading means more commissions and related costs.

- Use tax-reduction strategies. MSIs understand that taxes are part of the equation. Long-term investors usually pay a lower capital gains tax as compared to short-term investors.

We will flesh out other points in later chapters, but these are meant to show that being a successful stock investor involves adopting an approach that is a commitment to success.

Unsuccessful investors (USIs) have typical features as well. Many USIs:

- Choose stocks without research. They hear a great stock tip from a friend or a co-worker. Perhaps they heard a talking head on a financial show mention a favorite pick. Either way, they don't know (or perhaps don't care) about the stock's fundamentals and relevant market facts.

- Show poor money management. USIs do not have funds set aside for bills or unforeseen expenses. They treat their stock portfolios as a savings account. Their thinking is that if they need money, they'll just sell some stock.

- Have a short-term focus. The emphasis is on quick profits and fast growth—jump in and jump out, if necessary. This approach simply makes the broker richer, not the investor.

- Underestimate transaction costs. What profit is made is eroded by commissions and related fees. Short-term trades mean either losses or gains subject to unfavorable capital gains tax treatment.

- Enjoy an occasional success. USIs do make a good choice now and then, but it is usually overwhelmed by bad choices. If they choose a solid stock, this is usually because of luck. The lucky choice is viewed as prowess, which encourages the USI to make more choices, which may ultimately be financially harmful.

What to do before you start investing

Is there a way to increase your rate of return while minimizing risk? Yes. You can do it if you first implement two basic strategies:

1. Make sure that your "financial house" is in order. Aside from your investment assets and

capital available for investing, make sure
that you are financially secure.

Use risk capital only for aggressive or speculative investments. Risk capital is money that you
can afford to lose without affecting your
lifestyle. In other words, you don't use money
that is normally set aside for daily living
expenses or emergencies.

2. Increase your knowledge, experience, and discipline. These three elements will help you to
   tip the scales of risk and return in your favor.
   In any market, those who know what they are
   doing always do better than those who don't.
   This is because the majority simply don't spend
   enough time gaining knowledge, experience,
   and discipline. Far too many investors go on a
   hunch or advice from a friend or newsletter.
   The lure of a quick fortune is tempting; the
   loss of your money is sobering.

   Consider doing "paper trading" before you use
   your hard-earned money. To do this, simply
   make believe that you have invested a sum of
   money in one or more specific investments,
   and track their progress in the financial
   papers. Read the relevant news to see how
   prices react to various stories and reports in
   the media. Calculate your gains and losses.
   This will give you a feel for how markets operate. Tracking investments is easily done by uti-
   lizing *The Wall Street Journal* or the *Investors
   Business Daily.* Each market reported has
   explanatory footnotes so that you can understand the symbols and abbreviations used.

In addition, many Web sites such as www.nyse.com and www.nasdaq.com let you set up an imaginary portfolio that works like paper trading.

Determining your risk tolerance

A variety of techniques and strategies reduce overall risk in your financial situation: reducing debt, avoiding speculative investments, and so on. We can factor out unwarranted risk by looking squarely at the financial data and making reasonable precautions. (In Chapter 12, "Monitoring Your Investments," we will discuss risk-minimizing techniques such as investment allocation and diversification.) In spite of all that, another point about risk is important to emphasize: What is your personal risk tolerance?

To answer this question, you need to consider the "sleep factor." What is the sleep factor? Simply put, you should not be involved in an investment that's causing you to lose sleep.

What do you want to do? Make your own list, and then think about which goals are the most important to you. List your most important goals first. Decide how many years you have to meet each specific goal—when you save or invest, you'll need to find a savings or investment option that fits your time frame for meeting each goal.

What are the things that you want to save and invest for?

- A home (house, condo, or vacation home)
- A car
- An education for yourself or your dependents
- A comfortable retirement
- Seed money for your business
- Medical or other emergencies

> 66
> How foolish you would be to start on a journey without knowing where you wanted to go. Have you ever sat down and seriously drawn up a plan for your life? Have you ever deliberately mapped out where you want to go during your life's journey? Now, isn't your life infinitely more important to you than any journey you may take? Why, therefore, not devote the most earnest effort to plan your life, to set for yourself a goal? We are now at the New Year season. Isn't this a peculiarly appropriate time to look ahead, to indulge in solemn thinking, to formulate life plans, to lay down a definite course to follow?
> —B.C. Forbes
> 99

- Periods of unemployment
- Plans for children
- Care for parents
- Events such as a wedding

Just the facts

- Create your financial statements. Start off with your balance sheet, and make a cash flow statement. Analyze the numbers. Where are you starting from?

- What are your short-term goals? How about long-term goals?

- Understand what you are trying to accomplish. Realize that stock investing is a powerful part of your long-term investment picture.

Doing Your Homework

GET THE SCOOP ON...
What made certain stocks great picks? ▪ Will
they continue to do well? ▪ What lessons can
you take from identifying past winners?
▪ Learning from failures as well as success stories

Analyzing Past Winners

Chapter 4

The history of stock investing is rich with examples of great stocks, mediocre stocks, and bad stocks. History is a great teacher, and because stocks are constantly analyzed, monitored, and recorded, there's no shortage of information to review. We can easily identify the characteristics of stocks that have been big winners in the past and apply that information to today's stock selections. Bear in mind that a company doesn't have to possess all these winning characteristics—it would be difficult to find such a company. (If you do, buy all the stock you can afford!) The goal is to find a solid company with one or more of these winning characteristics.

What makes certain stocks great picks?

It's easy to recognize a successful stock once it's become successful, but it's very difficult for the investing public to recognize a successful stock before it starts to bloom. Usually this is because, in the beginning, a good stock is lost in the crowd. It

Bright Idea
Benjamin Graham
is considered the
dean of value
investing. He has
written two
books that are
considered clas-
sics: *Security
Analysis* and *The
Intelligent
Investor.* Many
investors,
including Warren
Buffett, have
gained knowl-
edge from his
investing insight.

takes on the characteristic of a winning stock only as
its success begins to differentiate it.

The process of choosing a winning stock is similar to the process of picking a winning horse at the
track. When 15 thoroughbreds leave the starting
gate, the winner and the losers are all neck-and-
neck, and the choice for bettors is a toss-up. Like
horse racing, choosing carefully greatly diminishes
your risk in the stock market. The data and research
are there for you to review, like the racing history,
odds, and breeding information of a horse.

But as the horse race continues, the winner starts
to break from the pack. At this point, it's too late for
bettors to change their bets; they have to watch as
their horses win or lose. Fortunately, stock investing
is different. You can invest at any time during the
life of the stock: as soon as the stock begins its trading life or when it reveals itself as a clear winner.
Your risk is measurable. You can invest sooner than
the crowd and take on greater risk, and possibly
make greater profits, or you can wait and accept lesser profit but expose yourself to less risk.

Fortunately, stock investing is different in the following way: Choosing carefully greatly diminishes
your risk. The data and research are there for you to
review. You can invest at any time during the life of
the stock—as soon as the stock begins its trading life
or when it reveals itself as a clear winner. Your risk is
measurable. You can invest sooner than the crowd
and take on greater risk and possibly make greater
profits, or you can wait and accept lesser profit but
expose yourself to less risk.

Looking at past stock market success stories, we
can identify characteristics that appear over and
over again. When you are researching stocks, keep
this list handy.

Characteristic 1: The company has a product or service that the public wants or needs

Whether a company is a large, public enterprise or a one-person, private entity, successful companies have similar traits. Does the company offer something of value that is not readily matched by competing companies? Is there uniqueness that delivers value to customers? Does the product or service generate excitement with customers as measured by growing sales?

You can't have a great stock unless you have a great company. You can't have a great company unless you please customers with value. This point makes it easier to select a stock because we are all customers who buy products and services from a variety of companies. The famed stock-picker Peter Lynch regularly invests in companies whose products and services he is personally familiar with. The reasoning goes that if you buy what the company offers and you are satisfied and then see that others are buying and are pleased, this is a company whose stock is worthy of further consideration as an investment.

Too many investors believe that picking stocks is a task best suited to the skills of Wall Street professional stock analysts. This is simply not true. Analyzing a company's stock requires common sense every bit as much as "crunching the numbers." Common sense and the company's numbers work together.

Coca-Cola has been a powerful stock for decades. It established strong brand name recognition that became difficult to compete with. Consumers enjoyed the taste, and they responded overwhelmingly. The Coca-Cola company had more than 70 percent of the market share while its main competitor, Pepsi Cola, was a distant second. Coca-Cola dominated the U.S. and international markets. It got to a point that restaurants and stores had to have the company's beverages as an offering to their customers or miss out on profits. Because of this, Coca-Cola has been a market leader since the 1960s.

Yes, there were (and are) alternatives. Many companies offered colas, but they couldn't replace Coca-Cola because it became a strong, differentiated brand. Coca-Cola's stock grew consistently through the 1980s and 1990s.

Characteristic 2: The company establishes a market presence with high barriers to entry by competitors
Microsoft is certainly one of the great stocks of the late twentieth century. Anyone investing in Microsoft when it emerged in 1986 would have experienced extraordinary returns on his investment. Several hundred shares bought at any point in the late 1980s and held for the long haul would have become a million-dollar investment. Investment newsletters and stock research services rehash the numbers constantly. Had you bought Microsoft in 1990, every $1 of your investment would have become $120 by February 2000.

Microsoft succeeded in the marketplace because the computer operating system that Bill Gates and his colleagues designed became an accepted standard in the computer industry. The Microsoft Disk Operating System (MS-DOS) was soon included in the vast majority of personal computers that consumers purchased. It beat out IBM's disk operating system (PC-DOS) and Apple's operating system as they competed for market dominance. Individuals and businesses accepted Microsoft's version overwhelmingly. Computer manufacturers sold millions of computers with MS-DOS already installed. This dominance set the stage for massive growth for the wide array of software products that Microsoft developed.

Investors saw Microsoft's dominance with MS-DOS as a foundation for further profits. Once Microsoft attained this leadership position in the software industry, other software companies had to accept Microsoft as a "gatekeeper." In other words, to gain access to customers, they had to design their software to work in Microsoft's operating system. Microsoft, however, was not content with simply charging fees to software companies as it worked to create products that interacted with MS-DOS.

Microsoft put its marketing clout and technical expertise into developing a multitude of products and services that sprung from the operating system. To compete with Apple's more graphical user interface, Microsoft created Windows. Windows became a graphical, feature-rich software program that made computing more user-friendly and more accessible to customers. Windows became the market's dominant choice over Apple's Macintosh interface mostly because Windows operated in conjunction with MS-DOS.

Microsoft went on to create more products that the marketplace embraced. Microsoft Excel is a spreadsheet program that leap-frogged over the then-market leader Lotus Development Corporation. Microsoft Word became the premier word processing software program, beating out previously dominant word processing software from WordPerfect and other competitors. Even if those competitors succeeded with their software products, they still had to work with Microsoft to comply with the operating systems that Microsoft controlled.

Watch Out!
Don't invest in a
company just
because it has a
highly marketed,
flashy Web site.
Instead, seek a
strong company
with established
sales and
earnings that is
launching a Web
presence.

Investors were rewarded with tremendous growth in Microsoft's stock price. In the 10-year period starting in 1990, the rate on investment for Microsoft investors exceeded 11,900 percent! The point bears repeating: Before the stock market embraces a stock, the company must first succeed with its products and services. Success as a company should always precede success for the stock.

Having a "high barrier to entry" is a critical competitive advantage. As investors poured their money into Internet stocks such as eBay, Yahoo!, and Amazon.com, they didn't realize that these stocks have a low barrier to entry. The barrier to entry point is embodied in this question: Can competitors get into that type of business easily?

Becoming an Internet company has few barriers to entry. Virtually any company that has a Web site address, computer equipment, and a minimal amount of working capital can get up and running as a dotcom. Literally millions of commercial Web sites have been launched worldwide from 1996 to 2000. eBay, a public auction Web site, is a good example of a business that can garner many competitors. eBay spawned many copycats. In 1999, more than 400 major public auction Web sites were launched. These competitors may not displace eBay's leadership position in the category of Internet auctions, but they have cut into eBay's share of the marketplace and reduced subsequent earnings. The increased competition will obviously diminish eBay's ability to grow at the same pace as it did during 1998–1999. The only way for eBay to continue to grow at its original growth rate is to either outdo its competitors or find new ways to generate profit. When choosing a stock, ask yourself whether it's easy or difficult for competitors to enter the industry.

On the other hand, the automotive and the utilities industries have a high barrier to entry. Both industries require intensive capital investment in plants and equipment as well as technological expertise. Resources are also necessary for ongoing marketing campaigns, labor costs, and so on.

What keeps these companies from being outstanding stocks is other considerations such as political and regulatory constraints. The automotive industry has high operating costs domestically and still must compete with companies from Europe and Japan.

Traditionally, utilities have been regulated monopolies. In this case, a utility is restrained from aggressive pricing by governmental watchdog agencies. Although utilities didn't offer much growth because of geographic and regulatory restraints, they were considered very safe investments for many years because they were defensive stocks (everyone needs electricity) and provided a large dividend income to shareholders. Utilities were considered "safe for widows and orphans."

This is changing as we have entered a period of gradual deregulation. Deregulation and the Internet are transforming the once-stodgy utilities industry into a more competitive and dynamic segment of our economy. Utilities such as Enron, for example, are providing more services for the Internet, such as more bandwidth (essentially greater capacity to carry more data and information services via our telecommunications infrastructure). These developments may carry greater risk

"
Buy low, sell
high.
—Unknown
Buy high, sell
higher.
—William O'Neill
"

for widows and orphans but will provide for more growth for our economy.

Characteristic 3: The company sells essential products and services to a megatrend

A megatrend is a major, established movement in society that will ultimately require goods and services to meet its wants and needs. A good example of a megatrend is the "Aging of America." The Internet is another acknowledged megatrend—no one refutes this. The Internet will touch all aspects of our lives as more people and organizations access its capabilities to disseminate information, make economic transactions, and so on. In Chapter 2, "The Stock Market Environment: Where Stocks Are Bought and Sold," we likened the Internet to the California Gold Rush. Those who made a lot of money in the Gold Rush were not those seeking gold—instead, those who sold the means to find the gold (the picks and shovels) got rich. What megatrends can you identify? What products and services will be needed? What companies will benefit from serving this megatrend, and can you buy their stock?

The Internet, during 1995–2000, was no different. Thousands of dotcom firms fell over each other to sell millions of products and services to the public. Internet commerce skyrocketed during those years, and the torrid pace continued into 2000. Yet, most of the Internet companies either made very little money or lost money. In spite of this, investors flocked to Internet companies. As one example, Drkoop.com (a health products Web site) saw its stock soar to $45 a share as it went public during 1999. By May 2000, however, DrKoop.com's stock fell to $1 per share. Another example, the Web site Ivillage.com, went public in 1999 offering information and products only for women. The company generated losses of $21 million in 1997 and $43 million in 1998. Although it racked up a loss of $93 million in 1999, however, its stock still shot up to a high of 67 that year. With expectations of losses in 2000, Ivillage.com's stock price fell to $6^3/_4$ by May 2000. The Web site could not excite investors and could not generate enough traffic to be profitable.

However, the companies that made consistent profits were ones that serviced those money-losing dotcom companies. Technology companies such as Dell Computers and Qualcomm serviced the Internet and those that wanted to connect to its power, and made a lot of money as individual Internet companies faltered.

Cisco Systems became the premier Internet company of the 1990s. The company's main business is manufacturing the hardware that makes the Internet operate. If you had invested $1,000 in Cisco when it went public in 1990, your investment would have surpassed $1 million by February 2000. It is acknowledged as a phenomenal success story because of its ability to generate profits in a competitive industry. Cisco didn't make money as a dotcom entity; it became dominant by selling the "picks and shovels" to the Internet industry.

The lesson for investors is to be aware of the world around you and see what major trends are strongly in place. The Internet is certainly a megatrend. Profitable companies that help businesses and consumers take advantage of the Internet merit our attention.

Another megatrend in place in our society is the "graying of America." The statistics are clear: There are more Americans over the age of 50 now than at

any other point in our history. Soon, we will have
more retirement-age men and women than ever
before. A record number of people will live past 100.
Companies that offer products and services to this
burgeoning market will do very well. As long as
investors choose stocks that have strong fundamentals in industries that are well-positioned to meet the
wants and needs of this growing market, they will
succeed.

Some industries that will do well with the aging
of America are financial services, pharmaceuticals,
and medical services. Clearly, common sense plays a
major role in selecting investments. Analyze the
megatrend and figure out what it will want or need.
Once you do that, find the leading companies that
provide products and services to meet these wants
and needs profitably.

Characteristic 4: The company is in strong financial condition

You can't avoid the fact that strong earnings, growing sales, and low debt are hallmarks of most successful companies. The strong financial condition
allows the company many options:

1. Many great companies with exciting products
    became history because of money problems
    that hurt them during slow periods. How many
    great ideas couldn't get off the ground because
    the company lacked financial backing (in good
    times, too)? Having low debt or extra cash in
    the form of bank accounts or saleable assets is
    a cushion during slow periods. Good credit is
    important, and it also has a direct effect on a
    company's earnings by lowering borrowing
    costs.

2. A strong financial position gives a company the ability purchase income-producing assets such as another company or a facility in a new market. Pepsi-Cola needed more outlets for its soda products, so during the 1980s and 1990s, the company bought franchises such as Kentucky Fried Chicken and Taco Bell. In addition to selling more soda through these new venues, the franchises were profitable enterprises in and of themselves.

3. A strong financial position gives a company the ability to reduce costs. In the early 1990s, the company TRW noticed that it was spending too much on printing. So it purchased printing facilities and did the printing in-house. The company's strong financial position helped it acquire an asset that cut costs, which increased its earnings. The printing division did so well that it became a profit center when TRW sold printing services to its customers.

4. A strong financial position can help launch new products and services. Minnesota Mining & Manufacturing (3M) is known for its ability to develop and launch new products, such as Scotchguard and Post-it notes. It has the clout to create and test the products, establish a distribution system, and finance the subsequent marketing campaign.

Characteristic 5: The company has excellent managerial leadership

Managerial excellence can best be measured through the financial output of the company. Many people feel that success means leadership that is charismatic or stands out in the crowd by some

Bright Idea
Use the Internet to get financial information on a company. Company Sleuth, at www.companysleuth.com, provides some excellent information on public companies.

❝

Stocks are simple. All you do is buy shares in a great business for less than the business is intrinsically worth, with managers of highest integrity and ability. Then you own those shares forever.

—Warren Buffett

❞

other barometer. When people think of managerial excellence, they may think of legendary corporate types such as Lee Iacocca or Jack Welsh.

But does charismatic leadership mean business success? Maybe, maybe not. From a stock investor's point of view, the reverse is more true: Business success means managerial excellence. Investors must determine how effectively the company's leadership is managing its resources. This is done by looking at financial measurements such as the return on equity and other ratios. (Chapter 7, "Value Investing," looks more closely at these internal factors.)

Characteristic 6: The company regularly introduces new products to the market successfully

This characteristic is true in industries that require research and development, such as technology, biotech, software, consumer goods, aerospace, medical products, and pharmaceuticals. Good companies are continuously looking at their customers' wants and needs, their competitors' products, and the marketplace to find more opportunities to sell more of what they offer. Good companies are also introspective: They look at their own products and constantly seek improvement.

Microsoft is an example of such a company. When the Windows program first hit the market, Microsoft sold millions of units. Windows 3.0 was hugely successful. Then there was Windows 3.1, followed by Windows 95, which was improved upon by Windows 98 and now Windows 2000. Microsoft developed programs that worked seamlessly with Windows, such as Excel, a spreadsheet program, and Word, a word-processing program. Resting on past success can mean fading into obscurity as competitors outdo you with their innovative products.

Characteristic 7: The company is a dominant player in a "sunrise" industry

A "sunrise" industry is a new or emerging industry that will be a strong and growing component of the economy. This is opposed to a "sunset" industry, an industry that either no longer grows or is in decline.

During the 1980–2000 period, our society witnessed a major shift in how our economy operates. New products, services, markets, and entire new industries have been introduced into our general economy and have revolutionized the way business is performed. This transformation created the struggle between the Old Economy—embodied by manufacturing and standard goods and services—and the "New Economy"—embodied by the Internet and new technological innovations. Sometimes success is simply doing something better than what people have gotten used to. People always used the Postal Service and United Parcel Service to ship packages. Yet an obscure company launched a new service in this established industry that caught on. Today Federal Express is certainly a successful billion-dollar business, yet most investors had not heard of it in the late 1970s when the company was in its infancy. The concept of "overnight" package delivery service took hold in the early 1980s and became a widely accepted business practice by the end of the 1980s.

A strong company doesn't necessarily need to have all seven of these characteristics to be worthy of your consideration. Indeed, it could do well with just one of them. But the more of these characteristics it has, the more profitable it will be as an investment over the long haul.

Timesaver
Here's a research shortcut to finding stocks in a particular industry. Consider reviewing the portfolios of sector funds. A sector fund is a mutual fund that limits itself to a particular industry or sector.

Unofficially ...
Increase your chances of success with your stock selection by sticking to industries that are growing at a faster rate than the market average. *Standard & Poor's Industry Survey* ranks the major industries and compares them with the general economy. Review the publication at the local library, or visit the Web site www. standardpoor. com.

Will the company continue to do well?

How do we know whether a company will continue to do well? We can only judge from the current data and from economic and market trends. We need to continue monitoring the stock, the company, the industry, and the general economy. We can track some of the things happening to the company directly and to the environment that it operates in.

Is the company continuing to improve financially?

Are key numbers in the company's financial position stronger than the year before? Are the following numbers significantly better than the year before?

1. Are sales increasing? (That means growing 10 percent or better than the prior year or, in the worst-case scenario, being equal to or greater than the rate of inflation.)

2. Are earnings growing? (Are they growing at a rate equal to or better than the sales rate? In other words, if sales are growing 12 percent per year, are earnings growing at least 12 percent per year?)

3. Are net assets growing? (Are they growing by at least 10 percent compared to the year before?)

4. Is total debt shrinking or low relative to assets? Is total debt as a percentage of total assets equal to or less than the year before? (If last year total debt amounted to 40 percent of total assets, is it still that percentage or less?) A greater treatment of company finances can be found in Chapter 7, "Value Investing."

Do the company's products/services continue to be noticed in trade magazines, trade associations, and/or the mass media?

You want to know whether a company's products and services are still being well-received in the marketplace. If the company is a software firm that creates and markets specialized software to small businesses, what do small business publications and associations say about the product? If the company or its offerings get good reviews from the very people and organizations that actually use the products, the company will continue to do well.

To find industry and trade associations, go to your library's reference section and check the *Encyclopedia of Associations*. To find trade publications and journals, check the *Gale Directory of Publications and Broadcast Media,* also in your library's reference section. Both publications are published by Gale Research.

Is Wall Street regularly following your choice?

As you chose a company using value-oriented analysis, sooner or later, others will notice your company as it continues to do well. This attention bodes well for your investment. As more brokerages, analysts, and financial show pundits turn to your company, more individuals and organizations will be buying your company's stock for their portfolios.

Are institutions showing interest in your stock?

Institutional sales are purchased by organizations such as mutual funds and pension plans. When a stock is noticed by the market, more institutional investors tend to purchase it. This is a very good sign that the stock is gaining acceptance. Because institutional investors are the biggest investors in

Unofficially ...
A *growth stock* maintains consistently faster growth of sales and earnings than the market (or industry) as a whole. Growth stocks tend to have higher P/E ratios than the overall stock market because investors expect more from them and are willing to pay more for reliable growth.

the market, their interest in a given stock will give a big boost to the stock price. Conversely, if a major mutual fund were to sell all their holdings in a particular stock, that single transaction would move the stock's price all by itself.

What percentage of stock purchases were made by institutions such as mutual funds and pensions? What was the percentage of sales from the most recent date available, and what was the percentage from one year ago? If the current percentage is equal to or greater than that of a year ago, this indicates that interest by money managers in the stock is high and still growing.

Conversely, if institutional interest is declining and purchases by small investors is increasing, this may indicate the stock has reached its peak. Typically, small investors tend to be the last ones to latch on to rising stocks. Institutional investors have a term for small investors: They call us "odd-lotters" because we tend to buy stocks in odd lots, 12 shares of Microsoft. 25 shares of GE, as opposed to the square lots of 1,000, or 10,000 or 100,000 that big investors purchase. Some large investors purposefully watch trading screens for hints of "odd-lotter" activity, and sell their stock when it hits a certain level.

But not all stocks react negatively to a surge of interest by small investors. For example, institutions normally don't look at micro-cap or penny stocks; they will look at companies that have achieved a strong record of performance. To check for institutional investor activity, you can check some sources on a regular basis either at the library or on the Internet, such as "Market Guide" and "Standard & Poor's."

What lessons can you learn from identifying past winners?

When analyzing past winners, you come across the time-tested approaches and formulas that could be applied to the task of picking the next winning stocks.

In recent years, two debates raged across the investment spectrum: "value versus growth" and "fundamental analysis versus technical analysis." The debates over which methods work are important to review so that you can learn from their application.

Value versus growth

We all seek a growing investment, but what do you look at first? What methods worked most consistently in the past that we can use to choose tomorrow's winners today? Do you choose a company that is value-oriented hoping that it will grow, or do you choose companies that already exhibit growth characteristics with only secondary emphasis on value? Judging from the performance of thousands of companies in a variety of industries over many years, the answer tends to be a combination of both value and growth. This will vary from industry to industry. For example, you may have two companies with similar financial conditions but with stock prices that act very differently because one is in a growth industry (such as biotechnology) and the other is in a stable industry (such as an electric utility).

It is important to point out that for long-term investors, a value-oriented approach in sunrise industries has been a consistent winning method in the past.

Unofficially ...
A *value stock* is considered "undervalued" by the stock market. On the most basic level, value stocks can be identified by analyzing the financial statements and looking at some key financial relationships or ratios. Does the stock have a reasonable price compared to the company's earnings (the price-to-earnings [P/E] ratio)? Is the market value of the company's stock anywhere near the book value of the company's net assets?

Fundamental analysis

Value investors generally use fundamental analysis when considering a stock investment. Analyzing a stock's fundamentals means looking at the inherent financial soundness of a company and its business plan. Fundamentals cover all the factors about a specific business that an investor might use in deciding whether to invest. These include its profitability, the strength of its balance sheet, the ability and experience of its management, the prospects of its industry, and so forth. Fundamental analysis need not be complicated; basic ratios such as price/earnings, debt/equity, and the quick ratio can be easily derived from a company's financial reports and are especially revealing when compared to the same figures for other firms in the same industry.

Fundamental investors also tend to seek firms whose management owns a significant stake, firms in businesses that others can't easily enter, firms in businesses that aren't heavily regulated, and firms in businesses that are easily understood and not continually roiled by technological change.

This approach sets fundamental analysts apart from technical analysts, who study previous trading patterns to forecast which direction (up or down) a stock or the market itself will head in the future.

Technical analysis

Technical analysis is the practice of trying to divine stock prices by examining trading patterns and comparing the shape of current charts to those from the past.

A cornerstone of technical analysis is Dow Theory, which states that in a true bull or bear trend, both the Dow Jones Industrial and the Dow Jones Transportation averages must be moving in

Timesaver
To find out how well great investors do, get the newsletter *Hulbert Financial Digest*. The editor, Mark Hulbert, has tracked the performances of investment newsletters for many years. *Hulbert Financial Digest* does the work for you—check out its Web site at www.hulbertdigest.com.

w Theory adher-
es higher than a
t goes below the

\f complex chart-
ost basic involve
k over time on a
rt is supposed to
ie stock is headed
lers pattern, for
; has topped out.
at have broken
n the upside). A
support level (on
d for further loss-
es. Critics deride technical analysis as only hocus-
pocus, not far removed from tealeaf reading.
Advocates insist that the stock market clearly moves
in broad patterns and that these can be recognized
by careful charting and a knowledge of history.
Whether or not technical analysis has any validity, it
has a good many adherents and, on that basis alone,
influences stock prices.

An important facet of technical analysis is assist-
ing investors in the art of "momentum investing."
Momentum investors look to buy stocks with rising
stock price and earnings momentum superior to
stocks in the general market. Publications such as
"Investors Business Daily" are proponents of this
approach.

Learning from failures as well as success stories

Learning from the past is more than knowing what
to do. It's also learning what not to do. Many

Watch Out!
Don't rely solely
on technical
analysis. The
past chart pat-
terns of a stock
can give you a
nice picture of
how well the
stock has done,
but they are
rarely a reliable
indicator of
future perfor-
mance. No mat-
ter what, you
should still look
at the company's
fundamentals.

Moneysaver
There's a big dif-
ference between
a cheap stock
and a bargain
stock. Cheap
means low in
price. Bargain
means that the
company has
value that
exceeds its stock
price; the stock
is "underpriced."

investors do things that ultimately cost them a lot of
money. You need to know what situations to avoid:

1. **Buying a stock when it's falling in price**—The
   strategy is that you can buy the stock at a cheap
   price and make money when it rebounds. All
   too often, however, investors just watch their
   investment continue to drop in value or sit
   there and do nothing. There is always a reason
   why a stock drops in price. Perhaps the company is losing money or is being hit with a lawsuit. Before you invest, find out why the stock
   price is falling. Frequently, it can be a great
   opportunity to buy, but as we have written
   before, the fundamentals are important. (We
   will cover financial analysis in Chapter 7,
   "Value Investing.") The bottom line: Don't buy
   a stock just because it's cheap.

2. **Using inadequate stock selection criteria**—
   Beginning investors don't know what to look
   for when purchasing a stock and often end up
   buying lackluster or poorly performing companies. "Adequate" stock selection criteria means
   doing the work: reading the company's annual
   report, analysts' published views, SEC reports,
   and so on. "Inadequate" selection means taking shortcuts by investing based on rumors or
   tips or just being lazy about doing research.
   "Adequate" means looking at multiple sources
   to verify the information about the company
   and its operations, prospects, and so on.
   "Inadequate" means stopping at just one
   source and making a hasty judgment.

3. **Buying companies because they have a familiar
   name or product**—Many of the best investments will be newer names that you may not

know very well but that you could and should know by doing a little studying and research.

4. **Acting on poor advice**—Most investors don't do their homework on a stock. Finding good information from a variety of sources is your first priority in today's market. Educate yourself; don't act impulsively on other peoples' opinions. Most rumors are false, and even if a tip is correct, the stock ironically will go down in price, in many cases. Why is that? If the rumor is positive, holders of the stock may see this as a selling opportunity and dump their holdings in the market. If buyers don't materialize, the stock price declines.

5. **Being afraid to buy a stock because it already went up significantly**—Investors may fear that they missed out on profits and feel that the current price is too high. If the company has strong fundamentals and is in a strong industry, buying it even at a higher price should not be a reason to avoid investing. It is better to overpay 10 percent on a winning stock than to buy a losing stock even at a 50 percent discount. Don't let fear dictate your investing.

6. **Stubbornly holding on to small losses when you could get out cheaply and move into a better performing stock**—Again, don't let your feelings run your portfolio. Frequently, investors may buy a stock that falters and stays in a narrow trading range. Perhaps they bought a stock at $50 per share and the stock fell to $47 and stayed in the range of $46 to $49 for a year (or longer). If the company is not providing a good dividend and offers no new activity (new products, deals, and so on),

it may be stagnant. If you don't sell and take a small loss, other investors will. You may end up holding on to a loser.

7. **Cashing in too soon**—If you see that you can nail down a good profit by cashing in your stock, there's nothing wrong with that. However, most investors cash in too soon. You should only cash in for one of two reasons: Either you need the money or the stock is no longer doing well. Obviously if you need the money, then cash in. Of course, if you cash in your stock because you need the money, that means that you didn't allocate funds for emergency needs (see Chapter 3, "Preparing to Invest in Great Stocks"). How do you know if the stock is no longer performing well? A good rule is to ask yourself whether the reasons you bought the stock in the first place have changed. If they haven't, and the company is still strong and the stock still a good value, don't sell.

   The best way is simply to protect yourself with a trailing stop to take the guesswork out of selling. Additionally, cashing in too soon may have tax consequences. Generally, long-term capital gains have a lower tax than short-term capital gains.

8. **Being diverted by ancillary concerns**—Taxes and commissions are certainly part of your investment picture. However, don't let them totally dictate your investment goals. Your no. 1 goal is making a profit. When you have made your money, you can then decide to realize your gains and deal with the taxes and transaction costs. Say that you buy a stock at $50 per

share and it goes to $100. Perhaps the company's financial situation has deteriorated and the news about the company's prospects are unfavorable. You refuse to sell your stock or even put in a stop loss order to protect your investment. Your reasoning is that selling the stock would mean paying capital gains tax. To avoid paying the tax, you watch your stock fall, wiping out most (or all) of your gain. In this case, it's better to take a gain and pay the tax then to avoid tax and watch gains evaporate.

9. **Seeking stocks for a quick profit**—Investors forget that they are investors and instead seek to speculate for short-term profits. This backfires more often than not. Seek big profits for the long term.

10. **"Buying on the dips"**—In a volatile market, investors see sudden drops in stock prices as a buying opportunity. If it is a stock that you were considering buying anyway, that's fine. If you see it as an opportunity to cash in quickly when the market rebounds, you are really gambling instead of investing.

11. **Using stock orders improperly**—Understand not only why you invest but also how to actually go about doing it. Some investors put price limits on buy and sell orders. This procedure can backfire because the investor is trying to save a little money rather than seizing the more important objective. If the stock is a great buy and the price is at 41½, some will put in an order at 41, hoping to save the half-point. The risk is that the stock could go to 42 or more, leaving your order behind. Your

Moneysaver
If you are unable to make up your mind about what stock to buy, consider parking your cash in a money market fund until you decide. Time after time, investors have lost money because they didn't do their homework and invested impulsively for many reasons except the right ones.

attempt to save money would result in losing even more money if you end up buying it later at a higher price.

12. **Investing emotionally versus objectively**—The main emotions are fear and greed, and both have ruled people and money for an eternity. Become disciplined and educated. Sell when emotions rule others. In other words, if the world is irrationally exuberant and buying up stocks, that may be a good time to sell. And if the world seems grim and everyone is selling their stock, that may be a good time to buy.

13. **Buying for the wrong reasons**—As we have written before, buying stocks for a short-term purpose is usually not a good idea. Investors often are influenced by things that are not really crucial, such as stock splits, increased dividends, and recommendations from brokerage firms.

What about the industry?

We have used the phrase "sunrise industry." It is always easier to pick a winning stock when its industry is also growing. Learning about the industry is another important step in the stock investment business research process. Some questions to consider include these:

- What are the industry trends and areas of growth?
- Who are the leading companies in the industry?
- What products and services are in the greatest demand?
- What new technologies are impacting the industry?

Analyzing an industry is easier than analyzing a company. If you are in an industry that is growing, your stock's prospects for growth are also enhanced. Some analysts would tell you that they would rather invest in an average stock in an above-average industry than an above-average stock in an average or below-average industry. Your chances for choosing a great stock are greatly enhanced when you choose one with solid fundamentals and in a growing industry.

It is an important point that it's easier to judge the success of an industry than it is to judge the success of an individual stock.

Some industry information resources you can turn to are listed here:

■ **Hoover's Industry Group Snapshots, www.hoovers.com**—Hoover's provide an overview of a variety of major industries with links to relevant sites in each area. Visit Hoover's Sector Analyses for detailed overviews and news articles on 28 sectors.

■ **Yahoo! Industry News, www.industry.yahoo.com**—Check industry press releases and current news. Corporate Information offers links to industry resources in more than 65 sectors.

■ **Dow Jones Business Directory, www.business.dowjones.com**—Dow Jones reviews major industry Web sites, including leading company home pages, industry associations, and reference and news sites.

■ **Fuld & Company, www.fuld.com**—Fuld & Company offers information and links to key sites in 27 industries.

Just the facts

- A value-oriented approach to stock investing has worked consistently well through good and bad markets.

- Study past winners in the marketplace. What made them successful?

- Learn as much as possible about the financial condition of the company you are considering.

- Find out what differentiates your choice from other stocks. What is its competitive advantage?

GET THE SCOOP ON...
Investor associations and investment clubs
■ Library resources: books and periodicals ■ The
Internet, TV, and radio ■ Financial advisers:
judging the views of analysts

Finding the Information

Quality information is your number-one tool in analyzing stocks. But no matter how good a source of information is, it's a good idea for you to look at more than one. When people are too quick to accept a tip from a TV financial show or broker, or a rumor at work, they can get burned. It's important to devote your time and effort to the task of investing.

The resources in this chapter are either free or at a low cost. Although more resources are available in Appendix B, "Investing Information Resources," those mentioned here should be the first ones you turn to before investing any money.

Investment associations

Associations pride themselves on being a concentration of knowledge on a given topic. The following associations (and others mentioned in the book) provide a solid learning environment for beginning and intermediate stock investors. They provide a

Bright Idea
Don't stop at one resource. No matter how good a publication, book, or Web site is, you need to look at as many sources as possible. Sometimes a stock hailed as a great buy at Web site A is given a negative rating at Web site B and a horrible review by publication C. Get many different points of view before you make a decision.

wealth of information on common stocks and related investments (such as mutual funds).

American Association of Individual Investors (AAII)
625 North Michigan Ave.
Chicago, IL 60611-3110
Phone: 312-280-0170
Web site: www.aaii.org/

AAII believes that individuals will do better if they invest in stocks that are not followed by institutional investors and avoid the effects of program trading. The association admits that most of its members are experienced investors with substantial amounts to invest, but it also has programs for newer investors. The AAII doesn't manage members' money—it just provides information.

Membership costs $49 per year for an individual; with the *Computerized Investing* newsletter, membership costs $79. A lifetime membership (including *Computerized Investing*) costs $490.

The AAII offers the *AAII Journal* 10 times a year and the *Individual Investor's Guide to No-Load Mutual Funds* annually. Also included is a local chapter membership (about 50 chapters exist), a year-end tax strategy guide, investment seminars and study programs at extra cost (reduced for members), and a computer user's newsletter for an extra $30.

The Investors Alliance, Inc.
219 Commercial Blvd.
Fort Lauderdale, FL 33308-4440
Phone: 888-683-1181
Web site: http://PowerInvestor.com

Investors Alliance was formed to enhance the investing skills of independent investors through research, education, and training. The organization claims membership of more than 65,000 investors in 22 countries.

Basic membership is offered at $49 per year and includes 12 monthly issues of the *Investors Alliance Investor Journal,* an educational newsletter packed with valuable information.

Computer membership is offered at $89 per year and includes a copy of *Power Investor for Windows* on CD-ROM and free daily modem updates of 16,000 securities in their database. New members at either level receive a free voucher for two zero-commission stock trades from a leading discount broker.

Investment clubs

Investment clubs offer investors the ability to learn about stock investing while actually doing it. This is very valuable experience. You invest and learn in a group environment with other investors. Stock selections are discussed and debated.

The National Association of Investors Corp. (NAIC), is a nonprofit organization operated by and for member clubs. The association has been in existence since the 1950s and states that it has more than 633,000 members. Membership costs $39 per year for an individual, or $35 for a club and $14 per each club member. The membership provides the member with a monthly magazine, details of membership, and information on how to start a investment club, how to analyze stocks, and how to keep records.

The NAIC also offers software for fundamental analysis, discounts on investing books, research information on member companies, and other educational manuals and videotapes. A network of more than 75 Regional Councils across the United States provides local assistance.

In addition to the information provided, NAIC operates a "Low-Cost Investment Plan." This program allows members to invest without a broker in participating companies such as AT&T, Kellogg's, Wendy's, Exxon, Mobil, and Quaker Oats. This also sometimes is known as a dividend reinvestment plan. Most company plans don't incur a commission, although some charge a nominal fee ($3–$5).

Of the 500 clubs surveyed in 1989, the average club had a compound annual growth rate of 10.8 percent, compared with 10.6 percent for the S&P 500 stock index. Its average portfolio was worth $66,755.

Contact the NAIC via these channels:

National Association of Investors Corp. (NAIC)
P.O. Box 220
Royal Oak, MI 48068
Phone: 810-583-6242
Fax: 810-583-4880
E-mail: service@better-investing.org
Web site: www.better-investing.org

Library resources

Many libraries carry one or more of the following resources in their reference or periodical section. Look at as many as possible, especially the Standard & Poor's materials.

American Stock Exchange Guide (directory)
Publisher: CCH Incorporated
Phone: 1-800-853-5224, 847-267-7000
Fax: 1-800-224-8299
Comments: Provides a directory, constitution, and rules of the AMEX. Published for the AMEX.
Issue frequency: Monthly
Subscription price: Individual $377

American Stock Exchange Reports (loose-leaf)
Publisher: Standard & Poor's Corp.
Phone: 1-800-208-1161, 212-208-8000
Fax: 212-208-1161
Comments: Details financial reports on all ASE-listed companies.
Issue frequency: Weekly
Subscription price: Individual $1,325

American Stock Exchange Weekly Bulletin (newsletter)
Publisher: American Stock Exchange
Phone: 212-306-1441
Fax: 212-306-2160
Comments: Provides news of membership changes, listings, dividends, meetings, and so on.
Issue frequency: Weekly
Subscription price: Individual $20; corporate $20

Annual Dividend Record (directory)
Publisher: Standard & Poor's Corp.
Phone: 1-800-208-1161, 212-208-8000
Fax: 212-208-1161
Comments: Gives complete dividend information on 10,000 listed and unlisted stock issues for a calendar year.

Timesaver
If your local library doesn't carry a particular resource in its reference section, ask if it is part of a library cooperative system. In many areas of the country, local libraries have set up a system so that all participating libraries can share resources to stretch their tight budgets.

Timesaver
To find libraries or databases using the Internet, try the following Web sites:
American Library Association www.ala.org
Big Yellow www. bigyellow.com
Internet Public Library www.ipl.org
This is like having the national Yellow Pages at one convenient site. Search by name, category, or geographical reference.

Issue frequency: Annually

Subscription price: Individual $40

Bank 13D Dictionary (directory)

Publisher: SNL Securities

Phone: 804-977-1600

Fax: 804-977-4466

Comments: Contains all active 13D filings and related filings for every publicly traded bank in the country, including those that trade on the "pink sheets." This directory also includes all expired filings made over the past year.

Issue frequency: Quarterly

Subscription price: Individual/corporate $495

Books of Wall Street (directory)

Publisher: Fraser Publishing Company

Phone: 1-800-253-0900, 802-658-0324

Fax: 802-658-0260

Comments: Provides a complete and thorough listing of books currently available on the stock market and investing; includes many hard-to-find titles.

Issue frequency: Annually

Subscription price: Free

Chartcraft Monthly NYSE and ASE Chartbook (loose-leaf)

Publisher: Chartcraft, Inc.

Phone: 914-632-0422

Fax: 914-632-0335

Comments: Provides point and figure charts on all NYSE/ASE stocks.

Issue frequency: Monthly

Subscription price: Individual $402

Driscoll Insider (periodical)

Publisher: Driscoll Industrial

Phone: 408-625-9026

Comments: Gives comprehensive listings of initial public stock offerings.

Issue frequency: Semimonthly

Subscription price: Individual $95

E-Z Telephone Directory of Brokers (directory)

Publisher: The E-Z Telephone Directory, Inc.

Phone: 212-422-9492

Fax: 212-483-8984

Comments: Lists all stock brokers and banks in the New York area.

Issue frequency: Semiannually

Subscription price: Individual $75; Canadian $85; foreign $90

Encyclopedia of Stock Market Techniques (loose-leaf)

Publisher: Investors Intelligence

Phone: 914-632-0422

Fax: 914-632-0335

Comments: Features the theories, methods, and thoughts on investment techniques of well-known analysts.

Issue frequency: Annually

Subscription price: Contact for info

Industry Review (periodical)

Publisher: Moody's Investors Service, Inc.

Phone: 212-553-0300

Fax: 212-553-4700

Comments: Gives comparative statistics and rankings of 4,000 leading corporations in 145 industry groups. Corporations are ranked by financial criteria and leading stock performance.

Issue frequency: Biweekly

Subscription price: Individual $450

Moody's Dividend Record **(periodical)**

Publisher: Moody's Investors Service, Inc.

Phone: 212-553-0497

Fax: 212-553-4700

Comments: Reports on current dividend data on more than 18,300 stocks; includes cumulative and annual supplement.

Issue frequency: Semiweekly

Subscription price: Individual $520

Moody's Handbook of Common Stock **(directory)**

Publisher: Moody's Investors Service, Inc.

Phone: 212-553-0300

Fax: 212-553-4700

Comments: Provides performance trends and full-page profiles on 950 NYSE and AMEX companies, with financial summaries on 750 additional companies.

Issue frequency: Quarterly

Subscription price: Individual $225

NASDAQ Fact Book and Company Directory **(directory)**

Publisher: The National Association of Securities Dealers (NASD)

Phone: 202-728-8000

Fax: 202-728-8882

Comments: Gives a year's conglomeration of statistical information about the Nasdaq stock market.

Issue frequency: Annually

Subscription price: Individual $20

Nelson's Directory of Investment Research **(directory)**

Publisher: Nelson Information

Phone: 1-800-333-6357, 914-937-8400

Fax: 914-937-8908

Comments: Serves as a complete and comprehensive guide to sources of fundamental stock research worldwide. Information on 9,000 companies is listed.

Issue frequency: Annually

Subscription price: Contact for info

New York Stock Exchange Guide (loose-leaf)

Publisher: CCH Incorporated

Web site: www.cch.com

Phone: 1-800-853-5224, 847-267-7000

Fax: 1-800-224-8299

Comments: Provides a directory, constitution, rules, and SEC-related material for the NYSE.

Issue frequency: Monthly

Subscription price: Individual $634

NYSE-Weekly Stock Buys (loose-leaf newsletter)

Publisher: Elton Stephens Investments

Phone: 1-800-553-5866, 219-291-3823

Fax: 219-291-3823

Comments: Lists blue-chip income and growth stocks.

Issue frequency: Weekly

Subscription price: Individual $390

Plunkett's Financial Services Industry Almanac (directory)

Publisher: Plunkett Research, Ltd.

Phone: 713-932-0000

Fax: 713-932-7080

Comments: Provides profiles on 500 leading corporations in banking, financial services, insurance, mortgages, online finance, credit cards, investments, and stocks.

Issue frequency: Every two years

Subscription price: Contact for info

Plunkett's On-Line Trading, Finance &
Investment Web Sites Almanac (directory)
Publisher: Plunkett Research, Ltd.
Phone: 713-932-0000
Fax: 713-932-7080
Comments: Saves you countless hours in your
research for data on investments, stocks,
bonds, commodities, banking, mortgages,
economics, trends, and more.
Issue frequency: Every two years
Subscription price: Contact for info

S&P 500 Information Bulletin (loose-leaf)
Publisher: Standard & Poor's Corp.
Phone: 1-800-208-1161, 212-208-8000
Fax: 212-208-1161
Comments: Is a monthly report detailing
price performance and composition of the
S&P 500 Stock Price Index.
Issue frequency: Monthly
Subscription price: Individual $185

Standard & Poor's Small-Cap 600 Guide
(directory)
Publisher: McGraw-Hill
Phone: 212-337-4062
Fax: 212-627-3811
Comments: Gives a complete guide to the 600
exciting, entrepreneurial companies that
make up Standard & Poor's highly acclaimed
index of small company stocks.
Issue frequency: Annually
Subscription price: Contact for info

Standard & Poor's Stock Guide (newsletter)
Publisher: Standard & Poor's Corp.
Phone: 1-800-208-1161, 212-208-8772
Fax: 212-208-1161

Comments: Contains statistical information
and data on more than 5,000 stocks. It also
indicates whether the company has a dividend reinvestment plan.
Issue frequency: Monthly
Subscription price: Contact for info

***Standard & Poor's The Outlook* (newsletter)**
Publisher: Standard & Poor's Corp.
Phone: 1-800-208-1161, 212-208-8786
Fax: 212-208-1161
Comments: Provides stock market and
finance research.
Issue frequency: Weekly
Subscription price: Individual $268

***Standard & Poor's Trendline Chart Guide*
(directory)**
Publisher: Standard & Poor's Corp.
Phone: 1-800-208-1161, 212-208-8792
Fax: 212-208-1161
Comments: Provides price action charts and
comparative data for 4,000 major stocks listed
on various exchanges as well as the Nasdaq.
Issue frequency: Monthly
Subscription price: Individual $160

***Standard & Poor's Trendline Daily Action
Stock Charts* (loose-leaf)**
Publisher: Standard & Poor's Corp.
Phone: 1-800-208-1161, 212-208-8772
Fax: 212-208-1161
Comments: Gives daily plotted charts on 728
leading stocks.
Issue frequency: Daily
Subscription price: Individual $676

Stock & Bond Brokers **(directory)**
Publisher: InfoUSA
Phone: 877-862-7700
Fax: 402-331-5481
Comments: Features information on more
than 13,000 stock and bond brokers.
Issue frequency: Annually
Subscription price: Contact for info

Stock Chart Service **(loose-leaf publication)**
Publisher: R.W. Mansfield Co.
Phone: 201-795-0629
Fax: 201-795-5476
Comments: Gives earnings and dividends,
relative strength, and moving averages for
each stock.
Issue frequency: Weekly
Subscription price: Individual $175

Stock Guide **(directory)**
Publisher: Standard & Poor's Corp.
Phone: 1-800-208-1161, 212-208-8000
Fax: 212-208-0400
Comments: Gives a monthly financial summa-
ry of more than 5,300 stocks.
Issue frequency: Monthly
Subscription price: Individual $128

Stock Price & Ratio Indexes **(loose-leaf
publication)**
Publisher: Standard & Poor's Corp.
Phone: 1-800-208-1161, 212-208-8000
Fax: 212-208-1161
Comments: Gives more than 100 industry
group stock price indexes, with ratios for
comparison with the market as a whole.

Issue frequency: Weekly

Subscription price: Individual $400

Stock Traders Almanac (report)

Publisher: Hirsch Organization

Phone: 201-767-4100

Fax: 201-767-7337

Issue frequency: Annually

Subscription price: Contact for info

Supertraders Reference Manual (directory)

Publisher: Market Movements, Inc.

Phone: 1-800-878-7442, 918-493-2897

Fax: 918-493-3892

Comments: Provides reference material for trading commodities and stocks; includes technical trading methods and explanations.

Issue frequency: Annually

Subscription price: Individual $144; foreign $164.

Vickers Directory of Institutional Investors (directory)

Publisher: Vickers Stock Research Corp.

Phone: 1-800-645-5043, 516-423-7710

Fax: 516-423-7715

Comments: Serves as a directory of international institutions (banks, insurance companies, and so on).

Issue frequency: Annually

Subscription price: Contact for info

Books

You can find thousands of books on the topic of stock investing. The following are insightful books that will help you become more knowledgeable as you start your stock investing career.

> **❝**
> There is no easy method of learning difficult things. The method is to close the door, give out that you are not at home, and work.
> —Joseph de Maistre
> **❞**

"
We live, and we
learn, as much by
unconscious
absorption and
imitation as by
systematic effort.
—Luella B. Cook
"

101 Investment Lessons from the Wizards of Wall Street: The Pros' Secrets for Running with the Bulls Without Losing Your Shirt
By Michael Sincere
Price: $14.99
Paperback, 256 pages
Publisher: Career Press, 1999
Comments: A concise, easy-to-read book free of technical jargon and suitable for all investors who want to reap the rewards of stock investing yet avoid the most common mistakes.

Austrian Economics for Investors
By Mark Skousen
Price: $9.95
Publisher: Pickering & Chatto Ltd., 1995
Comments: An economics book for stock investors on free market economics from economists that are considered the "Austrian School of Economics." Books such as this one apply the basic theories of the Austrian school of investing.

Buffettology: The Previously Unexplained Techniques That Have Made Warren Buffett the World's Most Famous Investor
By Mary Buffett and David Clark
Price: $14.00
Paperback, 320 pages
Publisher: Fireside, 1999
Comments: A detailed look at Warren Buffett's approach to investing. This style of investing is based on the work of Benjamin Graham and requires a quality that most investors lack: discipline.

Common Stocks and Uncommon Profits and Other Writings
By Philip A. Fisher
Price: $19.95
Paperback, 271 pages
Publisher: John Wiley & Sons, 1996
Comments: A well-respected book by Philip Fisher, acknowledged as one of the pioneers of modern investment theory. His work continues to be held in high regard by today's astute investors.

Dictionary of Financial Terms
By Virginia Morris and Kenneth Morris
Price: $14.95
Paperback, 160 pages
Publisher: Lightbulb Press Inc.
Comments: A nicely laid out A-to-Z publication for investors mystified by financial terms. It explains the important investing terms we come across every day.

Forbes Guide to the Markets
By Marc Groz
Price: $16.96
Paperback, 250 pages
Publisher: John Wiley & Sons, 1999
Comments: A very practical guide to the financial markets. It covers both stocks and mutual funds for beginners and experienced investors.

How to Buy Stocks
By Louis Engel and Henry Hecht
Price: $15.95
Paperback, 398 pages
Publisher: Little, Brown and Company

Comments: Considered a classic stock market primer that is regularly revised. Highly recommended for beginners.

How to Make Money in Stocks: A Winning System in Good Times or Bad
By William J. O'Neil
Price: $10.95
Paperback, 266 pages
Publisher: McGraw-Hill; 2nd edition, 1994
Comments: Guidebook for becoming an investment pro.

The Intelligent Investor: A Book of Practical Counsel
By Benjamin Graham and Warren E. Buffett (Preface)
Price: $30.00
Hardcover, 340 pages
Publisher: HarperCollins; 4th revised edition, 1985
Comments: A revised edition of the best-selling investment guide. This book takes account of both the defensive and the enterprising investor, outlining the principles of stock selection, explaining simple portfolio policy, and offering advice on a range of strategies.

The Neatest Little Guide to Stock Market Investing
By Jason Kelly
Price: $12.95
Paperback, 257 pages
Publisher: Plume, 1998
Comments: A combination of friendly guidance and sound financial expertise, giving readers a solid foundation on which to build

a profitable portfolio. It includes important tips from Wall Street masters Peter Lynch, Benjamin Graham, Warren Buffett, and others.

One Up on Wall Street: How to Use What You Already Know to Make Money in the Market
By Peter Lynch and John Rothchild (contributor)
Price: $14.00
Paperback, 320 pages
Publisher: Simon & Schuster, 2000
Comments: An easy-to-follow book in which Lynch offers directions for sorting out the long shots from the no-shots by spending just a few minutes with a company's financial statements. His advice for finding long-term, high-performing stocks is valuable. Lynch's no-nonsense, value-oriented approach is very educational for beginners. His other book, *Beating the Street*, is equally recommended.

Secrets of the Great Investors
Price: $14.95 per set; $295 collection
Publisher: Knowledge Products
Comments: A cassette tape series about investing. This series is narrated by Louis Rukeyser, famed host of the weekly TV series *Wall Street Week with Louis Rukeyser*, and edited by Mark Skousen. It contains 26 tapes in all (13 sets), covering a wide array of investment topics and principles.

Security Analysis **(Classic 1934 Edition)**
By Benjamin Graham and David L. Dodd
Price: $50.00
Hardcover, 735 pages
Publisher: McGraw-Hill, 1997

Comments: One of the most important and best-selling investment books of all time. Now twenty years after his death, Benjamin Graham, one of the greatest investment thinkers, still commands a loyal following. The original edition will appeal to purists who prefer to read Graham's work in its original form, undiluted by subsequent contributors, as well as to investors, security analysts, and portfolio managers.

The Wall Street Journal Guide to Understanding Money and Investing

Price: $15.95
Paperback, 160 pages
Publisher: Lightbulb Press
Comments: An excellent publication that clearly lays out how the financial markets work. The text and the graphics do a great job of explaining financial concepts and terms.

The Warren Buffett Way: Investment Strategies of the World's Greatest Investor

By Robert G. Hagstrom Jr. (preface) and Peter S. Lynch
Price: $6.99
Paperback, 313 pages
Publisher: John Wiley & Sons, 1997
Comments: An exploration into Warren Buffett's investing strategies. *Forbes* identifies Buffett as one of the richest people in the United States year after year. Of the more than 70 individuals or families worth more than $1 billion on the *Forbes* list, only Buffett acquired his wealth through investing.

Moneysaver
Use Amazon.com to acquire some of these hard to find titles. Amazon.com may not be a great stock (as of April 2000), but it is excellent for discount book buyers. Amazon.com also provides reviews from book buyers to help you make your decision before purchasing.

The Internet

The Internet, the information hunter's greatest tool, can access numerous resources, with literally thousands of Web sites whose quality ranges from excellent to awful.

Most of the Web sites listed in this section have extensive information available without a fee to log on. The following are worthy of your attention.

10-K Wizard
www.10kwizard.com
Full-text search engine for all SEC EDGAR filings. Data is available for download in formats for spreadsheets and word processors.

Allexperts Stock Market Q and A
www.allexperts.com/invest/stocks.shtml
Answers from professional analysts and others to questions about stocks, the stock market, and investment strategies.

Allstocks.com
www.allstocks.com
Free real-time news pages, stock picks, investor links, and much more.

Blue Chip Success
www.bluechipsuccess.com
Three investment strategies to beat the S&P 500.

CBS's MarketWatch
www.MarketWatch.com
A comprehensive look at the markets, news, and investments. This great overall Web site includes information for beginners and experienced investors. You can get a wealth of data on virtually any public stock, mutual fund, or industry.

Contrarian Investing.Com
www.contrarianinvesting.com
Market analysis and stock picks with a contrarian viewpoint.

Daily Stocks
www.dailystocks.com
Tools for charting, market commentary, news, and lots of fundamental content for U.S. stocks.

Disclosure-Investor.com
www.disclosure-investor.com
Access to financial information on thousands of companies for small business professionals and individual investors. The site contains SEC EDGAR filings, an index of SEC Paper Filings, and U.S. and international company financial reports.

EZresearch.com—Stocks
www.ezresearch.com
A great number of stock and investing-related links.

Fiend's SuperBear Page
www.fiendbear.com
Daily updates of stock market data along with commentary with a bearish bias.

Financial Engines
www.financialengines.com
Provides an extensive array of resources and links for investors. Provides long-range forecasts for investment portfolios, as well as an extensive array of other resources and links for investors.

FinancialWeb
www.financialweb.com
Market news, quotes, opinions, and research.

Unofficially ...
Having a solid grasp of economics is critical to your success as an investor. Great investors of the twentieth century acknowledge Ludwig von Mises as the premier economist. His works, including "Human Action" (a treatise on economics), have been very influential in investing circles. To find out more, visit the Ludwig von Mises Institute at www.mises.org.

FreeEDGAR

http://freeedgar.com/

Unlimited access to real-time SEC filings, free alert service, Excel spreadsheets of financial tables, fundamental financial data , and annual and quarterly corporate reports.

Investor.Net

www.investor.net

Access to EDGAR and links to several business publications for investor research. The investor can look up stock quotes and get charts.

InvestorPackages.com

www.InvestorPackages.com

Stock research database. It maintains more than one million news and information links for more than 8,000 publicly traded companies.

Market Guide Investor

www.marketguide.com

Information on more than 10,500 publicly traded companies on the NYSE, AMEX, Nasdaq, and OTC exchanges. It offers information in the form of quotes, news, charts, screening, and financial reports.

Microsoft's Moneycentral

www.moneycentral.msn.com

MoneyBrief

www.moneybrief.com

Daily briefing on the stock market and investing. This site includes a market commentary, technical analysis, and proprietary indicators.

Multex

www.multexnet.com

More than one million reports from more than 400 international brokerage firms and research providers, some for free but most for a fee. This site is geared to corporate finance, investment banks, and institutional and individual investors.

Multex Investor Network

http://multexinvestor.com

Full-text research reports from more than 200 brokerage firms, investment banks, and independent researchers, covering more than 200,000 firms.

Quote.com, Inc.

www.quote.com

A comprehensive analysis of investments. Features include broker research, earnings estimates, and an industry watch. This site also has an Investment Research Education Center.

Simply Stocks

www.simplystocks.com

Stock quotes, broker research, technical analysis, and stock market data.

Standard and Poor's

www.Personalwealth.com

Stock and Mutual Fund Evaluator

www.stockevaluator.com

A free stock evaluator tool for scoring your stock against all stocks in the market for strength and risk every day.

Stock Investor's Handbook from About.com

http://stocks.about.com

Daily features articles, educational material, a discussion forum, well-organized and annotated links, and scheduled chats.

Tech Stock Investor
www.techstockinvestor.com
Top 10 and top 50 lists of some of today's
fastest growing and most successful companies. The site is updated monthly.

Wall Street Links
www.wallstreetlinks.com
Thousands of links to business, financial, and
Wall Street Web sites.

Considering how dynamic the Internet is and
how often new Web sites appear, this list is not comprehensive. However, all the Web sites presented
have valuable information to offer all investors.
Again, don't take any one Web site as "gospel"—
look at many different sources before you make any
decision with your money.

Periodicals

Staying current on your investments, the markets,
and the economy means reading the publications
that investors consider the best sources for timely
information. You can read the following at your
library's periodical section, you can subscribe, or
you can visit their Web sites.

Newspapers

To keep track of your investments on a daily basis,
the best recommendation is to read one or all of
these excellent publications:

> *Barron's* (weekly financial newspaper)
> www.barrons.com

> *Investors Business Daily* (daily newspaper—
> weekdays)
> www.wsj.com

The Wall Street Journal (**daily newspaper—weekdays**)
www.wsj.com

Magazines

These magazines are available at most newsstands and offer excellent, comprehensive information for avid investors. Their Web sites typically offer information on the markets and investing in general as well as financial tools such as retirement calculators.

Bloomberg's Financial Magazine
www.bloomberg.com

Forbes Magazine
www.forbes.com

Fortune Magazine
www.pathfinder.com

Money Magazine
www.money.com

Kiplinger's Personal Finance Magazine
www.kiplingers.com

Smart Money Magazine
www.smartmoney.com

The following publications are not as readily available at your newsstand, yet they offer excellent information for stock investors.

Better Investing Magazine
Publisher: National Association of Investors Corp.
Web site: www.betterinvesting.org
Phone: 877-275-6242, 248-583-6242
Fax: 248-583-1984
Comments: Gives investment education, specific stocks and industries for study, investment ideas and techniques, news of

investment clubs, and legislative and regulatory items affecting investors.

Issue frequency: Monthly

Subscription price: Individual $20; Canadian $49; foreign $49

Bull & Bear Financial Newspaper (tabloid)

Publisher: Bull & Bear Financial Newspaper

Phone: 407-682-6170

Comments: Summarizes stock market advisory newsletters and provides investment information on stocks, gold commodities, mutual funds, currencies, economic trends, monetary survival, and real estate. It also includes stock selections by the leading investment advisers.

Issue frequency: Monthly

Subscription price: Individual $29; foreign $56

Current Market Perspectives (**magazine**)

Publisher: Standard & Poor's Corp.

Phone: 1-800-208-1161, 212-208-8000;

Fax: 212-208-1161

Comments: Provides monthly charts on more than 2,200 NYSE, AMEX and Nasdaq stocks.

Issue frequency: Monthly

Subscription price: Individual $260

Individual Investor (**magazine**)

Publisher: Individual Investor

Phone: 212-843-2777

Fax: 212-843-2792

Comments: Gives complete coverage of undiscovered stocks and mutual funds with high growth potential.

Issue frequency: Monthly

Subscription price: Individual $22.95

Unofficially ...
A great way to find publications on investing or business topics is visiting the Web site set up by Oxbridge Communications. Using a keyword onsite search engine, www. MediaFinder.com can help you find the right publication among thousands of magazines and periodicals listed.

Kiplinger's Stocks 2000: The Smart Investors Guide (**magazine**)

Publisher: Kiplinger Washington Editors, Inc.

Phone: 1-800-544-0155, 202-887-6400

Fax: 202-778-8976

Comments: Gives you everything you need to know about investing directly in stocks.

Issue frequency: Special

Subscription price: Contact for info

On Line Investor (**magazine, World Wide Web publication**)

Publisher: Stock Trends, Inc.

Web site: http://onlineinvestors.com

Phone: 1-800-778-8568, 914-949-4726

Fax: 914-949-8638

Comments: Covers personal investing for the digital age and connects you to the next hot stock tip.

Issue frequency: 10 times per year

Subscription price: Individual $19.95; corporate $24.95; Canadian $31.95; foreign $43.95

Online Investor: Sourcebook (**magazine**)

Publisher: Stock Trends, Inc.

Phone: 630-645-1730

Comments: Serves as an extensive resource guide to Web investing.

Issue frequency: Special

Subscription price: Contact for info

Personal Investing News (**magazine**)

Publisher: SMI

Phone: 407-629-9229

Fax: 407-629-6719

Comments: Provides personal investing news features on a broad range of financial and investment vehicles for the active investor, including stocks, bonds, mutual funds, commodities, and more.

Issue frequency: Monthly

Subscription price: Contact for info

Business and financial chats and boards

If you need to communicate with other investors or get answers to general questions on stocks and investing, there are many sites on the Internet where you can connect with like-minded people on financial and investment issues and concerns of the day. These are some of the more popular sites:

4-Lane.Com Business Chat Room
www.4-lane.com/businesschat/index.html

BrowseMaster.Com—Message boards
www.browsemaster.com

The Chat Site's Business Chat Room
http://thechatsite.com/business.htm

LoanValue.Com Loan Chat Room
www.loanvalue.com/in/46.HTM

MarketForum.Com—Futures & options boards
www.marketforum.com

RagingBull.Com—Message boards
www.ragingbull.com

SiliconInvestor.Com—Message boards
www.siliconinvestor.com

Snap—Chat & message boards
www.message.snap.com

Stock-Talk.Com—Message boards
www.stock-talk.com

Talk City
www.talkcity.com

Web Marketing Information Center Chat Room
www.wilsonweb.com/webmarket/chat.htm

World Wide Web Chat With Links
www.all-links.com/webchat/a-d.html

Yahoo!—Chat & message boards
www.yahoo.com/r/ms

Radio: Business stations and shows

As stock investing has become America's favorite pastime, financial talk shows have proliferated. These are a great way to be informed, but be careful. Just because an "expert" says something on a credible show doesn't mean you should believe it. Be sure to verify all information with other sources.

About.Com—Web radio
www.broadcast.com/shows/aboutcom/radioshow

AJR—U.S.A. Radio Networks
http://ajr.newslink.org/netr.html

AJR—U.S.A. Radio Stations
http://ajr.newslink.org/rad.html

Atlantic Broadcasting Service's live market update
www.abslive.com

AudioHighway.Com— Web radio
www.audiohighway.com

Capitalist Pig—WNEW, New York
www.capitalistpig.com

DailyRocket.Com—weekly radio show
www.dailyrocket.com

Entrepreneur Radio Network—KRRF 280 AM, Denver
http://ern.amradio.net

Expedia.Com—Web radio
www.expedia.com/daily/radio

EYada.Com—Web radio
www.eyada.com

MarketPlace Business Network
www.marketplace.org

"Money Matters with Larry & Steve"—KTOE 1420 AM, Great Lakes
www.efs-net.com/radio.htm

MSNBC's "High Noon on Wall Street with Chris Byron"—Web radio show
www.msnbc.com/news/313517.asp

Netradio.Com—online radios and shows
www.netradio.com

Radio.Com—Web radios directory
www.radio.com

RadioWallStreet.Com—online financial radio
www.radiowallstreet.com

"Sound Money"—Minnesota Public Radio (MPR)
http://money.mpr.org

"The Venture Guy's Big Biz Show"—KSDO 1130 AM, San Diego
www.broadcast.com/shows/mds/ventureguy/

WABCradio.Com—Web radio
www.wabcradio.com

Watch Out!
Investors should be wary of any information passed along in chat rooms and message boards. Although you can find great information in these places, a variety of scams and frauds perpetuated in these forums abound. Be skeptical of anything you read, and verify everything with other sources.

Television: Business stations and shows

Financial television shows have become very popular in recent years. These shows can give you a quick overview on the markets and the economy. The stock investment analysis offered is interesting but shouldn't be taken as fact without first doing your research, beginning with the resources in this chapter.

ABC Network Business News
www.abcnews.com/sections/business

**American Journalism Review—U.S.A.
Television Stations (great site)**
http://ajr.newslink.org/tel.html

**American Journalism Review—WorldWide
Television Networks**
http://ajr.newslink.org/neti.html

BBC Business News
www.bbc.co.uk/hi/english/business

CBS MarketWatch
http://cbs.marketwatch.com

CBS network
www.cbs.com

CNBC network
www.cnbc.com

CNNfn: The Financial Network
http://cnnfn.com

Emerging Company Report—cable television
www.emergingcompany.com/welcome.htm

FOX Market Wire
www.foxmarketwire.com

FOX network
www.fox.com

MoneyHunter—TV show
www.moneyhunter.com

MSNBC
www.msnbc.com

NBC network
www.nbc.com

Nightly Business Report
www.nightlybusiness.org

PAX network
www.paxtv.com

PBS Business Channel—Management Issues
www.pbsbusinesschannel.com

PBS' "Livelyhood" show—The show about the "daily grind"
www.pbs.org/livelyhood/

PBS' "Money Moves" show
www.pbs.org/moneymoves/index.html

PBS Online
www.pbs.org

PBS' "Working Stiff" show—worker issues
www.pbs.org/weblab/workingstiff/

UPN network
www.upn.com

WB network
www.thewb.com

"Wall Street Week with Louis Rukeyser"
www.mpt.org/mpt/wsw/home.html

Financial advisers

Advisers come in many varieties—there are good and bad of every type. Bear in mind that advisers are different from brokers (or at least they should be). A broker's primary duty is to implement the buy or sell transaction. They may or may not give advice, but if they do, it should be scrutinized. Brokers may render advice on securities they are selling. This may cause a conflict of interest because the advice could be related to generating commissions or other fees.

Make sure that the adviser you are considering discloses any financial arrangement that may affect the objectivity of her or his advice. It's better to use a fee-based financial adviser, which means that the adviser gets paid directly by you, the investor. This means the adviser should have a greater allegiance to you and your interests as opposed to any other party involved in the transaction.

To find a fee-only financial adviser, contact the National Association of Personal Financial Advisers (NAPFA). NAPFA is the largest professional association of comprehensive, fee-only financial planners in the United States. It has members and affiliates in 50 states.

National Association of Personal Financial Advisers

355 West Dundee Rd.

Suite 200

Buffalo Grove, IL 60089

Phone: 1-888-333-6659

E-mail: info@napfa.org

Web site: www.napfa.org

Another place to find a competent adviser is through the Financial Planning Association (FPA), the largest membership organization for the financial planning community. It was created when the Institute of Certified Financial Planners (ICFP) and the International Association for Financial Planning (IAFP) merged on January 1, 2000. Members include individuals and companies that have contributed to building the financial planning profession and all those who champion the financial planning process.

FPA members are dedicated to supporting the financial planning process to help people achieve their goals and dreams. The FPA offers services and resources designed to help the public understand the importance of the financial planning process and to connect consumers with local CFP professionals. Consumers can visit www.fpanet.org or call 1-800-282-7526 for this information. The FPA also believes that financial planners should be CFP licensees. To be licensed to use the CFP mark, an individual must meet the following stringent qualifications, as specified by the Certified Financial Planner Board of Standards, Inc. (the CFP Board):

■ **Examination**—An individual must successfully complete the CFP Board's comprehensive certification examination, which tests the individual's knowledge on a multitude of key financial planning topics.

■ **Experience**—Depending on the level of degree work completed in a collegiate setting, an individual must acquire three to five years of financial planning-related experience prior to receiving the right to use the CFP mark.

■ **Ethics**—An individual must voluntarily ascribe to the CFP Board's code of ethics and additional requirements as mandated. This voluntary decision empowers the CFP Board to take action if a CFP licensee should violate the code of ethics. Such violations could lead to disciplinary action, including the permanent revocation of the right to use the CFP mark.

■ **Education**—A CFP licensee must obtain 30 hours of continuing education every two years in the body of knowledge pertaining to financial planning areas such as estate planning, retirement planning, investment management, tax planning, employee benefits and insurance.

To learn more about the CFP designation and to find out if any CFP has been disciplined by the Board, contact:

CFP Board
1700 Broadway, Suite 2100
Denver, Colorado 80290-2101
Phone: 303-830-7500
Fax: 303-860-7388
E-mail: mail@CFP-Board.org
Web site: www.cfp-board.org

Interviewing the financial adviser

When you speak with a prospective adviser, you should ask some important questions:

- **What experience do you have?**—Find out how long the planner has been in practice and the number and types of companies that he has been associated with. Ask the planner to briefly describe his work experience and how it relates to his current practice. Choose a financial planner with a minimum of three years of experience counseling individuals on their financial needs. Ask what the adviser's specialty is as well—you want a planner with stock investing experience.

- **What are your qualifications?**—The title "financial planner" is used by many financial professionals. Ask the planner what qualifies her to offer financial planning advice and whether she holds a financial planning designation such as the Certified Financial Planner (CFP) mark. Look for a planner who has proven experience in financial planning topics such as insurance, tax planning, investments, estate planning, or retirement planning. Determine what steps the planner takes to stay current with changes and developments in the financial planning field. If the planner holds a financial planning designation, check on her background with the CFP Board or other relevant professional organizations. Ask if she teaches financial matters or has been published.

▪ **How will services be paid for?**—As part of your financial planning agreement, the financial planner should clearly tell you in writing how she will be paid for the services to be provided. Planners can be paid in several ways:

▪ A salary paid by the company for which the planner works. The planner's employer receives payment from you or others, either in fees or commissions, to pay the planner's salary.

▪ Fees based on an hourly rate, a flat rate, or on a percentage of your assets and/or income.

▪ Commissions paid by a third party from the products sold to you to carry out the financial planning recommendations. Commissions are usually a percentage of the amount that you invest in a product.

▪ A combination of fees and commissions, whereby fees are charged for the amount of work done to develop financial planning recommendations, and commissions are received from any products sold.

▪ In addition, some planners may offset some portion of the fees you pay if they receive commissions for carrying out their recommendations.

Moneysaver
If you're considering using an adviser, consider a fee-only professional who can assist you on an annual basis. Advisers that are commission-based may tend to have their decisions colored by how much they earn in transaction costs.

▪ Would a third party benefit from any recommendation you make? Some business relationships or partnerships could affect the planner's professional judgment, inhibiting the planner from acting in your best interest. Ask the planner to provide you with a description of his conflicts of interest in writing.

For example, financial planners who sell insurance policies, securities, or mutual funds have a business relationship with the companies that provide these financial products. The planner may also have relationships or partnerships that should be disclosed to you, such as business he receives for referring you to an insurance agent, accountant, or attorney for implementation of planning suggestions.

▪ **Have you ever been publicly disciplined for any unlawful or unethical actions in your professional career?**—Several government and professional regulatory organizations, such as the National Association of Securities Dealers (NASD), your state insurance and securities departments, and the CFP Board, keep records on the disciplinary history of financial planners and advisers. Ask what organizations the planner is regulated by, and contact these groups to conduct a background check. (See the listing provided in the following section.)

How to find a financial adviser in your area

When you don't have the benefit of knowing someone in the financial industry or can't get a reliable referral, the next best thing is to contact the relevant associations. Even if you do find someone, it's a good idea to ask what association that person

Bright Idea
Get a free copy of the CFP Board's pamphlet *10 Questions to Ask When Choosing a Financial Planner* by contacting: Certified Financial Planner Board of Standards 1700 Broadway, Suite 2100 Denver, CO 80290-2101 Phone: 888-237-6275 Fax: 303-860-7388 Web site: www. CFP-Board.org

belongs to. Most associations have a code of ethics, dispute resolution, and disciplinary procedures for members that the public has problems with.

American Institute of Certified Public Accountants—Personal Financial Planning Division
1-800-862-4272

American Society of CLU & ChFC
1-800-392-6900

Certified Financial Planner Board of Standards
1700 Broadway, Suite 2100
Denver, CO 80290-2101
888-237-6275
Fax: 303-860-7388
Web site: www.CFP-Board.org

Financial Planning Association
Atlanta; Denver; Washington, D.C.
Phone: 1-800-282-7526, 1-800-322-4237, 404-845-0011
Fax: 404-845-3660
E-mail: membership@fpanet.org
Web site: www.fpanet.org

National Association of Personal Financial Advisers
1-888-333-6659

Judging the analysts' views

Many analysts are interviewed on TV and radio financial shows. All are professionals, and all have what seems like well-reasoned opinions on the immediate outlook for the market in general and some stocks in particular. But analysts' views can be suspect. First, they usually have a short-term bias. Analysts too often look at how well the company did

Watch Out!
To check the disciplinary history of a financial planner or financial adviser, contact these organizations:
National Association of Securities Dealers
1-800-289-9999
Certified Financial Planner Board of Standards
1-888-237-6275
National Fraud Exchange (fee involved)
1-800-822-0416
North American Securities Administrators Association
1-888-846-2722
Securities and Exchange Commission
1-800-732-0330

❝
Most men believe
that it would
benefit them if
they could get a
little from those
who have more.
How much more
would it benefit
them if they
would learn a lit-
tle from those
who know more.
—William J.H.
Boetcker
❞

last quarter and how well they will do in the coming quarter. The emphasis is on earnings and sales in the current period. Second, analysts may offer views that are influenced by their employers or clients.

During the 1998–1999 period, despite the fact that the bull market was maturing and the majority of stocks were underperforming the major indexes, the majority of analysts issued positive reports on stocks. When the Securities and Exchange Commission reviewed the stock recommendations of Merrill Lynch during 1999, there was not a single "sell" recommendation. In other words, every stock recommendation they made was either "buy" or "hold." The interesting thing is that 75 percent of stocks actually hit new lows in 1999 as opposed to the higher-visibility minority of stocks that did tremendously well.

Frequently, the analyst receives pressure to put a positive spin on a particular stock. The stock may be a company that is a client to the analyst's brokerage firm. Perhaps the brokerage firm is underwriting the company's stock or bond offering, or has been contracted for other services. This type of influence may be benign, but it does affect the objectivity of the research.

Recently, I visited a Web site that tracked analysts' views on major stocks in the news. One company highlighted was an Internet company that had three straight years of losses and had no prospects of earnings for another three years. Yet a survey of 22 analysts showed 10 "strong buys," 10 "buys," and 2 "hold" recommendations—not a single "sell" recommendation! This is an example of herd mentality in a mature bull market. If the same stock had been analyzed early in a bull market or during a flat or bear market, the majority of analysts would have exhibited much different views.

The bottom line on analysts? If you listen to just one analyst, you are putting your money at risk. Listen to several analysts and do independent research before arriving at a conclusion, and you have a much better chance of making wise investment decisions.

Keep in mind that resources and prices are ever-changing, so check with their Web sites for the most current information.

Just the facts

- In the beginning, spend more time (versus money) on research. Use the library and the Internet.

- Purchase a batch of the best books for your personal library from proven authors that actually profited from stock investing.

- Make it a daily or weekly habit of tracking the economy and the markets by reading periodicals and watching or listening to financial programs.

- Gain practical knowledge in basic accounting and free market economics to form a solid foundation for your investing success.

- The more you learn, the less you will be dependent on the views of others. Also, the more you learn, the greater value you will gain from the advice of professionals (or the more you can determine whether their views make sense to you).

GET THE SCOOP ON...
Annual reports ▪ Financial statements
▪ Stock reports ▪ The SEC report ▪ A company's
prospectus

Reading the Essential Documents

Every public company has information about its activities that is easily accessible to investors. These documents are available either from the company's shareholder service department (such as annual reports) or from public sources like the Securities and Exchange Commission (such as the company's 10-K). These documents are where most organizations start to analyze the company's current business situation and financial condition. It's not sufficient to get your information second-hand through financial TV shows, analysts, and investment gurus. These sources are helpful, but the documents I discuss in this chapter give you a more complete picture of the company's operations.

Annual reports

The place to start is the annual report, as it's the principal document that most public companies use to disclose corporate information to shareholders.

❝
You are your greatest investment. The more you store in that mind of yours, the more you enrich your experience, the more people you meet, the more books you read, and the more places you visit, the greater is that investment in all that you are. Everything that you add to your peace of mind, and to your outlook upon life, is added capital that no one but yourself can dissipate.
—George Matthews Adams
❞

Also known as an *annual*, the annual report is usually a state-of-the-company report including a letter from the chief executive officer, financial data, results of continuing operations, market segment information, new product plans, subsidiary activities, and research and development activities on future programs. It can be obtained from the company's shareholder services department. If you're already a stockholder, the annual report will be automatically mailed to you.

The elements of the annual report

How you read an annual report depends on your purpose. As an investor, your purpose may be to assess profitability, survivability, growth, stability, and dividends (if any), and to learn of problems, risks, and other factors that may affect your investment. Reviewing a company yearly is the minimum diligence required   the annual report provides a convenient way to do this.

The annual report summarizes and highlights the company's activities for shareholders and interested parties. Primarily it's a public relations document, although it does contain vital financial and operational information for investors. It doesn't read like a book, and there is no single author. There's no need to read it cover to cover because there is no beginning and no end. Putting annuals together year after year creates a kind of never-ending story as the entity progresses, merges, closes, or is acquired.

Consider the following as you read through an annual:

- Is the report well written, clear, concise, and succinct?

- Are photos modeled or live? How well do they relate to the text of the report?

- How much discussion is there of competition?

- How clear are product plans?

- What does it tell you about the company's new product research and development?

- Could the report be made more interesting, understandable, or eye-appealing? How does it compare with others in the same industry?

Most annual reports are composed of nine identifiable sections. Not all reports will have all nine sections or the same type and level of information. Here's how these sections can help you in your research:

1. Read the chair of the board's letter (this is also sometimes written from the CEO). This letter should cover changing conditions as well as the goals the company has either achieved, missed or is currently attempting to achieve. Ask yourself these questions: What actions has management taken (or not taken) toward achieving these goals? Does the letter honestly communicate successes and failures of the past year? If the comparative financial statements in the annual show negative changes over the past year, such as decreased income or increased debt, are these explained in this letter? If there is a problem mentioned, how will the company resolve it and will that problem affect future growth or dividend payout?

2. How did the company do with sales and marketing? The annual report should cover what the company sells, which products or services sell best, and where and when the products

Timesaver
The Wall Street Journal has an Annual Reports Service, which is a free reader service. You can get annual reports for some companies by calling 1-800-654-2582 (or by faxing 1-800-965-5679), or you can order an annual report 24 hours a day through the Web site www.icbinc.com.

Watch Out!
If the letter from the chairman of the board or the CEO spends too much time on the company's future prospects and little time on the most recent year of operations, read the annual's financials to see if it was a bad year.

and/or services are sold. Do you get a clear indication about where the company presently makes most of its money, and does that make sense? Is the report clear about the scope of lines, divisions, and operations? Does it adequately and accurately portray the market share for the company's products and/or services?

3. Read the 10-year summary of financial figures. This will tell you the growth of profits and operating income over the last 10 years. If this isn't included, look for a 5-year or even a 3-year summary.

4. Read the management discussion and analysis section to gain a clear understanding of significant financial trends over the past two years. How candid and accurate is it?

5. The CPA's opinion letter, written by the company's accounting firm, provides you with their opinion on the company's financials. The important thing to look for here is what the firm is qualifying (holding back). For example, does the firm hold back on providing a definitive opinion on certain numbers, such as extraordinarily large income from the one-time sale of assets or from large expense items such as compensation to key personnel?

6. The financial statements (*financials*) provide information about sales, profits, research and development (R&D) spending, inventory, and debt levels, and compare these numbers with prior periods. Read the footnotes to ferret out any changes if they report these numbers. A good example is depreciation. If depreciating

methods have changed, this will have an impact on reported earnings. For instance, if the company accelerates depreciation or reports more earlier rather than later, this will make earnings lower now and higher later.

7. Look for information about the company's subsidiaries (both domestic and foreign) and the company's brands and other intellectual property, such as patents and trademarks? Where is headquarters? Is it clear what lines and brand names the company has, and what its overseas distribution network is?

8. Read through the list of directors and officers. How many outside directors versus inside directors are there? Are the directors well-known and respected? What are the outside directors' backgrounds? (It is a good sign if the outside directors are related to the company's industry.)

9. Look at the stock's price history. Is the stock's general price trend over time up or down? With which exchange is the company traded/listed? What is its stock symbol? What is its bonus/dividend history? If the company has a dividend, does the company offer a dividend reinvestment plan?

Reading the annual report

Start with the notes and read from back to front (the front is usually public relations copy written to shed the best light on the company). Look for items such as lawsuits that could harm the company and subsequently stock value, or accounting changes that inflated earnings. Use your findings to evaluate management. Read the sections that you may consider "boring," such as the accounting firm's notes on income statements or balance sheet items. This is especially important if you plan to hold the stock for long-term growth.

Look for notes to offer relevant details, not "selected" and "certain" assets. What is written about sales and operating profits of subsidiaries, geographical divisions, and so on? How does the company keep its books, especially as compared to other companies in its industry?

If the company manufactures or sells products, look at the figure for inventory. Did it go down because of a different accounting method? Which assets does the company own, and which are leased?

Financial statements

If you're going to be diligent about what company you're going to invest in, you'll have to look at the financial statements. The main documents are the balance sheet, the income statement, and the cash flow statement.

The balance sheet

The balance sheet offers you a snapshot of where the company stands financially at a given point in time. It details the equation of assets minus liabilities, to equal stockholders' equity.

Publicly traded companies are designed to make money. The conventional way of scoring this pursuit is by looking at the company's ability to make money: Operating earnings, pretax earnings, net income, and earnings per share are all common measures. However, this is not the only way to determine if there is real value in a company's stock.

A company's real earnings are the earnings that make it from the income statement to the balance sheet as a liquid asset. Shareholder value ultimately derives from liquid assets, the assets that can easily be converted into cash. A company's value is determined by how much in the way of liquid assets it can amass. There are two ways to think about this. The first is to look at terminal value, which assumes for the sake of calculating potential return that at some future point a company will close down its operations and turn everything into cash, giving the money to shareholders. The second is to look at where tangible shareholder value comes from—returns on invested capital generated by the company's operations. If a company has excess liquid assets that it does not need, it can deploy those assets in two ways to benefit shareholders: dividends and stock buybacks.

Knowing what is on the balance sheet is crucial to understanding whether the company you are investing in is capable of generating real value for shareholders. Most investors who look at company annual reports and SEC reports such as 10-Ks and 10-Qs (see the section "SEC Reports," later in this chapter, for more information) spend far too much time worrying about earnings and far too little time worrying about the balance sheet and the statement of cash flow. The balance sheet can tell you whether a company has enough money to continue to fund its own growth or whether it will have to take on debt, issue debt (through bonds) or issue more stock to keep on operating. Does the company have too much inventory? Is it collecting money from its customers in a reasonable amount of time? The balance sheet—the listing of all the assets and liabilities of the company—can tell you all of this.

Where do you find all this information about the balance sheet? Would you believe you can get it for free? The documents that the Securities and Exchange Commission (SEC) makes available to you online at the SEC's EDGAR Web site (at www.sec.gov) give you all sorts of balance sheet information in the 10-Ks and 10-Qs. The 10-K is a toned-down version of the annual report with more text and fewer pretty pictures that comes out once a year, containing the company's annual balance sheet. The 10-Q is a quarterly filing that a company makes with the SEC three times a year (the fourth filing is the 10-K in the fourth quarter) that also tracks the balance sheet through the course of the year. The advantage of the annual balance sheet over the quarterly 10-Qs is that the annual balance sheet was double-checked by accountants before it was filed with the SEC.

Armed with this information, you are ready to begin your journey through the balance sheet.

The income statement

The income statement tells you how well the company is doing in a given period in terms of income and expenses. The income statement is also referred to as the profit and loss statement (P&L) or the income and expense statement. This is where we see how profitable the company is. What is the company's net income or earnings? The income statement will even tell you whether the company is profitable at all.

Sales revenue = price × quantity

Revenues are the proceeds that a company receives for its merchandise or services. They are usually recorded at the time of the sale or completion of the service, providing that the earnings process is substantially complete and that the collectibility of the revenue can be estimated. Sales revenue equals the price of goods sold multiplied by the quantity of goods sold minus returns.

Earnings process

The earnings process is the sequence of events necessary to complete the sale of goods or services to be recorded on the income statement. The following criteria must be met to substantially fulfill the earnings process:

- The buyer and seller have agreed on the price of the merchandise or service. The buyer is not a middleman, withholding payment until a resale occurs.

- The product or service is delivered in full. The buyer and seller are not related (such as a parent and a subsidiary).

The cost of doing business

Running a business is an expensive endeavor. Whether you're selling balloons at an amusement park or selling delivery trucks to the U.S. Postal Service, running a business costs money. These expenses are listed on the income statement right below sales and revenues. Subtract total expenses from sales and revenues, and you arrive at taxable income.

The most substantial expense we encounter is usually cost of goods sold (COGS). These are the expenses of purchasing materials and preparing goods for sale, such as labor, materials, overhead, and depreciation.

Inventories have a strong relationship with COGS. If you add the inventory on hand at the beginning of the year with any inventory purchased during the year, that total will be split between inventory remaining at the end of the year, which is listed on the balance sheet, and COGS.

Sounds fairly straightforward, eh? If only it were so. The problem arises with the way a company can flow costs through the books, which may or may not resemble the way the goods were actually handled. When reporting sales, profit, and remaining inventory on hand, a company may use first-in, first-out (FIFO); last-in, first-out (LIFO); or the weighted average method.

With FIFO, the inventory acquired first is considered to be sold first. This is the way goods are typically sold by a firm (you don't want that spoiled milk left on the shelves). LIFO, conversely, lists items purchased most recently as those going out the door first. The incentive for using LIFO is twofold. First, LIFO usually results in higher income tax deductions. Also, if you consider that the cost to replace inventory will likely be equal or greater to that of the most recently purchased, LIFO is a closer representation of the current cost of business operations.

The final method is a compromise between how it probably happened and how it's best portrayed on the books. The weighted average method values both COGS and ending inventory using the weighted average cost of all inventory available for sale. If you purchased five units over time at costs of $2, $4, $6, $8, and $8, respectively, you would list each unit at a cost of $5.60 ($2 + 4 + 6 + 8 + 8 / 5 = 5.6$).

Using LIFO may lead to lower earnings than FIFO or the weighted average method, all else being equal. However, a company using LIFO will generally pay lower income taxes and therefore will

produce greater cash flows. Consequently, companies generally choose LIFO as the preferred
accounting method.

So why does the inventory accounting method a
company chooses matter when you're looking to
buy stock? In some cases, a company may choose to
use a certain method, such as FIFO, because they
are more concerned about inflating quarterly earnings numbers in the eyes of investors than they are
about paying lower income taxes. But this may be
bad for the long term because lower taxes would
produce greater cash flows, which can then be used
for investing in growth. What's most important,
though, is that the company is consistent in its use
of accounting methods. If it uses FIFO year after
year, chances are that's the best long-term method
for the company. It's when a company switches from
one method to another that you should sit up and
take notice, and look into why the switch was made.

Factory overhead consists of all indirect costs
associated with the production of goods. In other
words, all production costs other than direct labor
and raw materials fall under this heading. Included
in factory overhead is the payroll of supervisors,
plant maintenance, general supplies, depreciation
of plant and equipment, insurance, and electricity,
among other things.

Factory overhead and direct payroll are considered fixed costs because the amounts generally
remain the same over a production cycle. As production volume increases and fixed costs remain
the same, profits should rise.

Gross profit may or may not be listed next on the
income statement; often it's omitted. Gross profit is
the difference between net sales and COGS.

The final expense we run into is listed simply as operating expenses. Operating expenses may be further broken down into selling and administrative expenses. Selling expenses are those costs associated with producing sales, and administrative expenses are the costs of managing operations. A company usually will not list a specific breakdown of operating expense on the income statement. This category includes items such as salaries, benefits, amortization of goodwill, supplies, and equipment expense. Basically, any expense incurred in transacting normal business operations outside of interest, taxes, and cost of goods sold is an operating expense.

Collectibility of credit sales

If the collectibility of a sale cannot be estimated, revenues are recorded only as the customer makes payments. This deviates from the accrual basis of accounting—recording sales when the cash is received, rather than when it is earned. Two methods are used when recording revenue as the customer makes payments: the installment method and the cost-recovery method.

Installment method   Under the installment method, revenues—and, in turn, profits—are recognized in proportion to the percentage of the sale price collected in a given accounting period.

For example, if Big Bob's House of Beans, Inc. (BBHB), sells, for $5,000, a customer 1,000 cases of garbanzo beans with a total cost to the company of $4,000, to be paid in five annual installments of $1,000 each, BBHB would record annual revenues of $5,000/5, or $1,000 from this transaction. Given annualized costs of $4,000/5, or $800, BBHB would record annual profits of $1,000 minus $800, or $200.

Cost-recovery method   The cost-recovery method matches revenues with costs until all the costs associated with those revenues have been recouped. After that point, profits can be recorded on the income statement. Using the previous example, BBHB would need to collect $4,000 from the customer before any profits could be recorded. Annual revenues of $1,000 would match annual costs of $1,000 during the first four years. With the cost of garbanzo beans fully recovered at the end of the fourth year, profits of $1,000 will hit the income statement in the fifth year.

Again, the important thing to notice in the method a company uses in tracking its collectibility of credit sales is that the company is consistent quarter after quarter, year after year. Consistency lends credibility to their choice of methods, and it makes historical comparisons easier. But it's also important when comparing one company's books to another's. Let's say, for example, that you're thinking about buying stock in one of two e-commerce companies. Company A has stronger sales, but you notice they use the installment method. Company B, on the other hand, uses the cost-recovery method, meaning that even though its sales are lower, there are several million dollars in credit sales that haven't yet appeared on its books.

The same rationale can be used in looking at the differences in logging long-term contracts revenue, explained below.

Long-term contracts revenue

Companies that provide services on a long-term contract generally record revenue under the installment method. If dependable estimates of selling price, construction costs, and degree of completion are obtainable, revenues will be recorded as the work is performed. This is known as the percentage-of-completion method.

An example is a three-year contract to construct a warehouse that will house BBHB's products. The first year, we estimate that one-third of the project will be complete; therefore, the contractor will record one-third of the estimated total revenue from the contract in year one. Years two and three would be treated the same way.

If dependable estimates of selling price, construction costs, or stage of completion are not obtainable, revenue is not recorded until the project is completed. This is known as the completed contract method.

Unearned revenue

Unearned or deferred revenue is sales revenue for which the company has not completed the earnings process. For example, if BBHB has been paid to train future employees of the customer on how to prepare beans and has received cash for this training up front, the company will not record the sales until the time of service. However, BBHB will create a liability account on the balance sheet, such as Advances from Customers, to properly account for the cash that has been received.

Bad debt

Uncollected credit sales are accounted for as bad debt on the income statement, as well as a deduction of accounts receivable on the balance sheet. The amount of bad debt is estimated out of necessity because it must be recorded in the same year as the original sale. It will often be another fiscal year before actual determination of uncollectible debt is possible.

Statement of cash flow

This shows key portions of the Statement of Cash Flows.

Some investors consider this statement to be the most important because of the insight it provides into the financial activities of the company. It tells you exactly where the company generated its cash from and how it was used.

It always pays to analyze the largest numbers, especially when looking at the statement of cash flows. That will give you a good sense of where the money is going and what it is used for. Where is the money flowing to and from? In terms of money flowing in, is sufficient cash coming in from sales? How about outflow? Is money going out primarily for current expenses, or is it also used to pay off debt? The statement of cash flows (or simply, the cash flow statement) tells you how well a company is managing its money.

The statement of cash flow is divided into three sections. The operating section tells you how the company's basic business performed. The investing section highlights capital expenditures, purchase of investment securities, and acquisitions. This is how the company has invested its money for the future.

The financing section shows whether the company borrowed money or whether the company issued or repurchased shares. The net change in cash is equal to the net effects of what the company generates in operations, what it spends to invest for the future, and how it finances itself.

TABLE 6.1   STATEMENT OF CASH FLOW FOR BUCKETS-OF-CASH CORPORATION YEAR ENDING 12/31/99

Operating Cash Flow	
Net income from operations	$75,000
Depreciation and amortization	$13,000
Non-cash items	-$1,000
Other	$2,300
Operating cash in-flow total	$89,300 (A)
Investing Cash Flow	
Capital expenditures	$36,200
Other investments	-$3,350
Total investing cash flow	$32,850 (B)
Financing Cash Flow	
Dividends paid	-$3,900
Sale (purchase) of stock	-$21,700
Net borrowings	$5,400
Other financing cash flow	$2,000
Total financing cash flow	-$18,200 (C)
Net change in cash	$103,950 (D)*

Note: Money flowing in is a positive number, while money flowing out is a negative number.

*Net change in cash (line item D) is the combination of items A + B + C.

You want to see a company in which net income plus depreciation are greater than capital expenditures plus dividend payments. This is the definition of free cash flow. If a company has free cash flow, it can finance its growth and finance its dividend payments from internal sources. If a company doesn't have a positive free cash flow, it may have to sell equity—which will dilute your holdings—borrow money, sell assets, or use its working capital more efficiently. The cash flow statement provides insight into which of these sources funded the company's activities in the period(s) in question.

In Table 6.1 on the previous page, Buckets-of-Cash Corporation's statement of cash flow shows a healthy cash position. Its net income from operations plus depreciation is $88,000 ($75,000 plus $13,000), which exceeds the capital expenditures ($36,200) plus dividends paid ($3,900) by $47,900. Here are some items to look for in the statement of cash flows:

- The company should have positive and growing cash from operations.

- Large and growing capital expenditures means that the company is investing in its future.

- Repurchase of stock represented by a negative number (because it is a use of cash) is generally positive. Sales of stock (positive values) are generally negative unless explained by rapid growth that often requires additional equity capital.

- A negative number for net borrowings indicating a repayment of debt is generally positive. A profitable company with low financial leverage taking on some new debt may also be positive. A highly leveraged company taking on more dcbt can be dangerous.

What observations can you make regarding Buckets-of-Cash Corporation's statement of cash flow? Its statement provides a useful insight into company operations, but we don't stop there. Beyond the annual report and financial statements, we can gain further information from outside sources such as analysts' reports from the financial industry.

Watch Out!
Currency translation will impact companies with significant foreign operations or companies with significant import and export activities, so this represents an additional business risk of the company.

Stock reports

Stock reports generally are issued from two types of sources: brokerage analysts and independent sources (usually publishers such as Value Line and Standard & Poor's). Analysts from the brokerage industry are among the most closely watched sources of investment opinion. They frequently are interviewed on TV, and some have even reached celebrity status.

Analyst reports

Most companies have been examined and analyzed by one or more financial analysts. These professionals, most often employees of brokerage houses, will write reports that include the analyst's opinion of the stock as well as estimates of future earnings and target stock price levels. This information is public. Assuming that the company whose financial packet you've received has an analyst following it, one of these reports might be included in the packet. (If not, the company will provide you with analyst names and phone numbers so that you can call and make your own request.)

Reading analyst reports is a truly useful exercise. However, there's one part of the report that the analyst and the media think is very important and yet is highly suspect: the buy, sell, or hold recommendation.

Some of the most valuable information in the report is the estimated earnings per share figures. (The better reports print estimates by quarter.) By matching the analyst's quarterly estimates against the quarterly earnings announcements as they come out, investors can determine whether a business and its profits per share are meeting, exceeding, or underperforming analysts' expectations.

Recognize that analysts know a fair amount about how to evaluate a particular company's prospects for growth. And while you shouldn't accept every assertion made by any analyst, their analysis is a key ingredient to sharpening your understanding of companies and their stocks. More than 3,500 analysts working for the brokerage industry keep an eye on thousands of publicly traded companies. And when these analysts speak, institutional as well as individual investors tend to listen, driving stock prices sharply up or down, depending on the nature of the analysts' latest pronouncements.

Some analysts are more influential than others, of course, and none are infallible. But whether you rely on your own analysis or on outside analysis, it's important to know what the professional analysts are saying about stocks you hold or are considering for your portfolio.

Making sense out of stock analysts' recommendations

On December 29, 1999, a Paine Webber securities analyst issued a "buy" recommendation on Qualcomm, the wireless communications company, and established a 12-month price target of $1,000. Swayed by the rosy outlook, investors snapped up shares. Within two days, Qualcomm stock surged more than 30 percent from $562 to $740 per share.

Fast-forward to March 31, 2000. Qualcomm closed at $149, down nearly 20 percent from its December high of $185 (this price reflects a 4-for-1 stock split in January). Adjusted for the stock split, the analyst's 12-month price target of $250 seems a long way off.

When securities analysts talk, you may be interested in hearing what they have to say. But as those investors who bought Qualcomm at or near its

December peak may have learned, don't be too
quick to act on their recommendations. Basing
stock investment decisions solely on the opinions of
securities analysts can be a perilous way to manage
your investments. But if you can't have confidence
in an analyst's recommendations, why listen to anything they have to say?

Understanding analysts' recommendations is
important for investors who want to learn all they
can about a stock. Analysts conduct exhaustive
research on many different companies and industry
groups, making them highly qualified to offer
insights on the prospects of a business or sector.
Although no one can guarantee the performance of
a particular stock or sector, analysts want to make
the right calls because their credibility and long-
term success in the financial services industry are
ultimately dependent on the accuracy of their recommendations. Just remember that analysts do not
have a crystal ball that allows them to predict circumstances that may negatively affect a company's
stock weeks or months down the road.

"Buy" recommendations from analysts are more
common than trees in Yellowstone Park. Out of nearly 26,000 analyst recommendations tracked by
Boston-based research firm First Call Corporation,
less than 1 percent are "sell" ratings. See the section
"Understanding Analysts' Stock Recommendations,"
later in this chapter, for a breakdown on how they
arrive at their recommendations.

Keep a few good rules in mind:

▪ Check company press releases and announcements or other news to see if there is additional information related to the analyst's
  commentary. Does the company give an

adequate explanation for what has happened (good or bad)?

▪ Learn more, if you can, about the track record of the particular analyst whose work resulted in the upgrade or downgrade. Is the analyst an "axe," Wall Street lingo for those whose analytical record is so good that their comments carry disproportionate weight? How about the analyst's employer? An analyst with Merrill Lynch or Goldman Sachs will have greater credibility than one from the obscure firm of Ida, Noe, Watts, Goinon, and Company.

▪ What has been happening to the mean brokerage recommendation on the stock? Has it been trending up or down in the last one, two, or three months? In other words, if 10 analysts are tracking the stock and, in recent months, their "average" recommendation has gone from "buy" to "neutral," do further research before you commit your funds.

▪ What has been the stock's recent performance? If the stock's price has enjoyed a recent climb, you may be late in joining the party. Often the analyst has only identified a stock that was already on an upswing. By the time you're ready to buy, the stock's activity might have slackened.

▪ Are there reasons not to buy the stock, even though you are impressed with the analyst's recommendation? If the analyst recommends certain types of stock, such as small-cap stocks, and his or her firm derives a sizable portion of its income from marketing these securities, you may have reason to

Bright Idea
Before making any investment decision that takes into consideration an analyst's ratings or comments, you should understand the type of analytical approach that the analyst used to arrive at a decision.

wonder if the recommendations are really nothing more than a disguised sales pitch.

▪ Has the analyst's firm done any other business with the company recently that would encourage them to recommend the purchase of the stock over the next 6 to 12 months? Many securities analysts operate with an inherent conflict of interest. Their firm's investment banking division often has banking relationships with the companies that analysts are reviewing. For example, the investment banking division may have managed a company's recent initial public offering (IPO). An analyst who comes out with a negative opinion on a recent IPO may be jeopardizing his or her firm's chances of getting future business from that company, a risk many may be loath to take. So try to look for other positive reasons that would motivate the analyst to recommend the stock.

▪ If an analyst is recommending a stock, find out what the brokerage is doing with its own holdings of that stock. Frequently, the brokerage (through its analyst's well-publicized views) is telling the public to buy the stock while it (or its major clients) is selling the stock. If this is the case, you can find out by checking the SEC reports that the brokerage firm must file.

Ultimately, you are the judge when considering individual stocks. It's okay to conduct your own research and have confidence in your findings. Many investors are building sizable nest eggs by relying chiefly on their own research and investment prudence, especially with the wealth of information now available online. But don't neglect what the analysts are saying, particularly those with stellar reputations and good track records. Just remember to take their recommendations with the proverbial grain of salt.

Understanding analysts' stock recommendations

Ever wonder what analysts mean when they recommend that you "accumulate" a stock? Here's a translation of some of the common terms that analysts use when rating individual securities:

▪ **Strong buy**—This top recommendation is issued if the analyst is very optimistic about the company's future growth prospects. Keep in mind that a "strong buy" doesn't guarantee that the stock will increase in value; it simply means that this analyst has great expectations about the stock's price performance.

▪ **Buy**—A "buy" recommendation means the analyst believes that the underlying company has good prospects for future growth. For example, the company may have introduced a promising new innovation or a high-profile joint venture. A buy recommendation probably will not cause a buying stampede for the stock, but it does signal that the stock may start moving up. Some analysts use terms such as *attractive* or *outperform* as a similarly positive recommendation.

▪ **Accumulate**—An "accumulate" rating simply means that you may want to consider buying the stock if its stock price becomes cheaper. Generally, the analyst who recommends a stock for accumulation isn't crazy about the company's short-term prospects but thinks it has good long-term potential.

Bright Idea
Many Web sites track analysts' views and recommendations. Check the following:
CBS MarketWatch
www.marketwatch.com
Financial Web
www.financialweb.com
I-Exchange
www.iexchange.com
Market Guide
www.marketguide.com
Microsoft's Moneycentral
http://moneycentral.msn.com

Watch Out!
Watch carefully if an analyst's recommendation changes. Several types of analyst comments can influence stock prices. A change in an influential analyst's estimates of a company's future earnings and its earnings growth rate will affect its stock price almost instantly.

- **Hold**—A "hold" or "neutral" rating is usually a euphemism for "I'm not thrilled about the stock's potential performance, and the odds are that it will do poorly, but, what the hell— we already have it in our portfolio."

- **Sell**—A stock would have to be doing very badly before you hear this rare recommendation. In fact, the "S" word is said so infrequently that you have to wonder if analysts are either blind to bad stocks or are haunted by a phrase from their childhood, "If you can't say anything nice, don't say anything at all."

These subjective judgments may be slanted according to a blatant and unapologetic conflict of interest that exists in the brokerage industry. The same firms whose analysis you're reading also have built their businesses on financing the companies they're analyzing. You won't be surprised to hear that the first buy recommendations you'll typically read about a new company that just came public will virtually always appear from the very same firm or firms that underwrote the public offering.

Furthermore, and more importantly, if the brokerage firm analyst were ever to put an outright sell recommendation on a given company's stock, that company would probably never again consider doing any financing business with the analyst's firm. Thus, you'll almost never see a sell recommendation from Wall Street. In fact, Wall Street analysts who see a stock selling at $10, which they predict will go down to $5, will still often call their rating of the company "neutral" rather than "sell."

Stock reports from independent sources
Whether you go to your library's reference section or surf the Internet, you should get a balanced view

on a company by viewing reports not only from analysts, but from other sources as well. The following financial information publishers offer extensive information on individual public companies and provide ongoing reports and ratings.

Standard and Poor's Stock Guides (S&P)
Standard and Poor's Corporation
www.spglobal.com

Value Line Investment Survey
Value Line Corporation
www.valueline.com

Morningstar
www.morningstar.net

(Sample pages from S&P and Value Line are highlighted in Chapter 12, "Monitoring Your Investments.")

SEC reports

Probably the best source of information on a company is the legal documents that public companies must file with the Securities and Exchange Commission (SEC). These fairly comprehensive documents are freely available for public viewing at the SEC government offices but are best accessed through the SEC's extensive Web site at www.sec.gov. The database at this site is called EDGAR, which is short for the Electronic Data Gathering, Analysis, and Retrieval system. EDGAR performs automated collection, validation, indexing, acceptance, and forwarding of submissions by companies and others who are required by law to file forms with the SEC. Its primary purpose is to increase the efficiency and fairness of the securities market for the benefit of investors, corporations, and the economy by accelerating the receipt, acceptance, dissemination, and analysis of time-sensitive corporate information filed with the agency. Not all documents filed with the Commission by public companies will be available on EDGAR. Companies were phased into EDGAR filing over a three-year period ending May 6, 1996. As of that date, all public domestic companies were required to make their filings on EDGAR, except for filings made on paper because of a hardship exemption.

However, the SEC does not permit some documents to be filed electronically, which means that they will not be available on EDGAR. Other documents may be filed on EDGAR voluntarily, so they may or may not be available on EDGAR. For example, Forms 3, 4, and 5 (security ownership and transaction reports filed by corporate insiders) and Form 144 (notice of proposed sale of securities) may be filed on EDGAR at the option of the filer. Similarly, filings by foreign companies are not required to be filed on EDGAR, but some of these companies do so voluntarily. (Until recently, this was also the case with Form 13F, the reports filed by institutional investment managers showing equity holdings by accounts under their management. However, on January 12, 1999, the SEC released a rule requiring electronic filing of the form as of April 1, 1999.)

It should also be noted that the actual annual report to shareholders (except in the case of investment companies) need not be submitted on EDGAR, although some companies do so voluntarily. However, the annual report on Form 10-K or Form 10-KSB, which contain much of the same information, is required to be filed on EDGAR.

Filers may choose to accompany their official filings with a copy in PDF. To read a PDF document, you need an Adobe Acrobat reader (available at no charge at www.adobe.com). Please note the following information about unofficial PDF copies on the Web site. Only documents submitted to the EDGAR system in either plain text or HTML are official filings; PDF documents are unofficial copies of filings. Filers may not use the unofficial PDF copies instead of plain text or HTML documents to meet filing requirements. SEC rules require that an unofficial PDF copy of a document be substantively equivalent to the official filing of which it is the copy. That is, the PDF document must be the same in all respects except that the PDF document may be formatted differently and may contain graphics. It is the filer's responsibility to make sure of this. The EDGAR system cannot check to make sure that the two documents are the same. You should look at the official filing if you need to see what has been filed with the SEC.

Unofficial PDF copies are not subject to certain liabilities under the federal securities laws that are imposed only on filings. However, they are subject to most of the civil liability and antifraud provisions. In addition, PDF copies that are prospectuses retain prospectus liability under Section 12 of the Securities Act. Please note that EDGAR filings are posted to this site at least 24 hours after the date of filing.

General information on the EDGAR database

EDGAR currently supports two types of access:

- **Web browser (used by most visitors to the site)**—Go to www.sec.gov.

- **Anonymous FTP (used primarily by those who download filings in bulk)**—To use anonymous FTP, use your File Transfer Protocol software to connect to ftp.sec.gov, and log in as user

Anonymous with a password of your electronic
mail address. Large FTP transfer requests
(greater than five documents/filings) must be
performed after 9:00 P.M. Eastern Standard
Time.

Guide to corporate filings

The following is a short description of the most common corporate filings made with the SEC. Many of
these filings are now made on EDGAR and thus are
available on the SEC's Web site.

The guide cannot take the place of the SEC's
official rules and regulations; it is not to be used as
a legal reference document. Refer to the federal
securities laws and the rules and regulations (Title
17 of the Code of Federal Regulations, parts 200 to
end) for the official description of the forms mentioned. These are available at most law libraries and
may also be ordered through:

Superintendent of Documents
Government Printing Office
Washington, DC 20402

or

Securities and Exchange Commission
Publications Unit
Mail Stop C-11
450 Fifth Street, NW
Washington, DC 20549

Prospectus

A prospectus is a document issued by a company
that is about to sell stock to the public. Prepared
with the help of lawyers and investment bankers, the
prospectus is an important document for investors.
It discloses critical information regarding the business of a private company, much of it not previously

made public. This includes financial data, background on the top executives, information on pending litigation, details of the offering itself (what proportion of ownership is being sold and what will happen to the proceeds), and risk factors to consider before investing (competition in the industry, barriers to entry, and so on).

The prospectus constitutes Part I of a 1933 Act registration statement. It contains the basic business and financial information on an issuer with respect to a particular securities offering. Investors may use the prospectus to help appraise the merits of the offering and make educated investment decisions.

A prospectus in its preliminary form is frequently called a "red herring" prospectus and is subject to completion or amendment before the registration statement becomes effective. After that, a final prospectus is issued and sales can be consummated.

Form 10-K

This is the annual report that most reporting companies file with the SEC. It provides a comprehensive overview of the registrant's business.

The 10-K is one of the most important documents for investors to reference, so we should take a comprehensive overview of the information provided by the registrant. The report must be filed within 90 days after close of company's fiscal year and contains the items of disclosure detailed in the next sections.

Cover page

This section lists the fiscal year end, state or other jurisdiction of incorporation or organization, title of each class of securities, the exchange on which it is registered, and the number of shares outstanding

Timesaver
Spredgar 2000 software calculates and graphs 30 standard financial ratios from the 10-K and 10-Q filings stored on the SEC EDGAR database. It also generates cash flow analysis and plots ratios over time for "article 5" companies, which includes all companies except financial institutions and utilities. Go to Spredgar's Web site at www.spredgar.com.

Timesaver
hOTeDGAR soft-
ware converts
documents from
the SEC EDGAR
database into a
user-friendly
Excel work book
format. In con-
verting the SEC
document into a
workbook format,
hOTeDGAR nei-
ther adds to nor
subtracts from
the information
in the filing. The
content and
integrity of the
original SEC fil-
ing is thus
unchanged when
using hOTeDGAR.
Go to the
Hottools Web
site at www.
hottools.com

of each of the issuer's classes of common stock, as of the latest practicable date (this date is commonly the filing date, *not* the time period covered in the document).

Part I

Part I consists of the following sections:

- **Item 1: Business**—This section identifies principal products and services of the company, principal markets and methods of distribution and, if "material," competitive factors; backlog and expectation of fulfillment; availability of raw materials; importance of patents, licenses, and franchises; estimated cost of research; number of employees; and effects of compliance with environmental laws.

  If there is more than one line of business, a statement is included for each of the last three years. The statement includes total sales and net income for each line that, during either of the last two fiscal years, accounted for 10 percent or more of total sales or pretax income.

- **Item 2: Properties**—This section identifies the location and character of principal plants, mines, and other important properties, and tells whether they are held in fee or are leased.

- **Item 3: Legal proceedings**—This section gives a brief description of material legal proceedings pending.

- **Item 4: Submission of matters to a vote of security holders**—This section contains information relating to the convening of a meeting of shareholders, whether annual or special, and the matters voted upon.

Part II

The following items are included in Part II of the 10-K.

- **Item 5: Market for the registrant's common stock and related security-holder matters—** This section includes the principal market in which voting securities are traded, with high and low sales prices (or, in the absence of those prices, the range of bid and asked quotations for each quarterly period during the past two years) and the dividends paid during the past two years. In addition to the frequency and amount of dividends paid, this item contains a discussion concerning future dividends.

- **Item 6: Selected financial data—**This provides five-year selected data, including net sales and operating revenue; income or loss from continuing operations, both total and per common share; total assets; long-term obligations, including redeemable preferred stock; and cash dividend declared per common share. This data also includes additional items that could enhance understanding of trends in financial condition and results of operations. Furthermore, the effects of inflation and changing prices should be reflected in the five-year summary.

- **Item 7: Management's discussion and analysis of financial condition and results of operations—**Under broad guidelines, this includes liquidity, capital resources, and results of operations; trends that are favorable or unfavorable, as well as significant events or uncertainties; causes of any material changes

> 66
> I find that a great part of the information I have was acquired by looking up something and finding something else on the way.
> —Franklin P. Adams
> 99

in the financial statements as a whole; limited data concerning subsidiaries; and discussion of effects of inflation and changing prices.

- **Item 8: Financial statements and supplementary data**—Two-year audited balance sheets as well as three-year audited statements of income and the cash flow statement.

- **Item 9: Changes in and disagreements with accountants on accounting and financial disclosure**—Details any changes in accounting disclosure by company and disagreements with accountants' reporting.

Part III

Part III of the 10-K includes these sections:

- **Item 10: Directors and executive officers**—Name, office, term of office and specific background data on each.

- **Item 11: Remuneration of directors and officers**—List of each director and highest paid officers with aggregate annual remuneration exceeding $40,000. This also includes the total paid to all officers and directors as a group.

- **Item 12: Security ownership of certain beneficial owners and management**—Identification of owners of 5 percent or more of registrant's stock. This section also lists the amount and percent of each class of stock held by officers and directors.

- **Item 13: Certain relationships and related transactions**—Disclosure normally made via a proxy statement. In some cases, this may be made using Part III of Form 10-K.

"
People who think they know it all are especially annoying to those of us who do.
—Anonymous
"

Part IV

Part IV includes the following items:

- **Item 14: Exhibits, financial statement schedules,** and reports on Form 8-K—Complete, audited annual financial information and a list of exhibits filed. This also includes any unscheduled material events or corporate changes filed in an 8-K during the year.

Form 10-K schedules (when applicable)

The following are other schedules that may be attached depending on the individual company's reporting requirements.

I. Investments other than investments in affiliates

II. Receivables from related parties and underwriters, promoters, and employees other than affiliates

III. Condensed financial information

IV. Indebtedness of affiliates (not current)

V. Property, plant, and equipment

VI. Accumulated depreciation, and depletion and amortization of property, plant, and equipment

VII. Guarantees of securities of other issuers

VIII. Valuation and qualifying accounts

IX. Short-term borrowings

X. Supplementary income statement information

XI. Supplementary profit and loss information

XII. Income from dividends (equity in net profit and loss of affiliates)

Bright Idea
One of the best Web sites for investors who use SEC reports is the 10-K Wizard (www.10kwizard. com), which tracks company report filings along with SEC reports for institutional investors and insider trading reports. There is no charge for searching this comprehensive, indexed database of SEC reports.

Form 10-Q

Form 10-Q is a rep t reporting companies. financial
statements and ew of the
company's finan year. The
report must be three fiscal
quarters of the ı is due within 45 days of the close of the qu⸺

Form 144

This form must be filed as notice of the proposed sale of restricted securities or securities held by an affiliate of the issuer in reliance on Rule 144 when the amount to be sold during any three-month period exceeds 500 shares or units or has an aggregate sales price in excess of $10,000. This document helps the public track insider trading.

Forms 3, 4, and 5

Every director, officer, or owner of more than 10 percent of a class of equity securities registered under Section 12 of the 1934 Act must file with the SEC a statement of ownership regarding such security. The initial filing is on Form 3, and changes are reported on Form 4. The Annual Statement of Beneficial Ownership of Securities is on Form 5. The forms contain information on the reporting person's relationship to the company and on purchases and sales of such equity securities.

Just the facts

▪ Learn as much as possible about the company from a variety of sources before you invest in its stock.

▪ Read the company's point of view in its annual report and announcements to find out what it is doing, how well it is doing, and why.

▪ Become proficient in reviewing financial statements because they communicate the company's financial standing.

▪ Use reports from analysts to gain informed views to gain a balanced perspective on how well the company is doing.

▪ The company's SEC reports are a relatively accurate source of information because they must legally disclose relevant information about their activities.

Picking Great Stocks

GET THE SCOOP ON...
Growth at a reasonable price ▪ The company's
earnings ▪ The price/earnings ratio ▪ Other
important ratios ▪ Measuring management
effectiveness ▪ Income considerations

Value Investing

Chapter 7

Like many activities, stock investing is subject to fads and the ebb and flow of our changing economy. It was very unpopular in the late 1970s, but it became America's favorite pastime in the late 1990s. Every few years, a new philosophy emerges that captures the attention of investors. Virtually every investing philosophy works occasionally. As the adage goes, even a broken clock is right twice a day. But has any investing approach consistently worked throughout the years?

A value-based approach to stock analysis

The investing approach that has consistently done well through the decades is value investing. Although we can modify the approach to improve on it, the core of long-term stock-picking success lies in a value-investing approach. Value investing means looking at the underlying company and judging whether its stock is "undervalued" or "overvalued."

A value investor sees the company's value and compares it to the stock price. The higher the value of the company and the lower the stock price, the better for the value investor. However, a value investor doesn't buy a stock because it's cheap. That investor buys it because the stock is undervalued. The difference is crucial.

How do you judge the value of a company? First and foremost, you look at the fundamentals—its sales, earnings, assets, and other components of its financial strength. You look at how effective management is at running the business. You compare its financial condition with other companies in its industry. You check the company's track record: How well has it done growing the business during the most recent three-to-five-year period? How about the company's equity (assets minus liabilities)? Is the equity growing year after year?

Here's an example. If you go to a store to buy a pair of pants, which would you choose: a $50 pair of pants on sale for $19, or a $17 pair of pants selling for $17? How you answer that question can determine whether you are a value investor or just somebody looking for cheap pants. The value-oriented approach means that you would buy the $50 pants for $19. Those who buy the $17 pair of pants aren't interested in value—they just want something cheap.

Why aren't more people value investors? One reason is that value stocks are usually not the high-profile stocks that have caught everyone's attention. Also, many investors left these stocks to chase after others that get a lot of play in the market. Don't let this bother you. As these "momentum" investors leave the stock, causing its price to decline, value investors get the opportunity to buy a company's stock at a lower price.

The value investor looks at the company's numbers from three perspectives:

1. **What is the current financial standing of the company?** What are its assets and liabilities what it owns and what it owes? How does the current financial standing compare with a year ago? Three years ago? Is the company's book value close to its market capitalization?

2. **How is the company doing in terms of income and expenses?** How well did it do last quarter? How about last year? Are current sales higher than those of the previous period? How about from three years ago?

3. **What is the standing of the company versus other companies in the same industry?** Is the company doing better than, worse than, or just as well as other companies in the industry? Is the company ranked higher or lower in the industry (based on sales and earnings) versus last year? Three years ago? Five years ago?

The value investor tries to find winning stocks before the rest of the investing public. A value investor does this is by first finding the leading companies in industries that are growing faster than the rest of the economy and researching these companies.

As you review the following observations on analyzing a stock by its financial and business condition, understand that it is the rare stock that has *all* of these attributes. But the more attributes a stock does have, the better. If you find a stock with strong earnings and 70 percent of the attributes discussed in this chapter, it's a worthy investment.

Watch Out!
In the mature bull market of 1999–2000, many investors became attracted to "momentum investing." Momentum investing essentially is investing in companies whose stocks have risen sharply and very quickly. The danger here is that analysis is limited to the stock's short-term behavior, and the strategy can quickly backfire.

Growth at a reasonable price

Valuation is the first step toward intelligent investing. When an investor attempts to determine the
worth of shares based on the fundamentals, she or
he can make informed decisions about what stocks
to buy or sell. Without knowing the company's fundamental value, what is left is guesswork and gut
feelings. Yes, we want value for our investment dollar, but we seek companies that have the potential to
grow so that their stock can appreciate.

For many years, the debate of "value versus
growth" raged in the marketplace. However,
investors do not have to choose. The most assured
long-term success for investors has been to invest as
a growth-oriented value investor.

A growth stock is the stock of a company that
consistently maintains faster-than-average growth. If
the market average for earnings growth has been 10
percent per year for the past three years, and your
stock grew 15 percent per year during the same time
frame, then it is technically a growth stock. There
are different measurements for what constitutes a
growth stock, but typically the measurements are in
areas such as sales and earnings. On Wall Street,
"growth stock" tends to refer to some large, established firms whose identities or brands are household words. Growth stocks tend to have higher P/E
ratios (explained later in the section "The Price
Earnings Ratios") than the overall stock market
because investors expect more from them and are
willing to pay for reliable growth. The danger is that
a company's stock may become overpriced and subsequently exhibit slower appreciation. Often, a value
stock that hits its stride in sales and earnings
becomes tomorrow's growth stock.

Unofficially ...
The most impor-
tant single mea-
sure of worth
that value
investors look at
is the price-to-
earnings ratio
(P/E ratio). It is
also referred to
as the "earnings
multiple" or
simply the
"multiple." This
ratio establishes
a connection
between a
stock's price and
the company's
earnings.

"Growth at a reasonable price" (GARP) has gained popularity, and for good reason. The world according to GARP investors combines the value and growth approaches. It also includes looking at the company's financial ratios to get a true picture regarding its business potential. Investors look for companies with solid growth prospects and current share prices that are as low as possible.

Imagine that you want to buy and run an existing business. You look in the business opportunity classifieds section of your local paper and come across two in an industry that interests you. They are similar businesses in virtually every way—both have growing sales and earnings. When you look at the financial data, you discover that they had identical net earnings last year: $50,000. Which do you choose? There is one crucial difference: their price. The first business is being sold for $1 million, while the second has a price tag of $750,000. In this case, the second business is the better choice because you are paying less for the same earnings. The second choice epitomizes buying growth at a reasonable price. It also illustrates a lower P/E ratio.

Former Fidelity Magellan Fund manager Peter Lynch is GARP's most well-known proponent. One of the most common GARP approaches is to buy stocks when the P/E ratio is lower than the rate at which earnings per share can grow in the future. As the company's earnings per share grow, the P/E of the company will fall if the share price remains constant. Because fast-growing companies normally can sustain high P/Es, the GARP investor is buying a company that is fairly priced today and will grow strongly tomorrow. The first item we need to start looking at is earnings.

The company's earnings

Earnings is the single most important item in a company's financial picture. When we watch the financial shows on TV or read the financial papers, we often read about the company's earnings as expressed in the quarterly earnings report. Analysts ponder and debate the company's expected earnings versus actual earnings and how the earnings fared over the prior quarter or the same quarter last year.

Earnings per share

The earnings are usually reported as earnings per share (EPS). EPS is the company's net income divided by common shares outstanding. A company that earns $1 million for the year and has one million shares outstanding has an EPS of $1. This EPS figure, which represents how much of earnings each share is entitled to, is important as the basis for various calculations that an investor might make in assessing a stock's price and value.

Earnings will always be the most important barometer of success for a company. Although we occasionally get periods in our history when analysts say that earnings are not that important (such as with Internet companies in 1999), they really *are* that important. Looking at past earnings is the first place to start your analysis.

Important point about past earnings

The company should have earnings that have steadily increased over at least the past three years, and preferably over the past five. Each of the years should see the earnings increase by at least 10 percent over the year before. If fictitious company,

Bright Idea
Five major services compile earnings estimates by analysts and make them available online. Visit these sites: **First Call** (part of Thomson Financial and my personal favorite) www. thomsoninvest. net/FirstCall **The I/B/E/S** (The Institutional Brokers Estimate System) www.ibes.com Multex www. multexinvestor. com **Standard & Poor's (S&P)** www. personalwealth. com **Zacks** www.zacks.com

Candy Apples'R'Us Inc., had an EPS of $1 in 1999, it should have an EPS of at least $1.10 in 2000, an EPS of $1.21 in 2001, and so on. In strong economic times, the rate should be at least 15 percent per year greater than the year before.

Calculating the EPS growth rate

When we talk about growth rate, we're talking primarily about the projected future earnings per share growth rate. The most relevant numbers—earnings estimates—are the ones that haven't been reported yet. The financial industry spends a lot of time and effort projecting earnings. Analysts crunch the numbers based on a variety of factors, including past performance.

The future EPS growth rate for a single year is quite simple to calculate. Let's say that Candy Apples'R'Us has just reported an EPS of 90 cents this year, and analysts estimate that it will earn a $1.35 EPS for the upcoming year. The one-year growth rate, a straight percentage gain calculation, is 50 percent. This was calculated by using the following formula:

Earnings Estimate for Upcoming Year –
Current Earnings ÷ Current Earnings × 100 =
Growth Rate

This is easy math. All you have to do is plug in the numbers and subtract, divide, and multiply. In the Candy Apples'R'Us example, the earnings estimate for the upcoming year is $1.35 per share, and current earnings are 90 cents per share.

Plugging those numbers into the previous formula, you get a one-year growth rate of 50 percent:

$1.35 – $0.90 ÷ $0.90 × 100 = 50%

Quality of earnings

When looking at a company's earnings, you also need to check their quality; check to see whether the EPS is reported as diluted. Diluted earnings means a watering down in the ownership stake represented by a single share of stock, usually as a result of the sale of additional shares.

In the previous example, we calculated the EPS as $1 per share. However, diluted EPS takes into the calculation all shares of the company, not just the shares outstanding. The shares outstanding in this example number one million shares, but what if there are 100,000 additional shares that are held by the company but not outstanding? Ultimately, these shares must be part of the equation. The diluted EPS would be 91 cents per share instead of $1 (net income of $1 million divided by 1,100,000 shares = 91 cents EPS).

As you can see, diluted earnings (or dilution) means diminished value for investors; the company hasn't gained any new assets or changed its market position, yet suddenly the pie has been divided into more—subsequently smaller—pieces.

Say that the fictitious company Candy Apples'R'Us Inc., reported 1999 earnings as $2 million on sales of $18 million. A quick calculation tells us that its earnings are 11 percent of sales ($2 million divided by $18 million). What makes up the $2 million in earnings? Those $2 million are actual earnings what a company earned with all current revenue and all expenses included.

What investors may misunderstand is that actual earnings may include one-time events that could warp operational earnings, either positively or negatively:

■ The company may write off substantial bad debts in a given year. Or, the company may take extra depreciation or acquire an asset of another company or settle a lawsuit against the company. These events would decrease actual earnings.

■ A company may sell an asset such as a building or other substantial asset. The company may spin off a division and sell it as a separate company. These events would increase actual earnings.

Actual earnings can be subject to a good many judgments by both company management and outside accountants because the actual earnings figure is arrived at by subtracting all expenses from all revenues. The problem here is that total revenues and total expenses will include unusual items that will skew the numbers, giving investors a misleading picture of the company's earning prowess. Some expenses exist mostly on paper.

Net income also can be swollen by earnings from discontinued operations, meaning that net income will be much lower next year. Because of the many issues surrounding net income, many investors prefer to focus on other measures of profit that remove some of the smoke and confusion generated by taxes, depreciation, and other factors. Although the total actual earnings is an important number, it should not be looked at as the only number. Value investors don't even regard the actual earnings as the most important earnings figure to look at; the best number to look at is operational earnings.

Operating earnings includes only revenue and costs from ongoing operations. It excludes one-time non-operational charges, such as gains or losses on sales of assets, or one-time acquisition costs. Inventory write-downs and currency impacts are to be included in operating earnings (although the market often views them as special). Costs such as interest expenses and taxes are also ignored. Operating income gives investors an idea of how much money a company makes from its business activity. Why are operating earnings a better measure of the business's financial ability? Because they measure the company's core activity of producing and selling the products and services it has to offer.

What to look out for in company earnings

There is growing concern by the Securities and Exchange Commission (SEC) and some financial analysts that many companies are relying on creative accounting to bolster their earnings results. More companies are investing in other companies' stocks, for example, boosting their own earnings when they sell shares at a profit. Experts say such gains—including those recorded for the rising value of a company's pension funds or those helped by adjusting assumptions about the depreciation of assets—can obscure the results from a company's operations.

Yet with many stocks trading at sky-high multiples of their earnings, at least on a historical basis, figuring out a company's true financial position has never been a more important exercise for shareholders. The SEC is concerned about the diminished quality of financial reporting.

In recent years, the SEC has penalized increasingly more companies for inaccurate or misleading earnings reports. They warn investors that they should read each public filing and not rely on any particular document when making financial decisions. This can be an uphill battle, at least where the average investor is concerned. Poring over SEC filings is rarely anybody's idea of fun. Some specific items that you should be aware of are discussed in the next sections.

Stock sales

More companies that report impressive earnings today do so with a little help from the bull market. Because many companies have also bought stock, gains from the sale of securities have become a bigger piece of the earnings pie. For example, in its most recent quarter, Bank of America reported gains on stock investments of 8 cents a share, or 6 percent of its earnings of $1.33 a share. Investors should consider these types of gains as nice bonuses, but they shouldn't be counted on as a regular component of income.

A company with securities gains of a different sort is American Express (AXP). In 2000, AXP reported a pretax capital gain of $154 million on its sales of credit card receivables during 1999. It did not attribute any earnings to the sales, saying that it invested the gains in marketing and promotion programs to increase card use and the number of cards in force.

However, AXP's earnings would have been lower if it had not been able to cover those marketing costs with the proceeds of the securities sales. The sale of these receivables accounted for about 22 cents a share in earnings, or almost 4 percent of the company's net income for the year. Also, because these capital gains were a one-time, nonrecurring event, they should not even have been used to offset an ongoing expense such as marketing costs (which are a recurring cost).

Stock options

Stock options have become a very popular form of compensation in recent years. Usually, compensation is an expense item that gets reported on the income statement. However, accounting rules have allowed companies that issue stock options to report them in creative ways. Companies such as Cisco Systems and Microsoft booked stock options as liabilities on their balance sheets rather than as current expenses in reporting income to shareholders. However, they paid no income taxes. How could this be?

Microsoft, for example, took an options-related tax deduction of $11.4 billion in the first nine months of its fiscal year 2000, which meant a corporate tax savings of $4 billion. Yet, to shareholders, Microsoft reported earnings of $10.6 billion. Many companies have performed this accounting gimmick. Eventually, the numbers even out, however—sooner or later, the stock option compensation has to hit the income statement. However, the inevitable decreased earnings will hurt share prices, which will send investment portfolios plunging.

Investors are best advised to see how stock options are booked. At the point they are paid by the company, they should be included as expenses. If not, check the liabilities section on the balance sheet. In a subsequent period, they will shrink earnings, which will have an adverse impact on earnings.

Pension income

Corporate pension plans are another device for tweaking company earnings. The bull market of the 1990s boosted the value of many companies' pension fund assets. Under SEC-approved accounting rules, to the degree that investment growth swells a pension fund's assets beyond its liabilities—that is, what it is obligated to pay pensioners—the gains go directly into the profits of a company.

Although such profits are wonderful, shareholders cannot view them as favorably as income generated from a company's business operations. In other words, the income from pension gains should not be assigned the same multiple as, say, the income from a company's sales of goods and services. Pension gains can account for quite a bit of a company's net income.

In 1999, General Electric (GE), for example, had total pension gains of $1.4 billion, a 40 percent increase from 1998. That amounted to 9 percent of GE's pretax earnings. Without the income from its pension funds' growth, GE's EPS for 1999 would have been lower by nearly 7 percent.

Boosting sales

Because Internet companies are judged on their sales growth, that is where investors in such companies should be careful.

Webvan Group is an Internet-based grocer housed in California that went public in 1999. In January 2000, the company announced that its revenues for the fourth quarter were $9.1 million, up 136 percent from the previous quarter. Gross profit was $1.7 million, up sharply from the $350,000 that the company recorded in the prior quarter.

But according to Webvan's earnings release, some 8.3 percent of the quarter's revenues, $750,000 worth, came from purchases by the company's executives and affiliated companies of goods that were then donated to charity.

Although this was a generous act by the company executives, these donations got booked as sales by the company. Webvan reported gross profit that was 500 percent the amount reported in the previous quarter. Without these "sales," the company's gross profit would have been up about 300 percent. That's still impressive, but significantly lower than reported.

Webvan confirmed that the donations were booked as revenues, but said that they were part of a corporate giving program started to help local food banks.

When Webvan disclosed the $750,000 in purchases, the company's stock was trading at $16; it closed at nearly $6. As of the end of June 2000, Webvan was still trading below $8 per share. The short-term price decline was directly linked to the report on charitable payments.

But any investor perplexed enough by this odd transaction to sell saved himself or herself quite a bit of portfolio damage.

Inflated assets

Beware of companies that overestimate how much their assets, or the equipment they lease to customers, will be worth down the road. Optimistic assumptions allow a company to reduce the amount of depreciation that it reports on its income statement each year. That, in turn, makes earnings look better—and sets up investors for earnings-damaging writedowns in the future.

One company that may be doing this is IBM. In its financial statements for 1999, the company said that the salvage value of equipment that it leases— $737 million last year—was rising as a percent of the money owed on the leases (in accounting jargon, the net investment). Last year, the salvage value was 5.2 percent of the net investment, up from 4.8 percent in 1998 and 4.1 percent in 1997.

Customer financing

Competition is getting so tough among companies selling telecommunications equipment and other technology that many of them are pulling out all the stops to make a sale. An increasingly popular approach is to finance corporate customers' purchases of equipment over a period of years.

Cisco Systems, Lucent Technologies, IBM, and Hewlett-Packard are just some of the companies now doing this. Many of those buying the gear are small startups that lack the cash to buy the equipment outright. The problem, of course, is that such buyers may never have the cash.

Cisco, which said in its latest quarterly report that its financings were rising, acknowledged the danger. "Although we have programs in place to monitor and mitigate the associated risk," the report said, "there can be no assurance that such programs will alleviate all of our credit risk." The difficulty for investors in all this is that some companies do not specify what portion of their sales are financed.

The price/earnings ratio

Ratios are relationships between numbers. They can reveal a great deal about a company's financial health. Financial ratio analysis is a method that lets you make internal evaluations using current data from financial statements (and comparisons with past financial statements)—but perhaps more importantly, it is also a method to compare the company with competitors or other industry players. Ratios are a sort of common denominator for comparisons between companies.

One of the most important ratios is the price/earnings multiple, or the "earnings multiple."

The P/E ratio is the latest closing price divided by the latest 12 months' earnings per share. The *P* in P/E stands for the stock's price; the *E* is for earnings per share. This is one of the most important and most widely regarded barometers of a company's value.

The P/E ratio is important because it is one of the few ratios that establishes a direct relationship between the company's operations (its earnings) and the stock price. As noted in previous chapters, a stock could be schizophrenic, going up or down in ways that seem to bear no relationship to the company's success. Sometimes a company can do well, yet the stock goes down. Sometimes a company does poorly, yet the stock goes up. In the short term, the stock seems to have its own life, separate from the fortunes of the company. This is partly the reason why many analysts give little credence to the P/E ratio. So what makes it so important to value investors?

The massive body of research done over many years into the relationship between stock values and the company's success presents a conclusive point. For long-term investors, the P/E ratio is extremely important. In the long run, the stock's price always comes down to the earnings and the P/E ratio. Ignoring the P/E ratio is done at the investor's risk.

A high P/E is often a reflection of lofty expectations for a stock because no one would invest knowing that it would take 40 years just to make that money back. The idea is that earnings will grow. A high P/E can also reflect poor recent earnings. A low P/E can imply low investor expectations, an undervalued stock, or both.

Unofficially ...
Historically, the general market has had a P/E in the range of 10 to 15. In 1997, the S&P 500's P/E was a then-remarkable 23. As of February 2000, its P/E was 37, but the S&P 500's P/E has usually been in the mid-teens. Generally, the lower the P/E ratio, the safer the investment. Always compare your stock's P/E with its industry and the market as well.

A good way to look at the P/E is illustrated in the following example. Say that your friend wants to sell you a business for $100,000, and he says that the business has net earnings of $1,000. You have to make a decision about buying it. In this case, the price to earnings ratio is 100 ($100,000 divided by $1,000). This is a very high multiple. If you bought the business, it would take 100 years to get your investment back! Why buy the business if that's the case? Additionally, you could get a better return on your money elsewhere. What if you put that $100,000 in a savings account earning 5 percent? Your investment would earn $5,000, which is a safer bet and gives you a better return on your money as well.

When you invest in a stock, the same concept applies. In January 2000, eBay, the Internet auction company, had an astronomical P/E ratio of nearly 4,000. This means that it would take 4,000 years for investors to get their money back if eBay's earnings continued at the same pace. Could eBay sustain its high price with that high a P/E ratio? In the long run, it's extremely unlikely.

In the short run, the P/E ratio does not have much impact because investors jump in and jump out continuously.

If high P/E stocks offer the risk of overvaluation, why would investors buy them? The simple reason is expectation. They expect that the future prospects of the company will overcome the current overvaluation. Also, the P/E ratio is not a static number. What if the company's earnings rise this year and the next? That would bode well for the stock price, too.

Keep in mind that there are two basic types of P/E:

- **Trailing P/E**—This is the stock price divided by the most recent four quarters (12 months) of earnings. This is the most frequently quoted type of P/E because we are dealing with the most recent available data. The drawback of the trailing P/E is that past performance is not always indicative of future results. What if next year's earnings differ greatly from last year's?

- **Forward P/E**—This is based on analysts' projections or expectations of earnings. You calculate the forward P/E by dividing the current stock price by the earnings per share expected for the coming 12-month period. Many investors prefer this P/E ratio because the stock's price will move based on earnings expectations.

The informed investor looks at both P/Es to monitor the company's progress.

The P/E is useless for companies lacking earnings, of course. Nortel Networks (NT), for example, reported earnings losses in 1999. Hence, there's no P/E ratio for Nortel. That doesn't mean that investors shouldn't invest in companies unencumbered by earnings, but P/E won't help you evaluate them. Investors shouldn't rely on P/E alone when they value companies.

P/Es can vary from industry to industry, so what is high for one is not necessarily high for another. A company's P/E should be looked at against those of similar companies and against that of the stock market as a whole because different industries and even different companies are characterized by markedly different P/Es. In general, fast-growing technology companies have high P/Es because the stock price is taking account of anticipated growth as well as current earnings. High-tech companies often trade at P/Es above 40, or about double the overall market P/E (as of March 2000). Real estate stocks such as real estate investment trusts (REITs) have had P/Es in the range of 9 to 14.

In his book *Irrational Exuberance*, Robert Shiller shows four extremes in price/earnings ratios going back over history. The first occurred in 1901, when P/E ratios rose to approximately 25. The second was in 1929, when P/E ratios rose to about 33. The third was in 1966, when P/E ratios rose to about 24. The most recent year was 1999, when P/E ratios rose to 44. The research in Shiller's book points out that when the market's P/E ratio reached these levels, investors thereafter experienced very poor (or negative returns) on their stock investments for an extended period of time. His findings indicate that the total real, inflation-adjusted returns after 1901, 1929, and 1966 were .02 percent, 0.4 percent, and 1.9 percent, respectively. The remarkable point is that these abysmal returns came after holding the stocks for 20 years!

The warning is that 1999's P/E ratio is much higher and therefore could augur similarly disastrous investment results.

Price/earnings growth (PEG) ratio

PEG is the P/E ratio divided by expected per-share earnings growth over the coming year. A value of less than 1 implies that the stock may be undervalued; greater than 1 implies that it's overvalued. The ratio is used to help investors gauge whether a stock is expensive, fairly valued, or cheap, relative to a

Bright Idea
When a company doesn't have earnings, the next best way to value it is with the price-to-sales ratio. Whether or not a company has made money in the last year, there are always revenues.

company's expected future growth. In general, experienced investors prefer to buy a stock when its P/E is lower than the earnings growth rate or when its PEG ratio is less than 1.

Say that the fictitious company Website-O-Rama Inc. (WOI)'s stock is at $20 and earned $1.00 per share during the past 12 months. In the coming year, WOI is expected to earn $1.25 per share, with earnings continuing to grow at the rate of 25 percent per year for the next three years. The P/E on the stock, based on the current year's earnings forecast, is 16 (calculated by dividing the stock price of $20 by the estimated earnings per share of $1.25). The stock's PEG ratio is 0.64 (found by dividing the P/E [16] by the long-term earnings growth forecast of 25 percent, or $^{16}/_{25}$). Generally speaking, WOI would be considered attractive because the stock's earnings multiple is significantly below its anticipated growth, as demonstrated by the stock carrying a PEG ratio below 1.0.

Of course, there are exceptions. Companies that post consistent growth (particularly if accompanied by high returns on equity and assets) often merit a PEG ratio higher than 1. For example, blue-chip companies such as General Electric (GE) have high PEG ratios. So, while earnings might be growing 15 percent annually, if future earnings forecasts are considered readily achievable, the market will be willing to pay more for the stock. Also, bear in mind that PEG ratios are more commonly used when evaluating growth stocks, as opposed to defensive or cyclical stocks. PEG ratios are considered less useful in assessing cyclical stocks than those in industries such as banking, oil, or real estate, where assets are a more important indicator of value.

Timesaver
If you are having difficulty figuring out how to calculate and use the PEG ratio, try the Internet. The Motley Fool Web site has what they call the Fool Ratio (PEG) or PEGulator. Calculate PEGs online by simply inputting all the necessary information at www.fool.com.

PEG is considered particularly useful in valuing small-cap and mid-cap growth stocks, which typically pay no dividend. For valuing larger stocks, it is advisable to add a company's dividend yield to its projected five-year earnings growth rate. This is based on the accepted idea that large-cap stocks are valued by investors for their dividend yield as well as the potential for appreciation.

Other important ratios

Although it's important to look at ratios with the company's earnings, they give only a partial picture to investors. Different types of ratios exist, all of which are very useful in gaining a clear picture of a company and its financial strength.

Say, for example, that you are thinking about buying the stock of a company that has debt of $1 billion. That's certainly a lot of debt. You may ask, "Isn't that too much debt?" But the more appropriate question to ask would be, "Compared to what?" If the company has assets worth $3 billion, the debt amount is not too burdensome. The ratio of debt to assets would be 33 percent. In other words, the company has only 33 cents of debt for every dollar of assets. This is an acceptable debt-to-asset ratio.

But what if the company has assets valued at only $1 million? The ratio of debt to assets is 1,000 to 1. This is an unacceptable debt-to-asset ratio. Whenever the company's debt exceeds the value of its assets, this is a negative sign. Is it enough justification to avoid the company altogether? Not necessarily. The company may have other redeeming features, such as positive earnings. Also, as in earnings ratios, debt ratios vary from industry to industry, so it's best to compare the company against its peers.

66
You want to know a sure way to lose money? Buy what's popular and don't know what you are investing in.
—Marty Whitman (Yale University professor)
99

When you are considering a company, you should look at all the important ratios. A company doesn't have to be perfect. It would be almost impossible to find a company that positively meets or exceeds all the ratios mentioned in this chapter. (If you find one, buy as much of its stock as possible!) Generally, it should be as strong as possible according to widely used ratios that have become acceptable standards of measuring business success.

Financial ratio analysis is a time-tested method of analyzing a business. Wall Street investment firms, commercial bank loan officers, and savvy business owners use it to learn more about the financial health and potential of a company.

In the previous section, we discussed the P/E ratio and the PEG ratio, which fall into one of five categories of ratios: profitability ratios. The other four categories are listed here:

Watch Out!
Don't stop ana-lyzing your com-pany after you buy its stock. Even if the past three years showed good financial health as measured by its ratios, con-tinue to analyze the numbers at least once a year. If the com-pany's financial strength deterio-rates, the chang-ing ratios will warn you, and you'll be able to sell your stock before the market notices.

- Common size ratios
- Liquidity ratios
- Efficiency ratios
- Solvency ratios

Common size ratios

Common size ratios can be developed from both balance sheet and income statement items. This is a simple process that converts numbers on your finan-cial statements into information that can be used to make period-to-period and company-to-company comparisons. For example, if you wanted to evaluate your cash position compared to the cash position of your primary competitor, you would want more information than to simply know that you had, say, $12,000 and that he or she had $22,000. Common size ratios are one way to make comparisons more meaningful. Use Tables 7.1 and 7.2 to further understand the roles of common size ratios.

Common size ratios from the balance sheet

To compute common size ratios from your balance sheet, simply compute every asset category as a percentage of total assets and every liability account as a percentage of total liabilities plus owners' equity. Here is what a common size balance sheet looks like:

TABLE 7.1   SOUP-ON-A-STICK, INC.
COMMON SIZE BALANCE SHEET
FOR THE YEAR ENDING DECEMBER 31, 1999

ASSETS	$	$%
Current Assets		
Cash	$12,000	6.6%
Marketable securities	$10,000	5.5%
Accounts receivable (net of uncollectable accounts)	$17,000	9.4%
Inventory	$22,000	12.2%
Prepaid expense	$4,000	2.2%
Total Current Assets	**$65,000**	**35.9%**
Fixed Assets		
Building and equipment	$105,000	58.3%
Minus depreciation	$30,000	16.6%
Net buildings and equipment	$75,000	41.6%
Land	$40,000	22.2%
Total Fixed Assets	**$115,000**	**63.8%**
Total Assets	**$180,000**	**100.0%**
LIABILITIES		
Current Liabilities		
Wages payable	$3,000	1.6%
Accounts payable	$25,000	13.8%
Taxes payable	$12,000	6.6%
Total Current Liabilities	**$40,000**	**22.2%**

TABLE 7.1 (CONTINUED)

ASSETS	$	$%
Long-Term Liabilities		
Mortgage payable	$70,000	38.8%
Note payable	$15,000	8.3%
Deferred taxes	$15,000	8.3%
Total Long-Term Liabilities	**$100,000**	**55.5%**
Total Liabilities	**$140,000**	**77.7%**
Equity	$40,000	22.2%
Total Liabilities and Equity	**$180,000**	**100.0%**

In the example for Soup-on-a-Stick Inc., cash is shown as being 6.6 percent of total assets. This percentage is the result of the following calculation: 12,000/180,000 × 100. Multiplying by 100 converts the ratio into a percentage.

Common size ratios translate data from the balance sheet, such as having $12,000 in cash, into the information that 6.6 percent of Soup-on-a-Stick Inc.'s total assets are in cash. It also gives you the information that can be produced by adding percentages together, such as the realization that 11.7 percent (6.6% + 5.1%) of ABC's total assets are in cash and marketable securities.

The ability to pay current liabilities is also extremely important. Looking at the common size balance sheet for the Soup-on-a-Stick Inc., it is easy to see that the company can meet current liabilities. (Compare the line items of Total Current Liabilities [$40,000] with Total Current Assets [$65,000]—you can see that assets outnumber liabilities by $25,000.)

Common size ratios for the income statement

To prepare common size ratios from your income statement, simply compute all income accounts as a percentage of sales. This converts the income statement into a powerful analytical tool. Here is what a common size income statement looks like for the fictional Soup-on-a-Stick Inc.:

TABLE 7.2   SOUP-ON-A-STICK INC.
INCOME STATEMENT
PERIOD ENDING DECEMBER 31, 1999

	$	$%
Sales	$200,000	100%
Cost of goods sold	$130,000	65%
Gross profit	$70,000	35%
Operating Expenses		
Selling expenses	$22,000	11%
General expenses	$10,000	5%
Administrative expenses	$4,000	2%
Total operating expenses	$36,000	18%
Operating income	$34,000	17%
Other income	$2,500	1%
Interest expense	$500	0%
Income before taxes	$36,000	18%
Income taxes	$1,800	1%
Net Profit	$34,200	17%

Common size ratios allow you to begin to make knowledgeable comparisons with past financial statements for the company and to assess trends (both positive and negative) in your financial statements. The gross profit margin and the net profit margin ratios are two common size ratios to which investors should pay particular attention. On a common size income statement, these margins appear as the line items Gross Profit and Net Profit. For Soup-on-a-Stick Inc., the common size ratios show that the gross profit margin is 35 percent of sales. This is computed by dividing gross profit by sales (and multiplying by 100 to create a percentage):

$$\$70,000/200,000 \times 100 = 35\%$$

Even small changes of 1 or 2 percent in the gross profit margin can affect a business severely. All expenses should be analyzed, and no expenses should be taken for granted. Comparing expenses to sales puts them in perspective.

Compute common size ratios from the income statement. Look at the gross profit and net profit margins as a percentage of sales. Compare these percentages with the same items from the income statement from a year ago. Are any fluctuations favorable and/or explainable?

Liquidity ratios

Liquidity ratios measure a company's ability to pay off short-term liabilities with assets that can readily be converted to cash. The two most common liquidity ratios are known as the current ratio and the quick ratio. Both are based on balance sheet items.

The current ratio is a measure of financial strength. The number of times current assets exceed current liabilities is a valuable expression of a business' soundness.

This is the formula for the current ratio:

Current Ratio = Total Current Assets/Total Current Liabilities

Using the balance sheet data in the first table for Soup-on-a-Stick Inc., we can compute the following current ratio for the company:

65,000/40,000 = 1.6

This tells the shareholders of Soup-on-a-Stick Inc., that current liabilities are covered by current assets 1.6 times. The current ratio answers the question, "Does the business have enough current assets to meet the payment schedule of current liabilities with a margin of safety?" A rule of thumb puts a good current ratio at 2 to 1. Of course, the adequacy of a current ratio will depend on the nature of the business and the character of the current assets and current liabilities. Although there is usually little doubt about debts that are due, there can be doubt about the quality of accounts receivable or the cash value of inventory. A current ratio can be improved by either increasing current assets or decreasing current liabilities.

A high current ratio may mean that cash is not being used in an optimal way. If the company has a current ratio greater than 2, there might not be good cash utilization. That is, the cash might be better invested in equipment or research and development to create more products.

The quick ratio is also called the "acid test" ratio. The quick ratio looks only at a company's most liquid assets and divides them by current liabilities. Here is the formula for the quick ratio:

Quick Ratio = (Current Assets −
Inventory)/Current Liabilities

The assets considered to be "quick" assets are cash, stocks and bonds, and accounts receivable (all of the current assets on the balance sheet except inventory). The quick ratio tests whether a business can meet its obligations if adverse economic conditions were such that the company couldn't convert its inventory to cash in time to pay its bills.

Using the balance sheet data for the Soup-on-a-Stick Inc., we can compute the following quick ratio for the company:

$$(65,000 - 22,000)/40,000 = 1.07$$

This is an adequate quick ratio for the company. In general, quick ratios between .50 and 1 are

Moneysaver
Many free financial calculators are available on the Internet to help you calculate stock ratios. Try the following Web sites:
E-analytics
www. e-analytics.com
Investorama
www. investorama.com
Microsoft Moneycentral
www. moneycentral. msn.com

considered satisfactory as long as the collection of receivables is not expected to slow.

Efficiency ratios

This section includes information on five types of ratios that measure the efficiency of your company's operations: inventory turnover ratio, sales-to-receivables ratio, days' receivables ratio, return on assets, and return on sales ratio.

These ratios are just a sampling of the many ratios that can be compiled from a company's balance sheet and income statement.

Inventory turnover

The inventory turnover ratio measures the number of times inventory "turned over" during a time period. It is also known as the cost of sales-to-inventory ratio. This ratio is an indication of purchasing and production efficiency. The data necessary for this ratio comes from both the company's income statement and balance sheet. Here is the formula:

Inventory Ratio = Cost of Goods Sold/Inventory

Using the financial statements for the Soup-on-a-Stick Inc., we can compute the following inventory turnover ratio for the company:

$130,000/22,000 = 5.90

In general, the higher a cost of sales to inventory ratio, the better. A high ratio shows that inventory is turning over quickly and that little unused inventory is being stored.

Sales-to-receivables ratio

The sales-to-receivables ratio measures the number of times that accounts receivables turned over during the period. It also uses information from both the balance sheet and the income statement. The higher the turnover of receivables, the shorter the time between a sale and the collection of cash. The ratio is based on net sales and net receivables. (Reminder: Net sales equals sales less any allowances for returns or discounts. Net receivables equals accounts receivable less any adjustments for bad debts. Sales on the income statement are in fact net sales.)

The sales-to-receivables ratio is calculated as follows:

Sales-to-Receivables Ratio = Net Sales/Net Receivables

Using the financial statements for the Soup-on-a-Stick Inc., (and assuming that the sales reported on their income statement is actually *net* sales), we can compute the following sales-to-receivables ratio for the company:

$$200,000/17,000 = 11.76$$

This means that receivables turned over almost 12 times (11.76) during the period. This means that only a 12th of total sales remained uncollected at any given point in time, on average. This is a ratio that you will definitely want to compare to industry standards. Keep in mind that its meaning depends on the amount of cash sales that a company typically has. For a company without many cash sales, it may not be important. Also, it is a measure at only one point in time and does not take into account seasonal fluctuations.

Return on assets ratio

The return on assets ratio measures the relationship between profits being generated and assets being used. It is computed as follows:

Return on Assets = Net Income Before Taxes/Total Assets × 100 (Multiplying by 100 turns the ratio into a percentage)

Using the balance sheet and income statement for the Soup-on-a-Stick Inc., we can compute the following return on assets ratio for the company:

$36,000/180,000 × 100 = 20%

You can find more on this ratio later in this chapter (under management effectiveness).

Return on sales

Return on sales is net income as a percentage of sales. Return on sales varies widely by industry. The supermarket business, for example, usually has a low return on sales; the business is heavily dependent on volume. Like the price/cash flow ratio, return on sales can be useful in assessing cyclical companies that sometimes have no earnings during down periods, and firms whose business requires a huge capital investment and thus a great deal of depreciation.

Solvency ratios

Solvency ratios measure a company's stability and its ability to repay debt over the medium to long term. Solvency ratios will give a strong indication of the financial health and viability of the business. We'll discuss the following solvency ratios:

- Debt-to-assets ratio
- Debt-to-equity ratio
- Working capital
- Net sales to working capital

Debt-to-assets ratio (DAR)

The debt-to-assets ratio (DAR) is liabilities divided by assets. The DAR is a good indicator of the extent to which a business is leveraged. The lower this number, the more conservative the firm and the less likely it is to be knocked for a loop in hard times. On the other hand, the judicious use of leverage can result in a higher return on assets—in other words, increased profitability. Like so many ratios, this one varies depending on the industry a company is in. Generally, however, the debt of industrial firms should not exceed two-thirds of equity, or a debt ratio of about 66 percent. This ratio tends to be higher in the transportation and utility industries.

Debt-to-equity ratio (DER)

The debt-to-equity ratio (or leverage ratio) is an indicator of a company's solvency. It is a measure of how dependent a company is on debt financing (or borrowings) as compared to owner's equity. It shows how much of a business is owned and how much is owed. It is computed as follows:

Debt-to-Equity Ratio = Total Liabilities/Net Assets (Reminder: Equity = Total Assets Minus Total Liabilities)

Using balance sheet data for the Soup-on-a-Stick Inc., we can compute the following debt-to-equity ratio for the company:

$140,000/40,000 = 3.5

If the debt-to-equity ratio is greater than 1, the capital provided by lenders exceeds the capital provided by owners. Generally, investors will consider a company with a high debt-to-equity ratio to be of greater risk. Debt-to-equity ratios will vary with the type of business and management's risk attitude.

Working capital

Working capital is a measure of cash flow and is not a real ratio. It represents the amount of capital invested in resources subject to relatively rapid turnover,

> **"**
> Spend at least as much time researching a stock as you would choosing a refrigerator.
> —Peter Lynch
> **"**

such as cash, accounts receivable, and inventories, minus the amount provided by short-term creditors. Working capital is computed as follows:

Working Capital = Total Current Assets – Total Current Liabilities

Working capital should always be a positive number. It is used by investors to evaluate a company's ability to weather hard times. It is also useful for other calculations, such as net sales to working capital. Using the balance sheet data for the Soup-on-a-Stick Inc., we can compute the following working capital amount for the company:

$65,000 – 40,000 = $25,000 (Soup-on-a-Stick Inc. has $25,000 in working capital)

Net sales to working capital

The relationship between net sales and working capital is a measurement of the efficiency in the way working capital is being used by the company's management. It shows how working capital is supporting sales. It is computed as follows:

Net Sales to Working Capital Ratio = Net Sales/Net Working Capital

Using balance sheet data for the Soup-on-a-Stick Inc., and the working capital amount computed in the previous calculation, the following net sales to working capital ratio can be computed:

$200,000/25,000 = 8

Again, this is a ratio that must be compared to others in that industry to be meaningful. In general, a low ratio may indicate an inefficient use of working capital (that is, you could be doing more with your resources, such as investing in equipment, for example). A high ratio means that you may be vulnerable to creditors. This may be dangerous, especially if there is a drop in sales, which could cause a serious cash shortage.

A common size ratio means the one common number to which all the other numbers in that particular financial statement correlate. In the income statement, all the numbers are "common-sized" to the sales amount; the sales amount is assigned 100 percent, and every other number is a percentage of sales. If sales were $1,000, expenses were $750, and net income was $250, what would be the common size ratios for these numbers? Sales are 100 percent (of sales), expenses are 75 percent (of sales), and the net income is 25 percent. The common size ratio is also used to compare the numbers year to year. If the net income (as a common size ratio) is greater this year than last year, that's a good development because the company is squeezing more profit from sales.

The common size ratio in a balance sheet uses the total assets as the common number. Total assets represent 100 percent, and every other number plays off it. If total assets equaled $10,000, liabilities were $6,000, and stockholders' equity made up the remaining $4,000, the common size ratios are easily calculated. In this example, the liabilities are 60 percent (of total assets) and the equity is 40 percent. Comparing these with a prior year is useful because you will be able to see whether the company is improving its financial picture. What if in this example you learned that the liabilities were 20 percent of total assets in the prior year? Generally, it would indicate that liabilities tripled as a percentage of total assets (not a good sign unless it was debt that was profitably invested in assets that generated a return greater than the interest expense).

Financial ratio analysis is one way to turn financial statements into business tools. When confronted with financial statements, many investors may be somewhat baffled by the long columns of numbers. Financial ratio analysis offers a simple solution to numbers overload.

Measuring management effectiveness

It has often been said that the key to a successful business is management. How do you measure management's effectiveness? Ultimately, management is assessed by how well the company is increasing in value and profitability. Three key ratios can help you track management effectiveness: return on equity, return on investment, and return on assets. In all three, return is defined as the company's earnings. The differences reflect the fact that there are three ways to measure the amount of capital that management is using to generate that level of income.

Return on equity (ROE)

ROE is the most basic measure of how effectively management is using the capital entrusted to it by the shareholders. Equity represents that portion of the company's assets that would be distributed to shareholders if the company were liquidated and all assets were sold at values reflected on the company's balance sheet. In other words, if the company stopped operating and all liabilities were paid off, what would be left for the owners to divvy up? ROE measures the profitability the management is generating on that amount. The formula is as follows:

$$\text{Return on Equity} = \frac{\text{Earnings}}{\text{Shareholders' Equity}}$$

If Soup-on-a-Stick Inc., had actual earnings of $4,000 and equity of $50,000 (total assets minus liabilities), then its ROE would be $4,000/$50,000 = .08, or 8 percent. Eight percent is not bad but it's not great. As a general rule of thumb, a ROE of 1–10 percent is mediocre, 10–19 percent is good, and 20 percent or more is great. In other words, the higher the number, the better. And if management is generating a high ROE year after year, it would be a great investment showing both value and growth. When you are looking at the ROE, be sure about what constitutes "return." Some analysts consider it the company's actual earnings, while others use "operational earnings." The better measure of management effectiveness would be operational earnings.

Return on investment (ROI)

ROI is a key measure of profitability. This ratio shows how effectively management is operating the company's basic operations. ROI is expressed in the following formula:

$$\text{Return on Investment} = \frac{\text{Operational Earnings}}{\text{Assets}}$$

ROI measures how well the core business is doing versus the resources of the entire enterprise. Say that Soup-on-a-Stick Inc.'s prime activity is fast food, but it also rents out its property to generate more income. Although it's good to know that it makes additional income, we need to know how well management is running its primary business because that is its core competency. ROI measures this core competence. ROI yields of 0–10 percent are low, 10–20 percent are good, and more than 20 percent is preferable.

Return on Investment is as "Return on Invested Capital." The formal calculation is the current year's net income divided by long-term debt plus common stock equity plus preferred equity.

Return on assets (ROA)

ROA goes beyond shareholders' equity. ROA measures management's effectiveness in using everything at its disposal (equity, loans, accounts receivables, and so on) to produce profits. How well is management using credit? Is it investing excess cash from operations to generate further revenue? ROA is expressed in this formula:

$$\text{Return on Assets} = \frac{\text{Actual Earnings}}{\text{Assets}}$$

If total assets amount to $10 million and the actual earnings (or total earnings) are $1 million, then the yield is 10 percent ($1 million divided by $10 million). As before, the higher the yield, the better.

Income considerations

Throughout the chapter we have looked at the ways a company is valued, measured, and analyzed. The perspective presented has been for investors seeking value and appreciation. But what about income? Some investors will seek stock investments for dividends. As we have written in previous chapters, high-dividend stocks are a good consideration for those seeking income (as well as potential appreciation). Should the income investor be looking for useful ratios? Everything we have discussed so far is generally applicable to income investors as well. However, two additional ratios are relevant for income investors.

Timesaver
To help you compare your stock's ratios with industry ratios, check out Robert Morris Associates' Annual Statement Studies. The publication is available in book form, on disk, on CD-ROM, or online at www.rmahq.org. Ask your reference librarian, or call the company directly at 1-800-677-7621.

Dividend yield

Dividend yield is the ratio of return to shareholders as dividends. It is expressed in the following formula:

Dividend Yield = Dividends Per Share/Market Price Per Share

If you bought a stock at $40 per share and the dividend is $3, then the dividend yield is 7.5 percent ($3 divided by $40). Whenever investors are comparing investments, whether they are different dividend-paying stocks or a dividend-paying stock to another investment such as a bank account, the dividend yield makes it easy to compare. If you were deciding between a bank account yielding 5 percent or the aforementioned stock, you would probably choose the stock because the 7.5 percent yield is 50 percent higher than the bank account's yield. The only reason you might take the 5 percent account is because the bank investment would be less risky.

Dividend payout ratio

This is the latest indicated annual dividend rate divided by the latest 12 months' EPS. Basically, this tells you how much of the company's earnings are paid out in dividends. A company with a high dividend payout ratio can be attractive to investors seeking income, but by paying out so much of earnings, the company will have little left to finance growth or have a margin of safety. A high dividend payout ratio could be troublesome if earnings weaken or decline because it may force a dividend cut.

For most companies, the dividend payout ratio should not exceed 60 percent of earnings. Like most ratios, however, this one varies with industry. Utilities can comfortably afford a payout ratio up to 70 percent because they typically have a stable, high cash flow. Real estate investment trusts (REITs) pay

Moneysaver
Do you want
to find stocks
that have a
20 percent
average growth
rate over the
past five years
and that also
have a high ROE?
Many brokers
(such as Charles
Schwab at
www.schwab.com
and Etrade at
www.etrade.com)
have free stock-
screening tools
available at
their Web sites.
An excellent one
is at www.
nasdaq.com.

out 95 percent of their earnings because a provision in the law exempts them from taxes if they do so. By contrast, newer, faster-growing companies often pay no dividends at all.

The following publications will give you an industry standard or "benchmark" that will let you compare your prospective company with others. Most business libraries carry them in their reference section.

Almanac of Business and Industrial Financial Ratios

Publisher: Prentice-Hall

Comments: Gives financial and operating ratios for manufacturing industries. This information is based on IRS tax returns, so data is about three to four years behind.

Issue frequency: Annual

Analysts Handbook

Publisher: Standard & Poor's Corporation

Comments: Provides historical (usually 20–30 years) statistics on the sales, operating profit, profit margin, depreciation, taxes, earnings, dividends price, P/E ratio, dividends yields, book value, working capital, and capital expenditures of about 85 industries.

Annual Statement Studies

Publisher: Robert Morris Associates

Comments: Gives financial and operating ratios on nearly 30 lines of business, including manufacturers, wholesalers, retailers, services, and finance companies. It also includes an annotated bibliography of sources for financial to operating ratios in each issue.

Issue frequency: Annual

Business One
Publisher: Irwin Business & Investment Almanac
Comments: Reprints the ratios from Dun & Bradstreet and the quarterly financial reports for manufacturing corporations.

Chain Store Age Executive (magazine)
Publisher: Chain Store Age Executive
Comments: Publishes an August issue each year that includes operating ratios for major stores as well as types of stores (drug, convenience, home improvement, and so on).

Computer Industry Almanac (directory)
Publisher: Computer Industry Almanac
Comments: Covers a wide range of computer industry statistics.

Computer Industry Almanac (directory)
Publisher: Downe Communications
Comments: Publishes a May and June issue each year, with some operating ratios included.

Encyclopedia of Associations
Publisher: Gale Research
Comments: Gives information on trade associations for specific industries. Every trade association covers its industry in depth, and the research is usually available to the public.
Issue frequency: Annual

Finance and Accounting for Non-financial Managers
Publisher: Prentice Hall
Comments: An excellent primer that is also suitable for investors.

Financial Studies of the Small Business
Publisher: Financial Research Associates
Comments: Gives financial-to-operating ratio for about 50 lines of small retail, wholesale service, contracts, professional services, manufacturers-by asset size categories.
Issue frequency: Annual

Industry Norms and Key Business Ratios
Publisher: Dun & Bradstreet
Comments: Gives financial ratios for 800 lines of business based on the Standard Industrial Classification SIC codes. It includes private and publicly held firm information for all size ranges of corporations.
Issue frequency: Annual

Information About How to Use Financial Ratios
Publisher: U.S. Small Business Administration,
Financial Management: How to Make a Go of Your Business
Comments: A nice overview for investors even though it is geared to entrepreneurs.

Manufacturing USA: Industry Analyses, Statistics, and Leading Companies
Publisher: Gale Research
Comments: Gives information broken down by Standard Industrial Classification (SIC) codes. It includes a "Selected Ratios" table for each code.

Moody's Handbook of Common Stocks
Publisher: Moody's Investor Service
Comments: Provides financial ratios on more than 900 stocks of high investor interest.
Issue frequency: Quarterly

Service Industries USA: Industry Analyses, Statistics, and Leading Organizations
Publisher: Gale Research, Inc.
Comments: Includes 22 different ratios for 2,100 individual services that are grouped into 151 industries. Industries are based on the SIC code system.

Standard & Poor's Industry Surveys
Publisher: Standard & Poor's Corporation
Comments: For each industry covered, provides sales, operating income, profit margin, depreciation, taxes, earnings, dividend yielded, book value, return on book value, and working capital expenditures.
Issue frequency: Quarterly

Understanding accounting concepts is a "must" for the serious investor since stock value is ultimately tied to company performance and financial strength. The author also utilizes ratios as a mandatory pre-requisite in the stock selection process. Some points the author suggests:

Make sure that the company's sales are growing at an annual rate of at least 10 percent (preferably 15 percent or more) for the most recent three years.

Current assets should exceed current liabilities by a ratio of 1.25 (preferably 2) to 1.

Earnings should be growing at an equal or higher rate than sales over the most recent three years.

The ROE should be increasing at a minimum of 10 percent per year (preferably over 15 percent) over the past three years.

Look for a debt-to-equity ratio that is as low as possible. Less than one-to-one is preferred. In the year 2000, there are far too many companies with high debt-to-equity ratios (two-to-one or higher) and this could spell disaster if the economy slows down or goes into a recession.

Just the facts

- Value investing with an emphasis on growth has a long and proven track record of success.

- Analyzing earnings will help you select winning companies that you can invest in.

- Comparing your prospective company with its industry and the rest of the market will help you choose wisely.

- Ratios are critical tools for analyzing companies and industries.

- A strong, profitable company with consistent earnings growth is easy to locate when you understand the fundamentals.

GET THE SCOOP ON...
Economic news ▪ Leading economic indicators
▪ Political considerations ▪ Regulations that can
make or break a company ▪ News and events
that affect a company's prospects

External Factors That Affect a Stock's Performance

Chapter 8

E ver wonder why the stock market goes down on good economic news and up on bad? Why, for instance, can a report of soaring job growth send Wall Street into a tailspin, while a lazy rate of job creation can spark a rally? It's not mere perversity; the market's movements depend on myriad economic circumstances, even if the relationship sometimes seems to defy logic.

Several times a day, a government agency or trade organization releases a number that offers a glimpse into the state of the economy. Because the economy is cyclical, ebbing and flowing with shifts in supply and demand, indicators can show what phase the economy is in—and where it's headed. Of course, buying or selling stocks and bonds in response to changes in one indicator is a strategy best left to professionals. Still, investors are wise to note economic trends because share prices are primarily driven by two factors: earnings and interest rates. When the economy is expanding and interest rates are low, earnings—and, therefore, share prices—likely will rise.

What to look for in economic data

The successful investor realizes that buying stocks is not done in a vacuum. Stocks are greatly influenced by elements such as general economic, political, regulatory, and even cultural trends. You should be aware of the various government agencies that can affect the investing climate. The stock market can go up and down because the investing public can see positive and negative developments.

One example of how governmental factors can influence the stock market is interest rates, the amount of money you have to pay a bank to loan you money, or the amount it has to pay you to keep your money in their bank.

Interest rates that are high and rising generally make stock prices go down. This is the case for several reasons. First, if people can make a decent return on their money by keeping it in the bank or by buying bonds, they figure they shouldn't bother taking risks in the stock market. Also, if interest rates are rising, this increases expenses for companies, which in turn reduces their earnings and makes it harder for them to invest in growth opportunities. When earnings decline, this ultimately causes stock prices to fall. Conversely, falling interest rates bode well for stocks. The companies' earnings improve, plus stock prices increase as investors take their money out of interest-bearing investments to seek stock market gains. Interest rates are primarily controlled by the Federal Reserve (the "Fed"). This is why "Fed watching" is a popular pastime on Wall Street.

The Federal Reserve

The Federal Reserve System is the nation's independent central bank and arguably has the greatest influence on the stock market. Established in 1913, many decades after the previous central bank was closed down by Andrew Jackson, the system is governed by the Federal Reserve Board, whose seven members are appointed to staggered 14-year terms. The Fed plays a crucial role in the U.S. economy—and indeed the global economy—by virtue of its control over the world's premiere currency, the U.S. dollar.

The Fed can increase or decrease the money supply, which has a direct and powerful effect on our economy. The Fed buys and sells Treasury securities and alters reserve requirements for the nation's banks. Through its influence on interest rates, the Fed has a major impact on the rate of economic growth and the direction of securities markets. Alan Greenspan, the Federal Reserve chairman since 1987, is a closely watched official whose carefully crafted pronouncements are widely scrutinized for evidence of the Fed's intentions with respect to interest rates. In recent years, the Fed's primary concern, aside from the health of the banking system, has been fighting inflation.

Paying close attention to the daily stream of economic reports is the best way to stay one step ahead of the Federal Reserve. And staying one step ahead of the Fed can be very profitable.

Most investors analyze any fresh economic data by trying to figure out if the news makes the Fed more or less likely to change interest rate levels or monetary policy. The Fed endorses the view that inflation accelerates when unemployment falls so

Bright Idea
One of the best places to learn about economic statistics and how well our economy is doing is to visit the Dismal Scientist at www.dismal.com. The site offers comprehensive and timely economic analysis along with useful tools such as a stock market valuation calculator.

low that firms are forced to pay more to recruit and retain quality workers. Firms pass along the higher wages by charging more for their output. Inflation then spirals through the economy, the theory goes.

The Federal Reserve monitors and generally controls the money supply, the main ingredient in inflation. People forget that inflation is not the cost of goods going up, but rather the value of paper money going down. Therefore, if the money supply grows too fast, inflation will heat up and cause problems for the economy.

There are three measures of money supply: M1, the most basic measure, consists of currency, checking accounts, money market funds, NOW accounts, and travelers checks. M1 is what the Fed watches most closely and what it can most immediately influence by buying or selling Treasury securities. M2 is everything in M1 plus time deposits exceeding $100,000 and repurchase agreements. M3 is even broader, encompassing M2 as well as savings bonds, Treasury bills, commercial paper, Eurodollars, and more.

Employment Situation Report

The monthly jobs report (released the last Friday of each month) is one of the most significant economic indicators. It is among the first data released about any given month, it looks at the most important sector of the economy, it is conceptually sound, and it is based on surveys of thousands of businesses and households.

This report gives us the unemployment rate and includes a count of the number of jobs created (known as nonfarm payrolls) and the changes in wages and hours worked. The market typically responds to whether the number of new jobs comes in above or below the consensus estimate, which can be way off the mark. But investors should compare the index's three-month average with the average of the previous three months to spot trends. If fewer than 100,000 new jobs are created in each of several months, the economy could be headed for a slowdown; if more than 300,000 new jobs are created, and it could be overheating. The Federal Reserve wants to see the number of new jobs in the range of 150,000 to 200,000.

The Labor Department also gives a more detailed look at total compensation costs in the quarterly employment cost index, which includes wages and benefits.

Other indicators also give snapshots of the labor market. Every week, the Labor Department reports on unemployment claims. Private sources, such as the monthly survey of the manufacturing sector by the National Association of Purchasing Management (NAPM), the Conference Board's Help Wanted Index, and the Challenger report on mass layoffs, help paint a complete picture of the labor market.

Demand-based reports

To determine the demand for labor and other scarce inputs, economists look at dozens of reports that measure what demand for goods and services exists. Demand from consumers, who account for about 70 percent of final sales, is indicated by the Commerce Department's monthly income and spending report; from monthly or weekly reports on wholesale and retail activity from the Commerce Department, retailers, retail analysts, and automakers; and from consumer confidence surveys published by the University of Michigan and the

Conference Board. The Federal Reserve itself keeps track of consumer debt, a key constraint on consumer spending.

Investment in the housing and construction market, which is extremely sensitive to economic conditions, can be gleaned from the Commerce Department's housing starts, construction spending, new home sales reports, and private data from the National Association of Realtors and the National Association of Homebuilders.

Oddly, the investments that businesses make in new equipment, techniques, and skills are not tracked with any sophistication by the government or private sources. The best source of information about investment comes in the quarterly gross domestic product report.

Inventories, on the other hand, are tracked in several Commerce Department reports. Inventory levels can help predict future levels of output, employment, and spending.

Demand in the manufacturing sector, which also tends to rise and fall with the business cycle, can be seen in the Commerce Department's reports on orders for durable goods and factory orders, as well as the Fed's own report on industrial production and capacity utilization. The NAPM survey is closely watched because it offers a quick backward view at the previous month as well as an expectations index for future demand.

The international component is increasingly important to the U.S. economy. The Commerce Department reports on international trade with a significant time lag, but in considerable detail, at least for goods. The Labor Department reports monthly on import and export prices in a variety of sectors and with most of the nation's major trading partners.

The government sector is becoming less important over time as fiscal policy contracts. The Treasury Department's monthly budget statement contains valuable information on government purchases, transfer payments, and especially the amount of taxes that Washington has received.

Gross domestic product (GDP)

For the broadest view of how the economy is doing, check the gross domestic product (GDP), released four times a year by the Commerce Department during the final week of January, April, July, and October. The GDP measures the nation's total output of goods and services for the quarter.

The GDP report includes several inflation gauges, including the implicit price deflator. Each month, the Labor Department releases the better-known Consumer Price Index for goods and services at the consumer level and the Producer Price Index for prices of goods received by factories, farms, and mines. The CPI and PPI are timely and thorough, but they have been criticized for overstating inflation. They do not give an advance look at inflation to come.

To better understand inflation, the Fed looks at the quarterly productivity numbers from the Labor Department. Although productivity is conceptually the most important economic indicator of long-term economic growth, difficulties in measuring productivity limit the usefulness of this report.

Many economic reports suffer from various inaccuracies. The government reports on the GDP for each quarter three times, revising its estimates as better data becomes available. Besides being a helpful way of keeping up with the Fed and the general economy, government and private data can also help investors find healthy sectors to favor or unhealthy sectors to ignore.

Although quarter-to-quarter changes are too small to be useful, GDP figures over several quarters can reveal whether the economy is on an upward or downward course. That, in turn, helps investors determine whether cyclical industries—such as basic materials and energy stocks—will outperform as the economy nears the end of a recession or underperform when it begins expanding.

Although the GDP tells investors where the economy has been, several other indicators better predict where it is going. These indicators are the easiest for investors to interpret.

Building permits and housing starts

Statistics on building permits and housing starts measure the number of residential units on which construction is begun each month. A start in construction is defined as the beginning of excavation of the foundation for the building and is comprised primarily of residential housing. Building permits are taken out to allow excavation. An increase in building permits and starts usually occurs a few months after a reduction in mortgage rates. Permits lead starts, but permits are not required in all regions of the country, so the number of permits therefore tends to be lower than the number of starts over time. The monthly national report is broken down by region: Northeast, Midwest, South, and West. Be sure to analyze the regional data because these reports are subject to a high degree of volatility—the high volatility can be attributed to weather changes and/or natural disasters. For example, housing starts could be delayed in the Midwest because of increased tornado activity or in the Southeast by hurricanes.

Consumer Confidence Index

The Consumer Confidence Index is a survey released the last Tuesday of each month. Simply put, the better shoppers feel about their financial situations, the more they'll spend. And because more than two-thirds of U.S. corporate earnings are derived from consumer buying, whether people feel good has a direct impact on corporate profits. The Conference Board, a nonprofit research organization in New York, compiles the index from the responses of 5,000 households to questions about their current financial situations and their expectations for the economy during the next six months. The results are compared to a base year, 1985, which is set at 100. The Conference Board's consumer research center says that when the index is above 100, people feel positive about their economic situation and are likely to continue spending. When it falls below 80 for at least two consecutive months, a recession is likely to begin within three to six months. However, The Conference Board cautions against reacting to a one-month blip. In January 1998, for instance, the index fell sharply when the President and Congress reached an impasse over the budget that caused the government to shut down temporarily, but consumer confidence rebounded over subsequent months.

The report can occasionally be helpful in predicting sudden shifts in consumption patterns, although most small changes in the index are just noise. Only index changes of at least five points should be considered significant. The index consists

Timesaver
Housing starts and building permits are important indicators of economic activity because real estate and construction activity mirrors the growth of the economy. To get the latest information on these statistics and a wealth of other significant information, visit the Census Bureau's Web site at www.census.gov.

of two subindexes: consumers' appraisal of current conditions and their expectations for the future. Expectations make up 60 percent of the total index, with current conditions accounting for the other 40 percent. The expectations index is typically seen as having better leading indicator qualities than the current conditions index.

NAPM Index

Closely watched by Federal Reserve Board Chairman Alan Greenspan, this index is compiled by the National Association of Purchasing Management (NAPM). This index asks managers of 300 companies in industries across the economy about changes in new orders, prices, and supplier deliveries. Released the first week of each month, the index's results are compared to a base of 50, which means that a reading between 55 and 60 shows the economy expanding at a good clip, while a reading below 44 is considered a warning of recession.

The index's supplier delivery component may have the greatest impact on interest rates. Managers are asked if suppliers are delivering orders faster or slower than they did during the prior month. Long delivery times indicate that suppliers may be working to capacity and therefore have the leverage to raise prices. In 1994, when the Federal Reserve raised rates pretty consistently, a high supplier delivery number was one factor.

Consumer Price Index

Also known as the cost-of-living index, this is a government index that measures changes in the price of typical consumer goods. It is usually released the fourth week of each month. The Consumer Price Index (CPI) reflects changes in the prices of a fixed "market basket" of goods and services purchased by the typical urban consumer. Increases in the CPI, which is updated about every 10 years, generally are considered warnings of inflation. Although it has been criticized for not quickly taking into account changes in buying patterns and trends, this index remains a widely watched indicator. If the CPI rises by an annualized rate of at least 8 percent during a three-month period, an economic slowdown is likely.

Cyclical indicators

Business cycle indicators have proven to be useful tools for analyzing the alternating waves of economic expansion and contraction known as the business cycle. The indicator approach that makes extensive use of this data was originated in the mid-1930s by the National Bureau of Economic Research.

The Bureau established the notion that the economy can alternately expand and contract in a cyclical fashion, which we can track with reasonable accuracy by reading and interpreting the economic statistics as they are compiled and compared with prior periods.

Over subsequent decades, the approach was developed and refined, mostly at the Bureau. Starting in the late 1960s, the U.S. Department of Commerce produced publications after which business cycle indicators were modeled.

The cyclical indicators are classified into three categories: leading, coincident, and lagging, based on the timing of their movements.

Leading Economic Indicators

The Leading Economic Indicators (LEI), compiled monthly by the Conference Board, is an index of economic components, including manufacturing orders, interest rates, and new construction, making it a good all-in-one indicator. The LEI is usually released the first week of each month.

The Conference Board says that changes in the LEI signal turning points in the economy. If the LEI shows a decline of at least 1 percent during a six-month period, then the economy is headed toward recession. The LEI has predicted the past six recessions, although delays in compiling the data may make the warning time very short. The corresponding index for wholesale prices is the Producer Price Index.

The primary leading indicators are these:

- M1 Money Supply
- M2 Money Supply
- 3-Month Percent Change in Sensitive Materials Prices
- New Orders for Consumer Goods
- Contracts and Orders for Plant and Equipment
- New Housing Permits
- Ratio of Manufacturing and Trade Sales to Inventories
- Vendor Performance, Slower Deliveries Diffusion Index
- Index of Common Stock Prices
- Average Workweek in Manufacturing
- Initial Claims for State Unemployment Insurance
- 3-Month Percent Change in Consumer Debt

The leading indicators are those series that tend to shift direction in advance of the business cycle, and for this reason they get the lion's share of the attention.

Coincident economic indicators

Coincident economic indicators simply mirror in real time the ebb and flow of the economic cycle. While leading economic indicators tell us what to expect, coincident economic indicators merely confirm how the economy is at the moment. They work in the same way as the temperature gauge on your car's dashboard. That's the gauge that flashes "overheating!" as you watch the steam billows out from under your hood.

The main coincident economic indicators are these:

- Nonagricultural Employment
- Index of Industrial Production
- Personal Income in Manufacturing
- Manufacturing and Trade Sales
- Civilian Employment as a Percentage of the Working-Age Population
- Gross Domestic Product

Primary lagging indicators

Lagging indicators tend to warn us that the business cycle (up or down) has matured and is nearing an end. They can also signal the next turn of the business cycle. A good example is the Average Duration of Unemployment (ADU). As a primary lagging indicator, it gives observers clues about the maturity of that particular cycle. For example, if the ADU indicates that unemployed workers have been unemployed for a relatively short period of time (three months or less), this indicates that the economy is continuing to do well. When the economy is growing, more people have jobs, and those who lose their jobs tend to regain employment fairly quickly.

Moneysaver
The American Institute for Economic Research is a nonprofit organization that offers excellent information on financial topics and economic matters for investors free or at low cost. Its booklet "Forecasting Business Trends" gives investors some clear explanations and great insights on the business cycle. To get a copy, send $6 to: American Institute for Economic Research, Booklet BT, P.O. Box 1000, Great Barrington, MA 01230, or visit the Web site www.aier.org.

If the economy is languishing in a recessionary phase (the economy is in a down cycle), the ADU is longer (three or four months or longer), indicating that it is more difficult for workers to gain (or regain) jobs.

The primary lagging indicators are these:

- Average Duration of Unemployment
- Manufacturing and Trade Inventories
- Commercial and Industrial Loans
- Ratio of Debt to Income
- Percent Change from a Year Earlier in Manufacturing Labor Cost per Unit of Output
- Composite of Short-Term Rates

It is important to keep in mind that no single statistic is a reliable indicator of which way the economy is going. Reviewing all the available key indicators is always advisable because they will ultimately warn you about what environment will influence your stock-picking strategy.

It is important to look at those economic indicators that affect the region or sector most relevant to the company you are investing in. For example, if you were investing in a company that sells raw materials to the housing industry, then the statistics on housing starts and construction permits would affect the company's growth. If housing starts are strong and are expected to continue being strong, then the market would be very beneficial for any company that services this sector.

Composite indexes

Remember the indexes that we looked at in Chapter 2, "The Stock Market Environment: Where Stocks Are Bought and Sold"? Stock indexes gave us a useful snapshot of how well the general stock market or a particular industry is performing. The Dow Jones Industrial Average (DJIA) showed us how well a basket of 30 major stocks was performing. We didn't have to spend a lot of time looking at each individual stock; it was efficient just to look at the index. Economic statistics can be conveniently presented in the same manner. Why should investors look at all the economic indicators? Let economists look at the statistics; investors can get a quick look at the economy's health by looking at composite indexes. Composite indexes are compiled to represent the leading, coincident, and lagging economic indicators.

Making sense of composite indexes doesn't always have to be a laborious process because many organizations have done a great job of compiling and interpreting them. A good source is the non-profit American Institute for Economic Research; visit its Web site at www.aier.org.

Diffusion indexes

Diffusion indexes, which measure the proportion of a set of indicators that are rising, provide another source of useful but often neglected information about the business cycle. They tell us how widespread a particular business cycle movement (expansion or contraction) has become.

The government includes diffusion indexes over two different time spans, one month and six months, for the components of the leading, coincident, and lagging indexes and for employment in 356 industries. The one-month span indexes tend to be erratic; signals from six-month diffusion indexes are much more reliable.

The composite and diffusion indexes are not redundant even though both indexes are based on the same set of data. Occasionally, they move in different directions. The composite index differentiates between small and large overall movements in the component series, while the diffusion index measures the breadth of a general movement, not the size. The difference is often very useful when attempting to either confirm or predict cyclical turning points.

Recessions: when the economy shrinks

Followers of the cyclical indicators are keenly aware of problems that arise when interpreting the leading index. The long-standing rule of thumb that a three-month decline signals a recession has given at least one false signal during six of the last eight expansions. However, few economists actually use such an inflexible rule. Most require a significant downward movement in the index of at least 1 percent and declines in the majority of the component series.

The U.S. economy is continually evolving and is far too complex to be summarized by one economic series. Official recession dates are determined from a multitude of indicators, and there is no agreed-upon formula for setting peak and trough dates.

Why not replace all this agonizing over a multiplicity of measures with a simple formula—say, define a recession as two consecutive quarters of decline in GDP? Any single measure is sure to encounter special problems just when they matter the most. Forecasting a peak, which is usually considered more important than forecasting a trough, has to be considered an even harder task than determining one after the fact.

Even though the composite leading index has flaws and is not 100 percent reliable, it can be used along with the corresponding diffusion index to give useful signals about the likely direction of the economy. Historical analysis shows that a negative growth rate over a six-month period of between 1 and 2 percent for the leading index and declines in at least half of the components (that is, the six-month diffusion index falling below 50 percent) is a reasonable criteria for a recession warning.

Forecasting recessions with the leading index summary

Often, it is claimed that three consecutive months of decline in the leading index forewarns of a recession. But this simple rule of thumb produces too many false signals. Looking for a 1 percent decline in the leading index (from its cyclical peak) and concurrent declines in at least half its components produces a more reliable predictor of a recession. Although this rule is not infallible—it sometimes prematurely suggests an end to an expansion—it performs well in signaling when the risk of a recession is greatest.

The leading index, a composite or average of 10 components, tends to smooth out volatility in the individual series by revealing common turning point patterns within a set of data. Signals from the composite are often clearer and more convincing than movements in any individual component. However, the leading index has limitations:

1. It retains some erratic movement, especially in data for the latest month.

2. It exhibits timing irregularity—it has always proven too much to expect the leading index

to lead the general economy by a consistent interval.

3. It lacks a ready-made rule for translating its movements into a turning-point prediction.

Followers of the economic indicators are keenly aware that these problems arise when interpreting the leading index. It is often stated in the coverage and in academic articles that economists look for a three-month decline to signal a recession is imminent, without attributing this dubious and inflexible rule-of-thumb to a particular source. The Conference Board does not endorse this rule (which has given at least one false signal during four of the past five expansions), and few economists actually use it. Most require a significant downward movement in the index (of at least 1 percent) and declines in the majority of the component series.

Even though the leading index has flaws, and even though its simple rules are inadequate, it can be used in conjunction with the corresponding diffusion index to give early warnings of unfavorable changes in the direction of the economy. Diffusion indexes, which measure the proportion of rising indicators, tell how widespread a particular business cycle movement has become.

As we've mentioned already, composite and diffusion indexes are not redundant even when both are based on the same set of data. Sometimes they move in different directions because a composite index, unlike a diffusion index, differentiates between small and large movements in the component series. Deviations between the composite leading index and the corresponding diffusion index can be particularly useful. For example, a short but sharp decline in the composite index accompanied by continued high readings for the diffusion index would suggest that the weakness in the composite is traceable to only a few, and possibly only one, component. This type of decline, therefore, is less worrisome than cases in which both composite and diffusion indexes are simultaneously weak.

Historical analysis shows that a decline of 1 to 2 percent for the leading index, coupled with declines in at least half of its components, is a reasonable criterion for a recession warning.

Cautions and conclusion

Although previous business cycles have shown patterns that are likely to be repeated to some degree and that should be watched for when predicting turning points, recessions can start and end quite quickly for a variety of reasons. Just as economists continue to debate the relative importance of the various factors that affect aggregate demand and supply—such as monetary policy, oil price shocks, business confidence, and the manner in which business cycles are propagated—there is often a wide range of opinion among forecasters about the most likely trend for the economy. Therefore, it is unreasonable to believe that any single indicator or even set of indicators will always give true signals and never fail to foresee a turning point.

Other more technical issues must also be considered when analyzing the cyclical indicators. First, delays in the availability of data shorten the effective lead of the leading indicators. Second, many of the indicators are subsequently revised, so it is only much later that they give an unambiguous picture of what is happening in a particular sector of the economy. Third, some indicators occasionally skip a business cycle altogether or show an extra cycle (for

Timesaver
How does the stock market or a given stock perform against the economy's leading economic indicator? Marketwatch gives you the ability to see a stock's price movement in a chart that coincides with a general movement in the economy, such as the inflation rate or the Dow Jones Industrial Index. View it at www.marketwatch.com.

Bright Idea
To find out
about the lead-
ing economic
indicators, visit
the Web site for
the Conference
Board. This
data is updated
and released
monthly at www.
tcb-indicators.
org/.

example, the stock market in 1962 and 1987). These complications confound our ability to quickly perceive the development of a turning point in the economy.

Statistics resources

The following sources offer comprehensive information and statistics on the economy. You can learn about the general condition of the entire economy or just a specific industry. Investors can review an industry's (or the economy's) growth and performance in the most current year with the prior year.

> **Bloomberg's Washington bureau**
> www.marketwatch.com
>
> **Department of Commerce**
> www.stat-usa.gov
>
> **Econo-Finance**
> www.econofinance.com
>
> **Federal Interagency Council on Statistical Policy**
> www.fedstats.gov
>
> **The Federal Reserve Bank of New York**
> www.ny.frb.org

Political considerations

The power of politics can make or break a market or an economy. As history has shown, more often than not, politics has done harm to investments and economic conditions. To understand politics is to understand the most potent external factor in judging your company's prospects for success. Politics can affect our investment in two basic ways: systemic and nonsystemic.

Systemic means just that: The system is being affected, which in turn affects all the participants in

that system. Because politics deals with the imposi-
tion of taxes, laws, and regulations, the effects can
be beneficial or detrimental to all (or some) of the
participants. The effects of politics may be positive
or negative, but you will feel the effects if your
investment is affected directly. Nonsystemic means
that the system is unaffected, but the individual par-
ticipant or entity is affected.

For example, say that you decide to buy stock of
Lobster Galore, Inc., (LGI). You feel that the market
for lobster is very healthy and offers a solid potential for appreciation in its stock. How would politics
affect LGI?

If politicians felt that (rightly or wrongly)
Lobster Galore is a monopoly, as one example, then
this would limit the company's size and scope. Say
that industry research shows that LGI commands 90
percent of the lobster market and that it regularly
buys out competitors or uses its resources to over-
whelm smaller companies that are competing with
it. The politicians would encourage the government
to step in and curtail LGI's market practices.
Perhaps the government believes that LGI has
engaged in "predatory practices." Maybe officials
cite LGI's tremendous market share and conclude
that it is in violation of antitrust laws. If so, the government would initiate legal efforts to force a
change. This is an example of political risk associated with the individual company. The general marketplace was not materially affected. However, for
LGI's customers, vendors, and stockholders, the
potential problems are real. LGI's stock will decline
sharply.

Perhaps Lobster Galore will be broken up into
smaller entities to encourage market competition.

Perhaps the lobster industry will be regulated to control prices on behalf of consumers and small businesses. In our history, a number of companies have been targeted by the Federal government for antitrust violations. During the early 1900s, Standard Oil was deemed too powerful, and the antitrust laws were invoked as the government broke up the company to keep the oil industry from monopolistic control.

In the 1960s and 1970s, IBM grew so large and dominant in its industry that the government initiated an expensive, protracted lawsuit in an attempt to shrink IBM's power and influence. The millions of dollars spent by IBM to defend itself and the distraction the lawsuit provided ultimately harmed IBM as "Big Blue" was knocked off its perch as the dominant computer company in the early 1980s. Industry observers remark that the market itself did as much, or more, harm to IBM's success than the government's legal efforts. As personal computer sales skyrocketed during the 1980s, IBM's smaller competitors prospered during the decade of the PC. Although IBM eventually recovered and did well during the 1990s, it never regained its once invincible market presence.

The government's lawsuit against IBM is an example where the industry was not targeted but an individual company was. Short-term investors lost money when IBM experienced some tough years. However, because it was a quality company in a growing industry, patient investors were ultimately rewarded during the latter half of the 1990s. The lesson for stockholders was that it was better to avoid IBM until it regained its footing. Although IBM fought off both the government and nimble competitors, its stock price suffered.

Microsoft is another case that offers risks for investors. The Federal government has sought to break up Microsoft because of potential monopolistic practices. Although there were no complaints by investors or consumers, the government intervened and initiated a lawsuit based on anti-trust laws. Although, as of June 2000, the matter has not been resolved, the uncertainty poses problems for long-term investors. Until the matter is resolved, investors should be aware that investing in Microsoft stock becomes a speculative play. Even if Microsoft should prevail, the unresolved issue is whether the lawsuit has inflicted some harm that would diminish its ability to compete in the coming years as effectively as it has during the 1990s.

The government has massive resources at its disposal—it has literally trillions of taxpayer-provided dollars that it can use, along with statutory legal power that no private organization can match. Investors now understand that if the government targets a business, whether for good or bad reasons, whether for real or perceived offenses, it is better to avoid the business until the problem or difficulty has passed.

How about systemic political risk? How would that affect your investment? Two examples illustrate how politics could have either a positive or a negative effect on a particular industry.

During most of the twentieth century, American Telephone & Telegraph (AT&T) was a regulated monopoly. During the late 1970s and early 1980s, the government sought (and accomplished) the breakup of AT&T. For many years, AT&T was considered a safe, stodgy, predictable stock investment that was suitable for "widows and orphans." After all, it wasn't simply a major part of the telephone industry—it *was* the telephone industry! For stockholders, AT&T was a guaranteed investment because the government essentially protected it from competition. Then AT&T's status changed in 1984.

In a government lawsuit, the court ruled in favor of the government, and AT&T (then called "Ma Bell") was to be broken up into seven smaller regional companies, or "baby bells." As the lawsuit was concluding, the investment world publicly debated the fate of the stock. What should AT&T stockholders do: hold on to their stock through this uncertain transition, or sell the stock outright? All the financial magazines featured investment experts debating pro and con. It was a momentous event that had long-term ramifications for deregulating the telecommunications industry.

AT&T as a national, regulated monopoly came to an end, but the result was the beginning of seven regional telephone companies and a "new" scaled-down AT&T. For stockholders, each share of "old" AT&T became one share of "new" AT&T and one share of each of the new regional telephone companies.

Those who watched and listened to the court's ruling saw the breakup of AT&T as an investment bonanza. What many investors who sold their "old" AT&T shares didn't realize was this: Each of those regional telephone companies became a regional telephone monopoly! If you lived in the Mid-Atlantic states (such as New Jersey or Maryland), your new telephone company became Bell Atlantic.

It had no competitors for local service because it became a regulated local monopoly. Long-distance service was deregulated as the "new" AT&T competed with new long-distance telephone companies such as MCI and Sprint. Deregulation brought tremendous growth for the telecommunications industry as a wide array of telephone services became available to the public. Beepers, cell phones, and Internet services were not far behind. During the late 1980s and all of the 1990s, the telecommunications industry was one of the hottest industries in economic history.

Investors who held on tight to "old" AT&T as it became eight new companies were rewarded handsomely. By the early 1990s, investors' total returns (appreciation plus dividend income) exceeded 1,000 percent. For people who understood the political considerations involved, the verdict was clear; politics helped AT&T investors receive tremendous appreciation.

More often than not, politics, as manifested by laws and regulations, can have unintended negative consequences. Because politicians and government bureaucracies are shielded from the rigors of a competitive marketplace, they often do not understand what government actions can do to harm or undermine desired goals. It has become a cliché that the road to hell is paved by good intentions. This is nowhere more true than when politics mixes with business.

Consider our imaginary company, Lobsters Galore Inc., (LGI). What would happen to the company if the government became involved in its industry? What if legislators passed a law that had a systemic effect on an industry that the company depended on?

Perhaps politicians notice that only expensive restaurants serve lobster and that people in lower income brackets cannot as readily afford lobster as people in higher income brackets. They pass a law to "remedy" the situation. After much debate in the legislature, the fictitious law appears as follows:

> Law # 1234: Any restaurant in the restaurant industry that offers lobster on its menu must sell it at 50 cents per lobster to all customers.

At face value, it is a well-intended law. After all, it would be great to buy restaurant-prepared lobster for only 50 cents. What a deal! However, what would be the actual results (versus the unintended consequences)?

It is clear: Lobster would probably disappear from the restaurant industry. Why? It is uneconomical for restaurants to offer lobster for only 50 cents because it costs substantially more to purchase and prepare it. Practically overnight, the demand for lobster from the restaurant industry would plummet. What would happen to our investment in LGI? Well, Lobsters Galore would become "Lobsters No-More." With sales demolished, LGI would get into financial trouble, and stockholders would stop holding their stock. In this case, no law affected LGI directly; the systemic political effect on the restaurant industry had an adverse effect on LGI.

How about real-world examples? In 1990, Congress passed a tax act meant to decrease the federal budget deficit. Then-President Bush capitulated in negotiations with Congress to authorize a major tax increase. One of the provisions of the legislation was the poorly conceived "luxury tax."

According to the politicians that favored it, the luxury tax was meant to increase government revenue by charging a federal 10 percent sales surtax on luxury goods such as yachts, expensive cars, and related luxury goods. The idea was that the tax would simultaneously bring in millions of dollars while affecting only the rich. It was a politically popular idea. However, the designers of the legislation did not expect the unintended consequences. Politicians may understand politics, but that does not automatically translate into economic sense.

When the tax act became law, the immediate effects were negative. Instead of generating extra revenue, the luxury tax provision actually lost revenue for the government! How did that occur?

Government tax statisticians frequently use "static" projection methods when figuring expected revenue. What does that mean and how did it impact revenue? When the politicians asked the statisticians, "How much money will we get from the rich?" The statisticians did simple mathematical projections based on existing numbers that would not change. In other words, if 10,000 yachts (at $200,000 per yacht) were sold last year, then this year we expect the same results ($10,000 \times \$200,000 = \$2,000,000,000$) to be sold this year. With the same sales amount of $2 billion, we will collect a 10 percent tax. Therefore, with the luxury tax, the government will have made $200 million. The only thing wrong with the scenario is the scenario itself. It didn't work out that way.

When consumers of luxury items saw that an additional 10 percent tax would be tacked on, most of them decided to forego their purchases. The number of yachts and expensive vehicles plummeted.

Timesaver
To find out what laws are being passed (or being introduced or debated) in Congress, check out THOMAS, the service performed by the Library of Congress. It tracks bills at the Web site www.thomas.loc. gov. The Web site has a search engine allowing you to find any legislation pending.

Unofficially ...
Tax policy is
the government
policy on how
to extract taxes
from individuals
and organiza-
tions, and how
much to extract.
For further
information on
taxes, visit
the House of
Representatives
Web site at
www.house.gov.

In early 1991, most categories of luxury goods were down in sales drastically. The amount of tax money actually received was a fraction of the amount expected. The unintended consequence was that more than 250,000 jobs were lost. When cars and boats were not sold, those companies lost money. They had no choice but to cut expenses to stay in business. The great irony was that the luxury tax that was meant to be paid by the rich ultimately put many middle-class workers on the unemployment line. The federal and state governments lost income tax revenue because of the lower car and boat sales. In addition, these same governments spent more money for unemployment compensation to help out those folks who lost their jobs.

How about investors? Investors in companies such as Mercedes Benz and Hatteras (the boat-building company) saw their investments decline.

When companies become the target of government, regardless of the reason, the very fact of being targeted puts immense downward pressure on the stock's price. It is important to keep in mind that politics can artificially boost or tear down a stock price, either directly or indirectly.

People understand the direct implications when government targets a particular stock. However, there can be indirect effects as well. It is important for investors to stay informed about politics in general and the current changing political landscape in particular.

Unofficially ...
Monetary policy
has to do with
the creation and
management
of the money
supply. This is
primarily the
jurisdiction of
the Federal
Reserve Bank. To
find out more, go
to the Web site
of the Board of
Governors for the
Federal Reserve
System at www.
bog.frb.fed.us.

Regulations that can make or break a company

In 1993, the Clinton administration launched an initiative into the feasibility of the federal government taking greater control of the healthcare industry. Its healthcare commission, headed by Hillary Clinton, held private hearings with the objective of designing the government's plans for the healthcare industry. Many critics felt the commission's goal was really to "nationalize" healthcare or engineer a government takeover. With the prospect of strict bureaucratic controls for the world of medicine, the market responded negatively. During 1993–1994, health-care-related stocks plummeted. Pharmaceutical stocks such as Abbott Labs and Bristol Myers Squibb declined along with the rest of the industry. Investors wanted no part of a company that would not have the ability to grow. Government controls meant lost earnings and company operations stifled. Investors moved their money elsewhere.

The election of 1994 was a different story. The Republicans were voted into power. They became the majority in Congress, which provided an equalizer to the Clinton Administration. In 1995, pharmaceutical stocks staged a resounding comeback as the dangers of nationalized healthcare, real or perceived, passed. With Democrats and Republicans neutralizing each other's power, this left the marketplace essentially free from interference. From 1995 to 1999, political intervention in the form of new taxes and regulation was kept at a minimum. The marketplace became more conducive for growth, and the stock market soared.

Congress also moved on deregulating the telecommunications during the mid-1990s. Removing the political and regulatory constraints paved the way for new products and services. Cellular phones and Web TV experienced tremendous growth. The Internet became a major component of the economy. Hardware and software for the Internet became a hypergrowth industry.

Unofficially ...
Fiscal policy has to do with managing the government's budget. The White House and Congress grapple over the sources and uses of government money (taxpayer money, really). Find out about their activities at www. whitehouse.gov.

Watch Out!
Always check to
see if there are
Securities and
Exchange
Commission
(SEC) investiga-
tions and pro-
ceedings against
any company.
You can search
the SEC's data-
base for infor-
mation on any
public company
at the Web site
www.sec.gov.
Also check with
the National
Association of
Securities
Dealers at
www.nasdr.com,
which maintains
this Web site to
track violators of
securities laws
in the financial
markets.

The lesson derived from the 1990s was simple: Keep the burdens of taxes and regulations at a manageable level, and allow markets as much freedom as possible. Economic growth will follow.

Taxes

Taxes can make or break a company, an industry, or the economy. When taxes become excessively burdensome, economic growth and the stock market suffer. When taxes are reduced, more capital and earnings are freed up for reinvestment. These have been the lessons throughout history. Taxes are systemic, so they affect all people and companies within the scope of their impact.

Many economic historians point out that the Great Depression could have been greatly shortened had it not been for taxes and government spending policy. During the 1930s, the tax rate skyrocketed to 91 percent! This greatly discouraged economic activity, which subsequently prolonged the time it took to recover. Ultimately it took another political act—the waging of World War II—as a catalyst for renewed activity in the economy. The 1930s were primarily a bear market for stocks in general.

During the early 1960s, President Kennedy was successful in pushing through tax rate reductions through Congress. This was a major catalyst for economic growth and a major bull market during the mid-1960s.

In 1981, President Reagan successfully urged Congress to enact the Economic Recovery Tax Act. This lowered tax rates, indexed tax rates to the rate of inflation, and expanded the availability of the individual retirement account (IRA), among other tax-reduction initiatives. In 1982, the century's greatest bull market for stocks began.

History is clear on the point that stock investing can be helped or hindered depending on whether the investing environment is "friendly." It generally doesn't matter whether the people in power are Democrats or Republicans. What matters to stock investors is how government power is applied (or misapplied). Taxes and regulations are ultimately acts of government, which are ultimately based on politics.

Here are some resources that can help you with tracking politics and the economy:

AllPolitics (CNN/Time)
www.allpolitics.com
Includes news stories and analyses, political polls, and an informative Congress and Governor Guide.

Campaigns and Elections (Congressional Quarterly)
www.congressionalquarterly.com
Includes political news and commentary.

Current Political Headlines (Yahoo!)
www.yahoo.com
Includes links to news stories and current events.

Vote Smart Web
www.vote-smart.org
Includes links facts and statistics about office-holders and candidates, and maintains many links to educational and reference resources related to politics and political science.

The company you invest in does not operate in a vacuum. A great company could quickly become a bad investment if the political environment becomes hostile. The more time you spend learning

Moneysaver
Saving on taxes is more than just using tax-reduction strategies. Voting and writing letters to politicians is also a tax-reduction strategy. The following nonpartisan, nonprofit organizations can give you further information on taxes and how they affect you:
Americans for Tax Reform
www.atr.org
The Tax Foundation
www.taxfoundation.org

how economics and government policy interact will make your choices more profitable.

Just the facts

- When the general economy is doing well, the environment is more conducive for your stock to do well.

- Keeping track of the general economy is important in helping you choose stocks that will be in a better position to rise faster and higher in good times while retaining value in bad times. Politics in the form of taxes, regulations, and other government actions can harm companies or industries.

- Understanding government's role in setting policy and enforcing regulations will help you make wiser buy and sell decisions with stocks.

- Being alert about political issues and pending legislation, and being proactive by tracking government actions and communicating with political officials will make you a more informed citizen and investor.

GET THE SCOOP ON...
The trend is your friend ▪ Technical analysis
▪ Warning signs preceding a stock's rise ▪ When
to sell a stock ▪ Warning signs preceding a
stock's decline ▪ Going short ▪ Stock purchase
strategies

Succeeding in Both Bull and Bear Markets

Chapter 9

As a stock investor, you must accept the reality that you always invest in a market that is either bullish or bearish. The stock investing environment will either help or hinder your stock-picking strategy so it is to your benefit to understand market cycles. In the world of stock investing, it's always easier to pick a winning stock when there's a bull market. The obvious corollary is that it's tougher to choose a winning stock when there's a bear market. How do you judge what kind of market you're in?

Major financial publications such as *The Wall Street Journal* and *Investors Business Daily* monitor the markets on a daily basis. Usually a consensus develops, giving you a clear indication of which way the general market trend is heading.

Being aware of which way the markets and the economy are going is critical because successful stock investing is not done in a vacuum. Your choices are still subject to the rigors of the marketplace.

How about the individual stock? You did your homework, and the company has it all. It has strong earnings, growing sales, and leadership in its industry, and it has become the darling of analysts everywhere. But what if the economy is slowing down and the stock market is falling? What should you do? After all, the value of your stock is based on the market's expectations. Sometimes the stock of the best company can drop like a rock when millions of investors get nervous and sell. You can't avoid the fact that stock price is subject to the economics of supply and demand.

How do you know when to jump in or get out? Do you sell your stock when you read the headlines that the next bear market is imminent? When you watch your stock, and the market itself, the clues present themselves. The vigilant investor can do more than watch stock appreciate; he or she can also avoid or minimize losses. When your stock is doing well, you enjoy the ride as its price ascends. However, you don't leave the stock subject to guesswork regarding the market's direction. If the bull market starts to sputter and run out of steam, the prudent investor removes uncertainty by using the trailing stops that so few investors use.

The trend is your friend

The basic approach is simple. When the stock market is a bull market, stay fully invested. When the stock market is a bear market, sell your stock and park your cash in a safe alternative, such as a bank account or a money market fund. As the next bull market starts, slowly get back into the stock market.

Of course, this is easier said than done. But if you harness the power of these up and down trends, you can maximize your portfolio's performance. When the century's greatest bull market began in 1982, you would have done very well with stocks. With well-chosen stocks, you would have done far better.

Understanding whether it is a bull or bear market will be important, but regardless of the type of market, you should make a habit of regularly reading the financial publications in the popular press, such as *The Wall Street Journal, Investors Business Daily,* and *Barron's*. Magazines such as *Money Magazine, Forbes,* and *Smart Money* are also excellent. Surf the Internet for Web sites such as MarketWatch.com, Bloomberg.com, and PersonalWealth.com as well. These and many other publications and Web sites are listed in Chapter 5, "Finding the Information."

Although it can be difficult to judge the absolute end (or beginning) of a bull or bear market, both tend to run for long periods of time. Studies have shown that investors still made superior returns on their money even starting late in a bull market. The following points often indicate changes in the stock market's general direction.

"Buy and hold" versus "timing the market"

In the insurance industry, a long-running debate was "whole life versus term" insurance. In the mutual fund industry, it was "load funds versus no-load funds." In the adult beverage field, it was "tastes great versus less filling." In the stock market, the "buy and hold" versus "timing the market" debate rages to this day. As is often the case, the optimal course is a mix of both.

"Buy and hold" is the best strategy for a bull market, but certainly not for a bear market. Famed investors such as Louis Rukeyser and Warren Buffett are successful proponents of the "buy and hold" strategy. Richard Russell, editor of *Dow Theory*

Forecasts, and Robert Prechter, Jr., editor of *Elliott Wave Theorist*, are successful proponents of timing the market. What should you do?

History suggests that elements of both approaches are valuable. You should modify your portfolio during the market cycles. To illustrate this, imagine that you have allocated $10,000 to purchasing stocks (this assumes that you have additional money elsewhere, such as bank accounts, real estate, and so on, for proper diversification). Of that money, you should optimally have it deployed in the following way during market cycles:

1. The bull market has started according to economic and market indicators. Ideally, 100 percent of your $10,000 is in stocks, preferably proven growth stocks. You stay fully invested as the bull market continues.

2. Economic indicators show that the economy is starting to show signs of slowing. The stock market is starting to exhibit a high P/E ratio (over 25). Have 50 percent of your portfolio in growth stocks, and shift 50 percent into defensive stocks such as utilities and food stocks.

3. The evidence is that the economy has clearly slowed. The market gurus are starting to argue about whether the market is bullish. More market commentators are expressing concern about the bull market running out of steam. Modify your portfolio. Have 25 percent of your money in growth stocks, 50 percent in defensive stocks, and 25 percent in cash.

4. The market has ceased rising and has started to decline. If your stocks are still doing well, hang on to them, but put in trailing stop orders to protect your gains.

5. The market has clearly started to fall. As your stocks have declined, the stop orders have been triggered and the stocks are automatically sold. As the market continues to weaken, your portfolio becomes 100 percent cash and/or other conservative, short-term investments, such as a short-term bond mutual fund. You safely watch from the sidelines as the bear market kicks in.

6. As the bear market beats down stock prices, you start researching the market to find value stocks with low stock prices. Income stocks offer a good opportunity in a mature bear market as low stock prices give you the chance to pick up stocks with high dividends. As this point, your portfolio is probably 50 percent cash and 50 percent stocks with a low P/E ratio and high dividends. You wait and watch for the next bull market to begin.

This market cycle gives us a chance to touch on the second major debate in the marketplace: fundamental analysis versus technical analysis. Fundamental analysis looks at the company's financial strength, market position, and managerial competence. The fundamentals include the company's sales, earnings, financial ratios, and so on. This contrasts sharply with technical analysis, which primarily looks at the stock's performance using charts and share price history. Further discussion of technical analysis follows.

Using fundamental analysis as you look at individual companies is most highly recommended. Technical analysis is recommended for the market at large. This combination includes the best of both worlds. If you have a solid company with strong fundamentals (earnings growth and the like), you will do well in a bull market. In a bear market, a solid company will not see its stock price fall as badly as weaker companies.

In a growing economy with a rising stock market, stocks are the premier investment. They usually beat out competing investments such as bonds and certificates of deposit. In a recessionary economy with a stagnant or declining stock market, strong stocks will do better than weak stocks, but stocks in general will not do as well as bonds and certificates of deposit.

Those who favor fundamental analysis look at technical analysis as if it were a form of voodoo. After all, how could past stock patterns predict future movements of the stock's price? Technical analysis has questionable value for individual stocks. However, it can be very useful in tracking the general market.

Technical analysis

Technical analysis is the practice of trying to predict stock prices by examining trading patterns and comparing the shape of current charts to those from the past.

Technical analysts use a variety of complex charting techniques, but some of the most basic involve plotting price movements in a stock over time on a fever chart. The shape of the chart is supposed to reveal something about whether the stock is headed up or down.

Technical analysis can be very useful in spotting trends. Although it's questionable how useful technical analysis is in forecasting future price movement for a given stock, it's very useful in analyzing general stock market trends. When the market is moving in your favor, your stock has a better chance of performing favorably for your portfolio. Technical analysis can help you time your investing with the general market's up and down trends. Technical analysis offers a variety of tools and insights that the investor can use.

Advance/decline index (A/D index)

The ratio of advancing stocks to declining stocks, the advance/decline index, over time gives an indication of where the broad market has been going— a trend that is sometimes masked by indexes such as the Dow Jones Industrial Average, which contains just 30 stocks, all large industrial concerns whose fortunes don't always reflect the overall market.

The advance/decline index is simply a cumulative total of the number of advancing issues minus the number of declining issues. First, a large number is chosen, such as 20,000. Each day, the difference between the number of advancing issues and declining issues is added or subtracted. Usually, New York Stock Exchange data is used for the calculation.

The A/D index is useful to investors because it can indicate which way the market is heading. If more stocks are advancing than declining, that's a bullish indicator. Of course, if more stocks are declining than advancing, that's a bearish indicator. Watching the A/D index for a day or a week doesn't tell you much. However, over a month or two, it can give you a strong signal about the market's potential direction.

Upside/downside ratio

New York Stock Exchange data is used for calculating the upside/downside ratio as well. The upside/downside ratio is the volume of advancing New York Stock Exchange issues divided by the

Unofficially ...
Market timing is a technique used by investors or money managers who believe that they can predict when the market will change course. For example, a mutual fund manager might switch the bulk of his fund's holdings from stocks into bonds or cash when he thinks—based on analysis, his own gut feeling, or both—that stocks have peaked. If he times the market correctly, he could make a huge profit.

volume of declining New York Stock Exchange issues. This ratio measures buying and selling pressure. A 10-period moving average can be used to smooth the data. However, most technicians will try different lengths of moving averages for smoothing. This indicator works best for short-term moves in the market. Very high readings above 4 are considered bullish signals, and very low readings below .75 are considered bearish signals. Additionally, Martin Zweig of *The Zweig Forecast* has found that readings greater than 9 to 1 have preceded every bull market and many strong intermediate uptrends. This indicator doesn't give many signals, but the ones that it does generate seem to be reliable.

For investors, the upside/downside ratio gives further evidence regarding the market's general direction. Again, it may not mean much over a day or a week but over an extended period of time, it can further corroborate market direction.

Relative strength

Relative strength measures the price performance of a stock in comparison to all other stocks in the market. Many analysts believe that stocks with strong and improving relative strength tend to continue to outperform all other stocks, with all other things being equal.

The figure is obtained by calculating the percent price change of a stock over a particular time period and ranking it against all other stocks on a scale of 1 to 100, with 100 being best. Stocks that are ranked from 70 to 100 are considered to have good relative strength, while stocks ranked lower than 50 are considered to have poor relative strength. *Investors Business Daily* regularly tracks relative strength by reporting the number in its stock tables.

Moving average (MA)

Moving averages are one of the oldest (and most useful) technical indicators. A basic definition of a moving average is the average price of a security (or index, such as the S&P 500 Index) at a specific time. Because stock price movements can be very choppy as they go up and down on a daily basis, a moving average is used to decipher a general trend for the stock.

A moving average is the average price of a stock over the previous days or years. For example, a 50-day MA is the average price of a security over the past 50 days. This gives an indication of a security's price trend. For technical analysts, a 200-day MA is a standard longer-term measure; often this is compared with a 50-day or even 5-day MA in an effort to gain insight into the direction of a stock. When the short-term average moves above the long-term average, it's considered a buy signal. When the short-term average is below the long-term average, technical analysts consider it time to get out.

For example, say we have been tracking the closing price of Moving Experiences Inc., (MEI) for the past 100 days, and we want to create a 30-day moving average. First, we add the closing prices for the first 30 days. Then we divide this amount by 30. This is the first point we would plot on the chart. Then we add the closing prices together for day 2 through day 31. We then divide this amount by 30. This is the second point on the chart. Then we add the closing prices for days 3 through 32. We divide this number by 30. And this can go on forever. We connect all the points we plotted in a line and run it through the price bars.

Bright Idea
When you have found stocks that fit your criteria according to the indicators, do some paper trading before you commit your funds. Paper trading is simply tracking investments as if you'd bought them to see how well your choices would have performed without risking any money.

This moving average shows us the smoothed price trend. A valid buy signal is given when price crosses above the moving average and the moving average is directed upward. A valid sell signal is given when price crosses below the moving average and the moving average is directed downward. Valid buy and sell signals are not given when the moving average changes direction but price does not cross above or below the moving average.

Moving averages can become more powerful when multiple moving averages are plotted on a chart. One combination used is to plot a 10-day moving average and a 30-day moving average on the same chart. A valid buy signal is given when the 10-day moving average crosses above the 30-day moving average and both moving averages are in an upward direction. A valid sell signal is given when the 10-day moving average crosses below the 30-day moving average and both moving averages are directed downward.

The average itself can act as an area of support and resistance. Support and resistance levels are important concepts in technical analysis. In a support level, the chart patterns indicate that the stock price has a "floor," or a price level that it does not penetrate. This shows that the stock has strength at that level. If the stock price falls below the support level, it is considered a bearish indicator for the stock.

The resistance level is the price level that the stock is having difficulty breaking through. If a stock surpasses its resistance level, technical analysts, consider this a bullish indicator.

In an uptrend, the following conditions apply. Long positions are maintained as long as price remains above the moving average. If price crosses above the moving average, a buy signal is generated. If price falls to the 200-day moving average but doesn't cross it and then moves back up, a buy signal is generated. If price drops sharply below the moving average line, a rebound toward the moving average line may occur, resulting in a whipsaw action. In a downtrend, short positions are held as long as price remains below the moving average. A sell signal is generated when price moves above a declining moving average line. If price moves up to the moving average line but doesn't cross it and drops down again, a sell signal is generated.

Because false signals can be given when using moving averages, technical analysts always use other indicators to confirm the direction of price. Moving averages tend to be confusing when the stock price fluctuates in a broad sideways pattern.

Alpha and beta of a stock

The volatility of a stock's returns—that is, the risk associated with a given security—is composed of two parts: alpha and beta. Before we get into a discussion of weighted alpha, we need to look at the regular versions of beta and alpha.

A stock's beta measures the part of its return that results from market movements. A beta of 1.00 indicates that the stock moves in perfect tandem with the market. That is, a 5 percent rise in the market will lead to a 5 percent rise in that stock. Betas greater than 1.00 indicate that a stock's returns will rise faster than the market (and also fall faster when the market falls). If a stock's beta lies between 1.00 and 0, it will fluctuate less than the market, while a negative beta indicates that a stock will move in the opposite direction of the market.

Bright Idea
To get an excellent introduction to technical analysis and its tools (such as moving averages, price patterns, and stock charts), check out the educational primers at the following Web sites:
Investopedia
www.
investopedia.com
Stock Charts
www.stockcharts.
com

An alpha, on the other hand, measures the return that is completely independent of the market—that is, due solely to that particular stock's own merits, such as earnings surprises, market dominance, and investor sentiment. For example, a stock with an alpha of 1.25 is expected to increase 25 percent, regardless of whether the market rises, falls, or stays flat. Factors that could cause alpha to increase include takeover rumors, accelerating earnings expectations, and so forth.

Now, a weighted alpha is very similar to a regular alpha except that, when calculating a stock's returns relative to the overall market, recent price changes are weighted more heavily than past changes. This makes intuitive sense because the farther into the past we go, the less relevant the stock's behavior is to the present.

Keep in mind that, when the overall market's direction is questionable, stocks with a positive alpha might be a good place to start your investment search.

Resources for technical analysis

Technical analysis can be ... uh ... quite technical. You could drown yourself in reams of charts and graphs trying to decipher all the patterns as you prognosticate the direction of your stock. This book won't delve into this topic because technical analysis can have limited or questionable value for stock investors. Technical analysis can be summed up as follows:

- ▪ Technical analysis for a specific company has little usefulness. The stock's chart may give you a great picture of where its price has been, but it still amounts to guesswork for its future. For analyzing an individual stock, fundamental analysis is usually superior.

▪ Technical analysis used to detect general market trends can be very useful. The market, along with society and the economy, does ebb and flow. These "megatrends" or cycles can help or hinder your investing. Understanding these cycles will increase your chances for success.

Some excellent resources for technical analysis are listed in Appendix B, "Investing Information Resources."

A surprising "reverse" indicator

Sometimes the best stock market indicators are not complicated or esoteric. The country's mood as reported by the media gives you great insight regarding the direction of markets. It is amazing how often the media can be used as a reverse indicator. As odd as it may sound, you need to bet against the mainstream media to succeed. If major news magazines and TV shows report that the economy is doing well, that particular companies or industries are booming, look at selling your investments. If the mainstream media is very pessimistic about the economy or stock market, consider buying.

In 1929, the mainstream media issued many positive stories about how no end was in sight for the booming '20s. The most respected economist of the day, Irving Fisher, said the infamous words, "Stocks have reached a permanent plateau."

In January 1973, *Barron's* did a survey of stock market pundits regarding the direction of the market. Every single one was bullish on the market, "Not a bear among them." In reality, however, 1973

Timesaver
Many Web sites will give you basic technical data and indicators for the stocks on NYSE, AMEX, and Nasdaq. They have stock screening tools that actually track a stock's basic technical indicators. Check out the Web sites mentioned in this chapter as well as those in Chapter 5, "Finding the Information."

was the toughest bear market since the Great Depression. In the 1973–1975 period, the stock market as measured by the Dow Jones Industrial Average fell nearly 50 percent. Many lesser stocks fell even more. This bear market was ferocious in its breadth and intensity.

In 1979, *Business Week* had the famous cover heralding "The Death of Equities." The economy was in sad shape. Society was pessimistic. However, the greatest bull market of the century started in 1982. Anyone who started accumulating stocks when the notorious *Business Week* cover hit the newsstand was handsomely rewarded. Because the public stayed away from the stock market, value investors found solid stocks at very low prices.

Why is the mainstream media so far behind the curve on stock market movements? Primarily, the mainstream media reports what is currently going on. In effect, they report the "symptoms" of economic activity as opposed to the "causes" of economic activity. The media may give you a detailed report about how high gasoline prices are, but it didn't give you a report six months earlier. The media is a "lagging indicator."

A good example is when you see a TV news reporter down at the unemployment office doing a report about the tough labor market. If you'd gone three months earlier, you wouldn't have seen the same reporter interviewing a company CEO about how his or her company was struggling. Investors could have seen the warning signs by looking at the shrinking profit margins and dubious financial ratios gleaned from the company's SEC reports.

Alert investors can find out about a company's fortunes (or misfortunes) before they become visible to the mass media and the public. It can take months to catch up on a primary trend, but by then the market has changed. By the time the media finds out what's going on, it is already history. For alert investors, yesterday's lagging market indicator is today's leading market indicator.

When a bull market ends

Markets give you clues when they're ready to change. These general characteristics occur during the last stage of a mature bull market:

- As odd as it sounds, bull markets generally end during a time of great optimism. The stories are well documented of the buoyant optimism that was rife in 1929. The public and the investing professionals thought good times would keep rolling on indefinitely.

- The market as a whole hits a high P/E ratio. In March 2000, the Nasdaq Composite Index hit an all-time high of 5,048. This lofty level meant that Nasdaq's P/E hit a staggering 200. Historically, its P/E has usually been under 40.

- Stocks that have been market leaders start to "top out." In other words, when you look at the chart of a particular market-leading stock, its price movement begins to stall. A great example is the stock price of Cisco Systems during 1999 and into early 2000. During 1999, Cisco's stock price was on an uninterrupted upward trajectory. For investors, it was like riding a rocket. However, the rocket started to sputter around March 2000.

Defensive stocks begin to lead the market (utilities, food and beverage stocks, and so on). Defensive stocks are stocks of companies that produce goods and services that are needed and wanted by the market regardless of how poorly the economy is doing. After all, no matter how the economy gets, people still need electricity, food, and other necessities.

▪ Low-quality stocks begin running up or making new highs as a record number of inexperienced investors crowd into the market to buy "the next great stock." In a mature bull market, the "Don't-leave-me-out-of-the-big-money" syndrome kicks in.

▪ "Stock-Market-Get-Rich" type of books start to proliferate. In 1999, several books with titles such as *Dow 36,000* and *Dow 100,000* came out.

▪ Consumer confidence is high. This leads to more spending and more debt. It soon becomes "consumer overconfidence."

▪ The "It-must-be-because-I'm-a-genius" attitude kicks in. In a bull market, successful stock picking is not difficult. Investors feel that no matter what they invest in, they'll make money. This gives people a sense of invincibility regarding their knowledge and stock-picking prowess. This overconfidence leads them to making poor choices later and subsequently losing money when the next bear market hits the scene.

▪ Signs of excess. When people are doing well and feeling good about their economic situations, they tend to spend more. Either they buy more of something, or they buy or do expensive things. Expensive vacations and fancy cars bought with debt becomes commonplace. New car sales hit record levels. Consumer and mortgage debt grows to record levels.

■ Economic statistics show a slowing or contracting economic activity.

When a bear market ends

Equally odd-sounding is the fact that bear markets usually end in times of great pessimism. What's that? Does that mean that the best time to catch a bull market is when society is at its most negative? Believe it or not, yes. There tend to be more "gloom-and-doom" books out when the market, and public confidence is already at a low point. Although it's not 100 percent reliable, history has taught us that being contrarian with bull and bear markets will make you very wealthy (or at least help you avoid losses).

The twentieth century is loaded with examples of how a contrarian approach could have either made you rich or saved you a fortune. In 1932, the market hit rock bottom as investors avoided stocks like the plague. However, contrarians made huge profits by buying large-cap stocks at small-cap prices. The companies were fundamentally sound even though their stock prices were battered to bargain-basement prices. In the 1973–1975 bear market, most investors lost money and fled the market. Experienced investors saw this as a buying opportunity and picked up the stock of great companies such as General Electric and Coca-Cola at rock-bottom prices. Investors who bought stock during the Great Depression did well because the stock prices were beaten down to bargain levels.

The following is a list of warning signs that the market is ripe for a new bull market:

- The P/E ratio for the market as a whole is historically low. A P/E at 10 or lower means that stock prices are low relative to company earnings. Standard & Poor's tracks the P/E for its widely followed S&P 500 Index at www.spglobal. com. The Dow Jones Industrial Average (DJIA) is tracked by Dow Jones at www.indexes. dowjones.com.

- Market values of companies' stocks are very close to or parallel to their book values. If you see book values of strong companies exceed their market values, this is a strong sign that the market is undervalued and that their stock is poised to rise.

- If surveys of analysts in the financial press are primarily bearish, it's time to consider stocks. The same herd mentality that is evident in the public is equally true of analysts in both mature bull and bear markets.

- Leading economic indicators have reversed course and are showing improvement (have gone from negative to positive). They indicate at least two straight quarters of increasing growth in the economy.

As a bull market ends, the optimal strategy is to sell the bulk of your stock holdings. Bear markets are perfect for "shoppers" seeking values in stocks that have been beaten up by the market.

Warning signs preceding a stock's rise

Just as there are indications of whether a bull or bear market is starting, there are indicators for individual stocks. Although these indicators are not infallible, they have been generally reliable for choosing rising stocks:

- Insiders begin buying heavily. Insiders are people heavily and intimately involved with the company's operations. They may be "operational," insiders such as the president or the CEO, or they may simply be individuals who own 5 percent or more of the company's stock. If operational insiders are buying up the stock, this usually bodes well for the stock's price. The feeling is that the insiders see things happening at the company that will boost the company's value, such as a new product announcement or a beneficial pending merger or business deal. For more information on insider trading, see Chapter 10, "Going It Alone or Using a Broker."

- Positive news stories about the company or its industry are reported. Keep careful watch on what news is being reported regarding the company. The financial press will write about the company's activities regarding a new venture, market, or product. For information regarding news and bulletins about a specific company, check the sources in Chapter 10, "Going It Alone or Using a Broker."

- Earnings report exceeds expectations. In the long run, the bottom line is how profitable the company is. Watching the company's earnings reports gives you clues about the company's pending success.

- Institutional buying increases. When large institutional investors start to buy a stock, this is a good sign for the stock's price. Keep track

Bright Idea
What is usually required of investors in times of economic decline and pessimism is not superior analytical skills or clairvoyance. It is discipline and courage. In extreme markets (both up and down), most investors and analysts lack those two qualities because it means thinking and acting outside conventional wisdom. When everyone is optimistic and buying stock, it's a good idea to consider selling. When everyone is fearful and selling stock, it's a good time to go shopping.

"

It takes big
demand to move
supply up, and
the largest source
of demand for
stocks is by
far the institu-
tional buyer.
—William J.
O'Neil, *Investors
Business Daily*

"

of what mutual funds, pension plans, and other organizations buy or sell. Publications such as those published by Standard & Poor's and Web sites such as www.marketguide.com keep track of institutional investors.

When the major investors in the market act, they exert tremendous influence over stock prices. Institutions such as mutual funds and pension funds buy and sell stocks in large blocks. These large transactions tend to drive prices up or down depending on the degree of buying or selling. When demand for a stock increases, its price usually increases. Conversely, stock prices tend to fall when there is an ample supply of shares or decreased demand. Identifying stocks with heavy institutional buying activity is a crucial element in locating stocks poised for big price moves.

Investor's Business Daily tracks the flow of institutional money daily in its paper.

When to sell a stock

Most of us understand why we buy a stock. We buy it for gain, whether capital gain or income gain. But it's difficult to decide when to sell a stock. Many people agonize over when to sell. They agonize either over the general market or over the individual stock.

The only two reasons to sell a stock

Buying stock is easy. Selling stock is more difficult. However, you can make the sale easier and smarter. You can narrow your reasons to sell a stock to just two:

1. You sell your stock because you need the money. No matter how well or how poorly the

stock is doing, if you need the money, then you need the money. There is no mystery here. Typically, investors need the money because they haven't set aside money in an emergency fund. Stocks are not meant to be savings vehicles; they are long-term investments.

2. You sell your stock because its price is no longer rising (or is losing money). Most investors believe that this means you analyze the stock, its industry, its P/E ratio, and so on. But it's easier than that. Simply use stop orders with your broker that are good-til-cancelled (GTC). For example, if you buy a stock at $50, put in a GTC stop order at $45. If the stock falls and hits $45, the stop order is triggered and the stock is automatically sold. If the stock goes to $60, the stop loss order at $45 is cancelled and replaced with a stop loss order at $55 that is also GTC.

What happens if you bought Piano Repair Corporation (PRC) stock at $75, you have a stop loss order at $70 and the stock stays flat indefinitely? As we mentioned in the second previous point, you should sell a stock if its share price is not growing. You should set a minimum acceptable annualized growth rate for your stock. Because the stock market historically grows at the average rate of 10 to 12 percent, this is an acceptable minimum growth rate.

When you are measuring how well PRC is performing, you should use the total return concept (TRC). The total return concept looks at what return have you gotten on your investment—combined appreciation and income (if any)—on an annual basis.

For example, say that you have a stock that you bought for $30 per share and that has a $2 dividend. Assume that this stock reached $50 per share a year later. What is the total return on your money? The answer is 73 percent—appreciation of $20 ($50 − $30), plus $2 dividend means that your $30 investment gave you a return of $22, or 73 percent. This stock should hit a year-end target price of $34 to equate to a 12 percent rate of growth (not including the dividend, if any). Keep holding the stock as it appreciates.

Selling when the stock is falling

Frequently, the investor becomes married to the stock. This means that the investor holds on to a stock even though it's in a nonstop free fall. The psychology is interesting and presented in the following scenario:

Irv, the investor, buys stock in the company Buncha-Losers Corp. at $50 per share. The stock falls to $40. Irv will not sell. He rationalizes, "The stock is a long-term play. If I sell now, it means taking a loss of $10 per share. Besides, the stock will eventually rebound."

Buncha-Losers Corp. falls to $30 per share. Irv thinks, "If I sell now, I'll have to admit that I made a mistake. Selling means locking in a loss. Perhaps this is a buying opportunity instead. I'll buy more today at $30." Buncha-Losers goes to $25 per share. Irv scratches his head. "Buncha-Losers doesn't have much downside risk at this point," she says. "I'll hold on because selling means taking a big loss."

In this scenario, emotion took over and discipline lost. If a stock is purchased and it falls 50 percent, this means that it will have to rise 100 percent just to get back to the original price. Irv would have

Watch Out!
Martin Zweig, a top investment adviser, said, "You can be right on your stocks only 40 percent of the time and still do fine—if you cut your losses short." Most investors get either greedy or overconfident and watch losses mount. Losing some money is inevitable. No investor buys only winners.

been better off selling earlier and reinvesting the proceeds in another stock. Limiting losses is tough for novice investors. The undisciplined investor would rather lose money than admit defeat and move on.

Investors must understand that selling stocks at a loss is far more common than they realize. The most successful investors (MSIs) always limit their losses and protect the bulk of their investment. MSIs understand that taking small losses is more than off-set by the winners you "let ride" that grow exponentially. If you have done your homework, you'll have winners in your portfolio. MSIs know that time is lost as they bide their time waiting for their losing choices to rebound. The quicker they get out, the quicker they can shift money to another potential winning stock. Consider the following example:

1/1/1999		1/1/2000		
	Original Invested Amount $	Gain/Loss %	New Market Value $	Gain/Loss Amount $
Stock 1	$2,000	−10%	$1,800	−$200
Stock 2	$2,000	−10%	$1,800	−$200
Stock 3	$2,000	−10%	$1,800	−$200
Stock 4	$2,000	−10%	$1,800	−$200
Stock 5	$2,000	−10%	$1,800	−$200
Stock 6	$2,000	+100%	$4,000	+$2,000
Totals	$12,000	+8.3%	$13,000	+$1,000

Result: Even with choosing five losing stocks out of six, one winning stock can still make the entire portfolio perform positively. In this case, the portfolio did a respectable 8 percent ($1,000 gain divided by the original investment of $12,000). But what if even one of those stocks were allowed to

❝

Now I'm in real
trouble. First, my
laundry called
and said they
lost my shirt,
and then my
broker said the
same thing.
—Leopold
Fechtner

❞

keep sinking? You would see your entire portfolio value plummet.

Clues preceding a stock's decline

Just because you have a stop loss order on a stock doesn't mean that you should stop looking at the company. The stop loss order is designed to protect you from only severe downside risk. You should still be alert if anything could affect your stock. If you can sell it before it hits the stop loss order, you are that much ahead of the game. What are some of the things you should be looking out for?

- Heavy insider selling is a big clue to the stock's potential problems. If "operational" insiders sell en masse, you should do the same. Operational insiders include the chief executive officer, (CEO) or president, the chief financial officer (CFO), vice presidents, and other key managers in the company. These insiders know better than anyone else how the company is really doing. (For more information on insider trading, see Chapter 10, "Going It Alone or Using a Broker.")

- Negative news stories about the company or its industry sometimes can have an indirect effect. For example, brokerage stocks plummeted in late May 2000 because the stock market fell dramatically. Nasdaq went from over 5,000 in early March to under 3,400 by mid-May. This 34 percent drop wiped out a lot of day traders. It also diminished the issuance of IPO financing. This caused a major drop-off in trading volume and volume of private companies doing initial public offerings (IPOs) during the same period. Because brokerage firms gained revenue from stock trading commission and IPO underwriting fees, they took a big hit as earnings fell from declining business revenues. Chapter 5, "Finding the Information," and Chapter 10, "Going It Alone or Using a Broker," will help you with information sources.

▪ If the company experiences significant deterioration in their sales, profitability, or other barometer of financial health, consider selling its stock.

▪ Perhaps the company is losing market share. When it was first in its industry, then second, then third, it's time to sell.

▪ Prospects for the industry might have dimmed. Say that you are invested in the market leader of the photography developing industry. With the advent of digital cameras, traditional photography will be adversely impacted. If the company is innovative, you may stay with them. But if the innovation is coming from outside the industry, consider getting out.

▪ Consider selling if a stock's P/E ratio rises more than 40 percent above its annual average for the past 10 years. For example, if the price historically is about 20 times earnings per share but suddenly climbs to 28, that may be the time to retreat. You can get these figures from a broker or from the *Value Line Investment Survey* (available at many libraries).

▪ The stock is targeted by government agencies such as the Securities and Exchange Commission.

Keep in mind that a company having problems may not always be a bad thing. Sometimes, you'll be thrilled to see a stock's price plummet, especially if you're shorting it.

Profiting from a stock's decline—going short

Short selling is selling a stock before you actually buy it. To sell short, you first borrow stocks from a broker. The broker will lend you the shares from his own inventory or borrow them from another customer or from another broker. Then you sell them immediately on the market. You keep the money that you earned from selling the stocks and wait, hoping that the price for the stock will drop.

If the price for the stock does drop, you can buy back the stock and give them back to your broker. You will then have made a profit because you sold them for more than you bought them. For example, say that you borrow 100 shares at $50 per share and sell them in the market; you have $5,000. If you wait a while and the price of the stock decreases to $30 per share, you can buy 100 stocks for $3,000. You then return the 100 stocks to the broker, pay some interest, and keep the $2,000 as profit.

Unfortunately, selling short does not always end as well as that. Consider if you borrow 100 shares at $50 per share again. You then sell them and get $5,000. You wait a few weeks, but the price of the stock continues to increase. Before you know it, the price of the stock is $60. You have to give the broker his stocks, and you have to pay him interest. This means that you have to pay $6,000 dollars to get the stocks back (to "cover" the position), but you just lost $1,000.

Moneysaver
If you short a stock, use a stop limit order to protect you from mounting losses that can occur if the stock price rises. If you short a stock at $50 and the stock goes up, you lose money. The more it rises, the more you lose. Put a stop limit in at 10 percent over your stock's price. If the stock hits $55, you lose $5 per share, but you limit your loss.

Most short sellers attempt to pick stocks that are fundamentally overpriced. They short stocks with high price/earnings ratios, high price/book value ratios, and low dividend yields—the opposite of those that value-oriented investors would buy. These include stocks that are currently fashionable that they feel will soon go out of fashion and stocks that should get hurt under an anticipated economic scenario. Shorting can be a good strategy, but shorting based on market timing or traditional parameters of value offers no certainty of profit.

Some resources on short selling include these:

Overpriced Stock Service (newsletter)
Publisher: Murenove, Inc.
Phone: 650-726-8495
Comments: Short selling recommendations.
Issue frequency: Monthly
Subscription price: Individual $495; foreign $525

Short on Value (newsletter via fax)
Publisher: Short on Value
Phone: 404-233-0120
Comments: Recommends overvalued U.S. stocks for short selling.
Issue frequency: Monthly
Subscription price: $240

Tulips and Bears (online newsletter)
Publisher: Tulips and Bears
Web site: www.tulipsandbears.com
Phone: 212-420-1405
Comments: Provides contrary investing opinion for thinking traders. Global stocks and markets are covered with both long and short picks. This newsletter is written by traders for traders.

Timesaver
Many brokerages and financial Web sites have free e-mail newsletters and e-mail alert services to warn you about new developments regarding your stocks. Companies such as Gomez Associates track brokerage firms and their services. Find out more about how your broker stacks up by going to the Web site www.gomez.com.

Issue frequency: Biweekly

Subscription price: Free

Web sites for bears and short-sellers include these:

Bear Market Central
www.bearmarketcentral.com

Investech
www.investech.com

Fall Street
www.fallstreet.com

Fiend's Super Bear
www.fiendbear.com

ProFunds
www.profunds.com

Short Boy
www.shortboy.com

Mutual funds that make money in bear markets (using techniques such as short selling) include these:

Bear Guard Fund
www.bearguard.com

Prudent Bear Fund
www.prudentbear.com

Stock purchase strategies

When the stock market fluctuates, the long-term investor is best advised to follow a disciplined plan to accumulate wealth. This can be done with one of several methods. Dollar-cost averaging, constant dollar, constant ratio, and variable ratio are four of the most popular time-tested strategies for succeeding with the market cycles.

These plans were developed to help investors gain some protection and cushion the blow if they purchase the stock at an unfavorable price. These methods can also be used for purchasing other investments, such as mutual funds.

Dollar cost averaging (DCA) plan

This is probably the simplest plan among the four. You can turn market cycles to your advantage with dollar-cost averaging. DCA consists of investing a constant dollar amount in common stocks over a long period of time at fixed intervals. The fixed intervals could be weekly, monthly, annually, or some other time period as long as it remains the same. For example, a person might invest $250 per month in common stocks or $25 per week. Or, this same person might invest $3,000 every six months. The idea is to invest smaller amounts of money on a regular, long-term basis. The theory is that stocks can always be sold on the average for more than they cost.

The investor must have a steady amount of income coming in and be willing to invest over a long period of time. This system also shouldn't be used on just one stock; the investor may want to choose five or six stocks to invest in this way. One or two different stocks could go down constantly, but a properly diversified portfolio will go up eventually.

This system doesn't mean that you should keep underperforming stocks in your portfolio. By all means, get rid of the dogs. One school of thought says that an investor should not purchase stocks with this program when they reach very high (over-bought) conditions. However, when a person does this, he or she may spend the money elsewhere, it is difficult to tell when stocks are too high, and the investor may not continue the program. I recommend that if stocks are at a level at which they may be too high, the money should be invested in stocks that do well in a declining market. An example is utility stocks.

Advantages of DCA

The average cost of shares purchased is usually less than the actual market price. The investor eliminates the possibility of buying too many shares when the price is too high. Also, periodic declines in the stock market provide buying opportunities at lower prices.

Disadvantages of DCA

Risks come into play when the time comes to sell your accumulated stock if stock prices are low. This could cause a portfolio loss. One way to minimize this danger is to plan to liquidate the portfolio several years before the actual liquidation time. This gives the investor time to pick and choose the best times to liquidate each holding. Another disadvantage is that the investor's income might not be as steady as would be hoped.

This could curtail purchases at times that are attractive for additional purchases. Another disadvantage is that the investor might try to time the purchases. This turns him into more of a speculator than an investor. Another disadvantage is that the person may be tempted to use the investment money for something important that comes up (such as a new car or a home repair).

A long-term plan not only makes it easier to ride out the ups and downs of the market, it also lets you take advantage of some basic investment strategies that have proven successful over the years.

Example of DCA in action over six-month period
Important note: This example illustrates buying a stock through a dividend reinvestment plan (DRP). A big plus of DRPs is that most do not charge brokerage commissions. For more details, see Chapter 10, "Going It Alone or Using a Broker."

Example	Investment per Month	Share Price	Shares Bought	Cumulative Holdings
1	$50.00	50	1.00	1.00
2	$50.00	40	1.25	2.25
3	$50.00	30	1.67	3.92
4	$50.00	35	1.43	5.35
5	$50.00	40	1.25	6.60
6	$50.00	45	1.11	7.71
Result after six months	$300.00	45	7.71	7.71

$300 total amount invested

$347 market value (7.71 shares × $45)

15.60% absolute growth percentage in six months

31.20% annualized growth rate

Dollar cost averaging (DCA) works best in a dividend reinvestment plan (DRP) or through a mutual fund to minimize transaction costs. In this example, the investor is buying stock through a DRP and is investing only $50 per month. Even though the share price fluctuated and was actually lower than the original purchase price during the investment period, the DCA method overcame it. DCA gives you the ability to buy more of a stock when it goes down and less of the stock when it goes up. Had the stock gone to $100 per share, the $50 investment would have bought only half a share.

The interesting phenomenon to be observed in this example is that even though the stock price dropped from $50 to $45 in six months, the total investment actually appreciated by more than 15 percent. This happened because the investor bought a batch of stocks at a price significantly below $45. When the stock rose in value, the total return increased because of the low-priced stock purchased.

This example did not take into account dividends or techniques such as stop orders, to keep it simple and clearly depict the concept of DCA. The key to DCA is discipline, something many investors do not cultivate. It also illustrates the concept that successful investing is more than just what you invest in; it is also how you do it. Methods such as DCA help overcome the uncertainties of market movements.

Constant dollar method

The constant dollar method is one in which the amount invested in stocks remains constant. A well-diversified portfolio should be used in this case. For example, an investor may have $100,000 invested in stocks. If the value of the portfolio rises a certain amount, say to $110,000, the additional $10,000 would be pulled out and invested in securities other than stocks. Or, the investor may choose a time period interval to pull the funds out, such as six months or one year.

Conversely, if the portfolio falls in value below $100,000, the investor would add capital to the portfolio to bring it back up to $100,000. Again, this might be done on a percentage basis (say 10 percent) or on a time period basis (once or twice a year).

Two advantages of this system are that stocks are sold when they are rising, and they are purchased when they are declining. The disadvantage to this type of system is that a certain degree of timeliness is involved in determining when to initially set up the system. Also, a period of constantly rising or declining prices doesn't work well. The system works best when prices fluctuate above and below the original level.

Constant ratio method

This method has the investor maintaining a constant 50/50 ratio in his or her portfolio between stocks and bonds. As stock prices rise, some are sold and bonds are purchased. As stock prices decline, bonds are sold and stocks are purchased. Profits can be made if stock prices fluctuate above and below the 50 percent line.

I have found little evidence that this plan performs better than any other plan. In fact, I have found little evidence that this plan works all that well. Also keep in mind that in the mid-1990s, this plan would not have performed well at all. It is a contrary investing strategy that aims to take advantage of the overall direction of the stock or bond market by increasing stock holdings when the market is weak and increasing bond or cash holdings when the market is strong.

Constant ratio investing is another timing method that works in concert with the market. Basically, you change your portfolio with the market. When the stock market goes up, you lower your equity exposure by selling a part of your shares and moving your funds into cash. For example, if your overall asset allocation is 60 percent cash and 40 percent equities and the market drops by 10 percent, you would increase your percentage equity exposure.

Proponents of the constant ratio investing method say that it helps you follow the golden rule of "buying low and selling high." That's because every time the market takes a big drop, you buy more stock at a discounted price and are well positioned when the market moves higher again.

However, if you're locked into a formula that calls for increasing your stock position as the market gets weaker, the value of your overall portfolio will also probably decline. And if the market is heading higher, a policy of increasingly shifting out of stocks will mean that your returns will suffer if the bull market lasts for months or even years.

Variable-ratio method

The variable-ratio method is a contrary investing strategy that aims to take advantage of the overall direction of the stock or bond market by increasing stock holdings when the market is weak and increasing bond or cash holdings when the market is strong.

The variable-ratio method works in concert with the market. You change your portfolio as the market changes. If the stock market goes up, you decrease your stock holdings by selling a part of your shares and moving your funds into cash. For example, if your overall asset allocation is 50 percent bonds and 50 percent stocks, and the market drops by 10 percent, you would increase your percentage stock exposure.

Proponents of the variable-ratio method say that it helps the investor to buy low and sell high. That's because every time the market takes a big drop, you buy more stock at a discounted price and will be well positioned when the market moves higher again.

However, if you're locked into a formula that calls for increasing your stock position as the market gets weaker, the value of your overall portfolio will also probably decline. And if the market is heading higher, a policy of increasingly shifting out of stocks will mean that your returns will suffer if the bull market lasts for months or even years.

Just the facts

- Staying informed about the economy and the market cycles is crucial for investing success.

- Avoiding big losses is something that every successful investor should be constantly on guard against.

- Discipline is an important trait that investors should cultivate.

- Sophisticated investors see profit opportunities, even in bear markets, by going short.

- Having a long-term, disciplined approach helps investors succeed no matter what the gyrations of market cycles and fluctuations are.

The Purchase

GET THE SCOOP ON...
Using brokers ▪ Types of brokerage accounts
▪ Types of stock orders ▪ Using trailing stops
▪ Stock trading using margin ▪ Direct purchase
programs and dividend reinvestment plans
▪ Joining investment clubs

Going It Alone or Using a Broker

Using brokers

When it comes time to make that purchase (or sale), in most cases you will turn to stock brokers. There are several types to choose from.

Types of brokers

Broker firms can generally be divided into the following categories:

1. **Full-service**—This type of broker is for people who care less about fees and more about attention and guidance. An experienced account executive is assigned to your account to help you understand investment choices and strategies and to implement them for you (Example: Merrill Lynch).

2. **Full-service discount**—This broker provides services almost indistinguishable from a full-service broker such as Merrill Lynch, but at about half the cost. These provide local branch offices for personal service, newsletters, a

personal account representative, and plenty of literature (Example: Charles Schwab).

3. **Discount**—This is the same as a full-service broker, but discount brokers usually don't have local branch offices and as much literature or research departments. Commissions are about one-third the price of those of a full-service broker (Example: TD Waterhouse).

4. **Deep-discount**—This type of broker executes stock and option trades only; other services are minimal. Often these brokers charge a flat fee (for example, $25) for any trade of any size. They have a lower fee because they primarily specialize in large-volume transactions (Example: Brown & Company).

5. **Online**—An online broker is the same as a deep-discount broker, but it is designed mainly for computer users (either dial-up or via the Internet). Note that some online brokers also offer the option of doing trades by telephone with a broker at a higher commission (Example: Etrade).

General information on brokers

All brokerages, their clearing agents, and any holding companies they have that can be holding your assets in "street name" had better be registered with the Securities Investor Protection Corporation (SIPC). Stock held in street name means that the stock is not registered in the name of the stockholder, but in the broker's name. This is done to make it easy for brokers to exchange stock during buy and sell transactions. The stockholder is still the legal and beneficial owner.

"
Too many people are apt to redeem their profits too quickly. In a huge bull market, they wind up with piddling profits, only to watch their former holdings soar. That usually prompts them into making mistakes later when, believing that the market owes them some money, they buy at the wrong time at much higher levels.
—Martin Zweig
"

Street name is really just for more convenient conveyance of stock between brokers. However, it could be a problem if a broker goes bankrupt. SIPC is the brokerage industry's equivalent to banking's FDIC. You're going to be paying an SEC "tax" (up to $3) on any trade you make anywhere, so make sure that you're getting the benefit; if a broker goes bankrupt, it's the only thing that prevents a total loss. Investigate thoroughly!

In general, you need to ask carefully about all the services the broker offers, your needs for services, and any fees associated with them. Ask about fees to transfer assets out of your account, inactive account fees, minimums for interest on non-margin cash balances, annual IRA custodial fees, per-transaction charges, and their margin interest rate, if applicable. Some will credit your account for the broker call rate on cash balances, which can be applied toward commission costs.

You may have seen that price competition has driven the cost of a trade below $10 at many Web brokers. How can they charge so little? Discounters that charge deeply discounted commissions either make markets, sell their order flow, or charge other fees. Being a market-maker means providing investment banking services and receiving underwriting fees. Selling an order flow essentially means generating transaction fees from other brokers or serviced agents that process the orders. Discount brokers also generate revenue by ancillary activities such as margin interest or advertising revenue from third-party sources seeking access to the broker's client base. These sources of revenue enable the cheap commission rates because they profit handsomely from trading with your order or selling it to another broker.

A discount broker offers an execution service for a wide variety of trades. In other words, you tell that broker to buy, sell, short, or whatever, and it does exactly what you requested and nothing more. This service is primarily a way to save money for people who are looking out for themselves and who do not require or desire any advice or hand-holding about their forays into the markets.

Discount brokering is a highly competitive business. As a result, many of the discount brokers provide virtually all the services of a full-service broker with the exception of giving you unsolicited advice on what or when to buy or sell. Then again, some do provide monthly newsletters with recommendations. Virtually all will execute stock and option trades, including stop or limit orders and odd lots, on the NYSE, AMEX, or Nasdaq.

Most can trade bonds and U.S. treasuries. Most will not trade futures; talk to a futures broker for this. Most have margin accounts available. Almost all of them will pay you interest on uninvested cash in your account by "sweeping," or transferring, your funds into a money market account, often with check-writing capability. All can hold your stock in street name, but many can take and deliver stock certificates physically, sometimes for a fee. Some trade precious metals and can even deliver them!

Many brokers will let you buy no-load (that is, having no commission or sales fee) mutual funds for a low (around 0.5 percent) commission. Increasingly, many even offer free mutual fund purchases through arrangements with specific funds to pay the commission for you; ask for their fund list. Many will provide free 1-page Standard & Poor's stock reports on stocks that you request, and 5- to 10-page full research reports for $5 to $8, often by fax. Some provide touch-tone telephone stock quotes 24 hours a day; some even allow you to make trades this way. Many provide computer quotes and trading; others say this service is on its way.

Evaluating brokers

Brokers can vary in a number of ways, ranging from price to service. Typically, a highly rated broker one year falls from grace the following year. Here are a few sources to help you get current information and ratings on brokers:

Deja.com
www.deja.com
Gives ratings of numerous products and services, including brokers. The ratings are done by users of the system. The site also has a search engine for newsgroups. You can check the newsgroups for complaints and compliments about brokers.

Don Johnson's Site
www.sonic.net/donaldj.html
Doesn't have impressive graphics, but does give very extensive information on numerous brokers, including several different broker rankings. (No, it's not *that* Don Johnson.)

Gomez Associates
www.gomez.com
Does extensive research on online brokers. Regularly rates them and reports customer satisfaction.

Bright Idea
You can request a free report on a broker's background from the National Association of Securities Dealers by calling 1-800-289-9999 or by visiting the Web site www.nasdr.com.

Invest FAQ
http://invest-faq.com/links/trading.html
Gives comments and ratings, and maintains links for online brokers.

SmartMoney.com
www.smartmoney.com/si/brokers
Gives its own ranking of brokers, and also includes a program that displays the ranking of online brokers based on how you specify the importance of various factors, such as price, service, and reliability.

StockZoo
www.stockzoo.com
Ranks some online brokers.

XOLIA.com
www.xolia.com
Has a broker comparison tool that lets you compare brokers side by side on a number of points. You can compare up to three brokers at a time. XOLIA.com also has DecisionMaker software that will interview you and then recommend brokers based on your answers. This site has an extensive list of online brokers (more than 50 as of May 2000).

Directory of brokers

The following is a list of the most popular online brokers. Visit their Web sites for more information on rates, service, and so on.

Accutrade
www.accutrade.com

American Express
www.americanexpress.com/trade/

Offers free trades (buys) for accounts with at least $25,000, and buys and sells for accounts with at least $100,000.

Ameritrade
1-800-326-7507
www.ameritrade.com

Brown & Company
1-800-776-6061, 201-435-9655
www.brownco.com

Charles Schwab & Co.
1-800-435-4000
www.schwab.com

Datek
1-800-823-3835
www.datek.com

DLJ Direct
www.dljdirect.com

Dreyfus
www.edreyfus.com

Etrade
1-888-388-7200
www.etrade.com

Fidelity Brokerage
1-800-544-7272
www.fidelity.com

InvesTrade
www.investrade.com

JB Oxford
www.jboxford.com

Morgan Stanley Dean Witter Online
www.online.msdw.com

Moneysaver
How low can commissions go? How about *free*. Free Trade, a subsidiary of Ameritrade, offers commission-free trading as long as you open an account with a minimum of $5,000. The catch: There are charges for ancillary services such as stop loss orders. Find out more at www.freetrade.com.

Timesaver
Keep this in
mind regarding
online trading: If
there's technical
difficulty in the
market (heavy
trading volume,
capacity prob-
lems, and so on),
you'll need a
second venue to
transact your
trades.

Muriel Siebert
877-327-8380
www.msiebert.com

My Discount Broker
1-888-882-5600
www.discountbroker.com

National Discount Brokers
www.ndb.com

Quick & Reilly
www.quick-reilly.com

Scottrade
1-800-619-7283
www.scottrade.com

Sure Trade
www.suretrade.com

TD Waterhouse Securities, Inc.
1-800-934-4407
www.waterhouse.com

Web Street
www.webstreetsecurities.com

Full-service brokerages with information-packed Web sites include the following:

Merrill Lynch
www.merrill-lynch.com

Prudential Bache Securities
www.prusec.com

Solomon Smith Barney
www.smithbarney.com

Timesaver
With online trad-
ing, it's okay to
try to get the
cheapest rates.
Just make sure
that the broker
has alternatives
to Web-based
trading in case
there's a problem
(customer service
numbers, local
branches, and
so on).

Brokerage account types

Brokerage firms offer clients a number of different accounts. The most common ones are a cash account, a margin account (frequently called a "cash and margin" account), and an option account (frequently called a "cash, margin, and option" account).

Basically, these accounts represent different levels of credit and trustworthiness of the account holder as evaluated by the brokerage firm. A cash account is the traditional brokerage account (sometimes called a Type 1 account). If you have a cash account, you may make trades, but you must pay in full for all purchases by the settlement date (three days after the date you executed the transaction).

Cash account

Just about anyone can open a cash account, although some brokerage houses may require a significant deposit (for example, $10,000) before they open the account. Fortunately, with competition very keen in the brokerage industry thanks to the Internet, most online brokers can open your account with as little as $1,000 or even $500.

Margin account

A margin account is a type of brokerage account that allows you to take out loans against securities that you own (sometimes called a Type 2 account). Because the brokerage house is essentially granting you credit by giving you a margin account, you must pass its screening procedure to get one. Even if you don't plan to buy on margin, note that all short sales (Type 5) have to occur in a margin account. If you have a margin account, you will also have a cash account. For a detailed treatment of margin trading, see the section "Stock Trading Using Margin," later in this chapter.

Timesaver
Do online trading at night or at off-hours when fewer customers are accessing the Web site. When trading hours begin, your order will be among the first to get implemented.

Timesaver
Make sure that your Internet service provider (ISP) has enough capacity to handle heavy online activity. It's not uncommon for an ISP to have interrupted service on high-traffic days. If so, have a second Internet access service available to prevent you from wasting time.

Option account

An option account is a type of brokerage account that allows you to trade stock options. To open this type of account, your broker will require you to sign a statement that you understand and acknowledge the risks associated with options and related derivatives. This is actually for the broker's protection and came into being after brokers were successfully sued by clients who suffered large losses in options and then claimed that they were unaware of the risks.

For example, you will almost certainly have a bit of cash in some type of brokerage account, perhaps because you received a dividend payment on a share held by your broker. This cash balance may be carried along as pure cash (and you get no interest), or the cash may be swept into an interest-bearing money market account. Presumably, if you have a margin account, the cash will appear there and not in your cash account.

Types of orders

After you have decided whether you plan to buy or sell a stock, the typical order (or "instructions" you give to the broker) you make will give you a few more choices. You can choose between a market order, a limit order, a stop order, and a stop limit order.

You can also make the order a "day order" (good only for the day) or a GTC order (good-til-cancelled). Each of these choices has its own implications.

Market order

This is an instruction to buy or sell a stock at the best market price available at the moment. For example, you may want to buy 100 shares of Merrill Street Corp. If the current market for it is 50 bid and 50⅛ ask, you may or may not get the stock at 50⅛. Market orders will definitely be filled, but you cannot be sure of the price. Prices will vary with market conditions, and these conditions are not always reflected at the Web site at that given moment. The final price at which your order is filled may be slightly better or worse than you expected.

Limit order

A limit order lets you place a price restriction on your order. It indicates that you are willing to buy or sell a stock only at a certain price or better. Your order is not filled unless the stock trades at that price. Placing a limit order, however, is not a guarantee that your trade will be executed at your limit price. Fortunately, it eliminates the risk that your order will be filled at a price worse than you expected.

For example, if you want to buy XYZ stock at $50 a share once again, and the market price is 50 bid and 50⅛ offer, your order cannot be filled immediately. If someone comes to sell the stock at $50, your order will be filled if it is next in line for execution. If more buyers enter the pit and drive up the stock price, your order will not be filled.

Stop order

A stop order is an order to buy or sell a stock at the market price when the price reaches or passes through a specified point, called the stop price. This type of order is generally used by people who own a stock and want to make sure that they sell out if the stock price starts to drop. The stop price placed on a sell stop order must be below the current bid price of the security.

Unofficially ... Just because a company is great doesn't mean you should pay a high price for its stock. Many successful investors will use limit orders to purchase a stock at a better price than the current market price. If your research and analysis suggest that the stock of a particular company is worth only $50 per share instead of the current price of $75, then put in a GTC limit order to buy it at $50. When the stock falls during this period, you will have bought a great company at a reasonable price.

For example, if you buy 100 shares of Hokey Smoke Corporation (HSC) at $35 a share and you want to protect yourself from a potential loss, you might place a stop order. If you placed a stop order at $30 a share, the moment HSC traded at $30, your order would become live and the broker would sell it to the highest bidder. If the market is particularly volatile, there is no guarantee that the order executed will be at the stop price. Once triggered, your order essentially competes with other incoming market orders.

Stop limit order

Stop orders can be placed for purchases as well. The stop price specified for a buy order must be above the current asking price. A stop limit order performs like a stop order with one major exception. When the order is activated (by the stock trading at or "through" the stop price), it does not become a market order.

Instead, it becomes a limit order with a limit price equal to the former stop price. For example, say you place a stop limit order to sell stock with a stop price of $67.50 a share. As with the stop order, when the stock trades at $67.50, your order is triggered. However, the broker cannot sell it below $67.50 a share no matter what happens. The advantage of this order is that you set a minimum price at which your order can be filled. The problem is that your order may not be filled in very volatile market conditions. In this instance, if the stock keeps moving down, you will keep losing money.

GTC versus day order

Good-til-canceled (GTC) orders remain in effect until they are filled, until you cancel them, or until the last effective day of the term adopted by that particular broker. For some brokers, GTC is for 60 days; for others, it is longer. At Ameritrade, for example, a GTC order placed on a given day left unfilled and uncanceled would be canceled automatically by the end of the following month. If you placed an order October 10, it could stay in effect until November 30. Make sure to check with the broker of your choice.

A day order is a limit order that will expire if it is not filled by the end of the trading day. If you want the same order the next day, you must place it again.

Final notes on orders

After a stock split or a dividend payout, the price on all buy limit orders and the stop price on sell stop and sell stop limit orders is adjusted. For example, if you place an order to buy Merrill Street Corporation at $100 a share and the stock splits 2 for 1, your order will automatically be adjusted to show that you want to buy Merrill Street Corporation at $50, reflecting the split.

You can put other restrictions on your orders if you wish:

- All-or-none (AON) is an optional instruction that you can use if you are placing an order of 300 or more shares. AON indicates that you do not wish to complete just a portion of your trade if all of the shares are not available.

- Do-not-reduce (DNR) means that the order price should not be adjusted in the case of a stock split or a dividend payout.

- Fill or kill (FOK) is an instruction to either fill the entire order at the limit price given or better, or cancel it.

66
If we don't
discipline our-
selves, the world
will do it for us.
—William Feather
99

The trailing stop

You can employ any one of a hundred different successful stock-picking strategies to pick a great stock. Or, maybe you threw a dart at the financial pages to make your pick. Maybe you surveyed a roundtable of stock-picking geniuses—or a chimp. No matter how you chose a stock, there is one thing you should do to protect your money regardless of your analytical style or prowess: use trailing stops. If you read the previous section, you now should be familiar with the stop order. However, you must actively manage that stop order to maximize your profits.

Say that you buy Moon Rocket, Inc., (MOON) at $50 per share. After reading the previous section on types of orders, you put in your good-til-cancelled stop loss order at $45. Now you know that you are protecting 90 percent of your investment with a stop loss order at 10 percent below your purchase price. You can rest assured that there is no upside limit for MOON's stock price. More importantly, it was bought with a GTC stop order. This ensures a disciplined approach that limits your risk.

Now say that MOON shot up to $75 per share. Now what? Cancel the original stop loss order at $45, and replace it with a new GTC stop loss order at $67.50. What happened? Again, you've left the upside open. For MOON, the sky is still the limit. But the floor has been raised to $65. Now you have not only protected 100 percent of your original investment of $50, but you also have protected $15 of your profit. If MOON falls, your profits won't crater along with it.

What happens if MOON goes to $100 per share? Again, you would cancel the $67.50 stop loss order and replace it with a $90 GTC stop loss order. If

MOON goes to $150, the GTC stop loss order goes to $135, and so on. The stop loss order trails the market price like a tail. The trailing stop is a very important tool for any investor.

How far from the market value should the stop loss order be? If you are a value investor and you chose stocks with a low beta (see Chapter 9, "Succeeding in Both Bull and Bear Markets") or volatility, set the stop 10 percent under the market price. If the price is $25, the stop order should be for $22.50. If your stock is a growth-oriented, volatile or high beta stock, set the stop order 20 percent under the market price. In any case, make sure that the stop order trails the stock as it rises.

During 1999–2000, many stocks shot up to stratospheric levels only to fall 70 percent, 80 percent, or more within a matter of a few weeks or months. Internet stocks are a great example. Microstrategy Inc., shot past $310 in February 2000. After some problems with sales and the SEC, the stock fell to under $25 that May. As amazing as that was, it was not an isolated case. Ivillage.com, Etoys.com, DrKoop.com, and many other Internet sensations have charts that look like mountains, with prices shooting up and then plummeting in spectacular fashion. Billions of dollars of market value were created in months, and billions were lost.

If that was your $10,000 stock market investment in 1972, your success would have been dramatically improved by a number of sophisticated techniques. One simple technique is using trailing stops. How would trailing stops help you?

Using trail stops to protect against a bear market
For the sake of this example, let's say that your investment in 1973 (just before to the start of the

toughest bear market since the Great Depression) was only one stock: 100 shares of Hindenburg Corporation at $100 per share. If you had this investment and a crystal ball, the obvious thing to do was to sell it and lock in your gain. That way, as the stock market tumbled, you would have preserved your $10,000 investment. At that point, even investing it in a interest-bearing savings account would have been better than having it skewered in such a rough bear market in which even the blue-chip stocks fell over 45 percent. But what if you didn't have a crystal ball?

Obviously, few of us could have foreseen how bad the market was going to be during the record-breaking year of 1972. However, disciplined techniques such as trailing stops would have been almost as good as a crystal ball.

If you were that investor with the $100-per-share Hindenburg Corporation, you could have asked your broker to put in a GTC stop loss order at $90. The stop order would have left you with your total investment value intact at $9,000, while others watched their investments nosedive. Later, when stocks hit rock bottom, you could have bought stocks at great prices and still have had money to spare. If Hindenburg Corporation fell to $57 per share in 1974, you could have then picked up 100 shares for only $5,700 (not including commissions) and still have had $3,300 remaining from the proceeds of the original $9,000 stock sale.

What if Hindenburg Corp., went up in price, even if only temporarily? If the stock went to $125 per share, you would have canceled the $90 order and replaced it with a new GTC stop loss order of $112.50 (90 percent of $125). As you watched the market fall, your stock would have fallen to $112.50 per share. While someone else's $10,000 stock investment would have dropped by $4,500, you got out of Hindenburg Corp., with a nice profit before it crashed and burned with the bear market.

How many investors use trailing stops? Not many. How many advisers and analysts use or recommend stop orders? Not as many as should. In an uncertain stock market (which is usually the case), trailing stops are a safety net.

Stock trading using margin

Brokers are only too happy to lend you money to buy stocks and bonds if you open a so-called margin account. You have to put up only part of the securities' price, and your broker lends you the rest. You just sign a couple forms, and your broker runs a routine credit check on you. Brokers are eager to approve your application because margin accounts lead to more business and higher profits for them.

You can come out ahead in rising markets because you put up only 50 percent of the cost of your stocks and 25 percent of the cost of your bonds. So, your money works at least twice as hard for you. The interest that you pay on your margin loan is not only relatively low, but it is also deductible from your taxable income, up to the amount of your net investment income for the year. In mid-1995, interest rates on margin loans ranged from 9 to 11 percent, compared with about 9 percent for personal secured loans at a bank.

Sound easy? Margin accounts can be a lot riskier than you might expect. Let's say you want to buy 100 shares of a $40 stock. Normally you would pay $4,000 plus commissions. But with a margin account, you have to put up only 50 percent of the

Bright Idea
When you accumulate stock through your DRP, take the stock out of the plan and deposit them with your broker using the margin account. When the stock is there, you don't have to use it to only buy stock. You can borrow up to the limit for other purposes. Because the rates are so low (secured loan rates are usually lower than unsecured loan rates) use your margin account to wipe out high-interest credit card debt. Ask your tax adviser about the tax benefits, too.

price, or $2,000. Your broker lends you the remaining $2,000, and the stock that you bought acts as the collateral for your loan.

If your stock rises, great! If it rises enough, you could sell some shares, pay off the loan, and come out ahead. But if the gains in your stock don't cover your interest payments, you lose money. And if the stock price falls, you could suffer in two ways. Not only would your investment dwindle, but you also could receive a call from your broker—a so-called margin call—to put up more cash. A margin call occurs when the value of your collateral falls below a certain percentage of your total purchase price— usually 30 to 35 percent. If the worth of your holdings drops under that level, your broker will demand that you deliver enough cash or other securities to bring your collateral back up to the required amount. If you can't deliver—sometimes by the next day—the broker will sell your stock, take back what he or she lent you, and collect interest.

Before you decide to borrow on margin, ask yourself this key question: Do I believe in the company so much that I would be willing to borrow money to buy their stock? If not, a margin account is not for you.

You can use margin loans to buy more than stocks or bonds. Say that you want to buy a house or a condo that costs $200,000. If you are fortunate enough to own $400,000 worth of stocks, your broker will lend you $200,000 against them. You continue to own those securities, and you avoid much of the up-front costs that you would have to pay on a mortgage loan. For a $200,000 mortgage, those so-called closing costs—for taxes, origination fees, lawyers' fees, title search, and the like—can easily run $6,000 to $10,000. Just remember that you ultimately have to pay off your margin loan, and you will have to pony up more securities if their price drops in a falling market. Check with your tax adviser: Investment interest is tax-deductible as an itemized expense.

In effect, investors have found that you can invest more money than you have and double your profit by borrowing from the broker, or by buying on margin. Of course, the possibility of also doubling losses is usually not considered because it's not an acceptable alternative, even though it's real.

Through its policy-setting Federal Open Market Committee, the Federal Reserve System determines how much brokers and investment banks can lend their clients against their investments. This percentage is called the margin rate. At present, the rate is set at 50 percent. This means that for every dollar in actual value an investor has in his account, he can borrow another dollar. If an investor has 100 shares of fully paid IBM shares in his account, he can in effect purchase another 100 shares just by using margin.

Of course, this is not a freebie. The extra funds are a loan from the firm to the investor, and the investor is charged interest on this balance on a monthly basis. The rate is usually tied to the broker call loan rate.

Rules governing margin trading will vary from one firm to another. Some may require that an account have a minimum balance level before granting margin. Some may not lend the full 50 percent or might require that some additional assets be kept on deposit and some may charge a higher loan rate.

Watch Out!
In recent years "day trading" has become popular. Traders try to profit by small moves in the security as it fluctuates. A stock could be bought and sold in a matter of minutes. If the market moves in your favor, you can make a small fortune very quickly. If it moves against you, you can lose a small fortune just as quickly. Day trading is extremely risky and speculative. A recent SEC study pointed out that 70 percent of day traders lose money, and 50 percent of these lose $50,000 or more.

One of the key elements of a margin account is the fact that it is repriced, or "marked to market," every night. If the value of the investment has declined from its initial purchase level, the amount of borrowed money will suddenly represent more than 50 percent of the total value of the assets. In such a case, the client will be subject to "maintenance margin" requirements imposed by the NASD, the NYSE, or the brokerage firm.

If the amount of equity relative to the amount borrowed falls below the maintenance level, the investor will quickly receive a call from the broker informing her that she must come up with additional cash to cover the margin shortfall. If she can't provide additional cash, the firm will sell a sufficient number of shares to cover the difference. If the decline is severe enough, the investor will be called upon to make successively larger payments to maintain the position, even as losses mount.

Conversely, if the price of the shares increases, the investor may use the paper profits to increase borrowings and obtain more leverage. But what must be kept clearly in mind at all times is that the amount borrowed on margin is constant. Whether the price of the shares goes up or down, the loan stays the same. For its part, the firm extending the credit must ensure that the total value of the portfolio (the shares purchased with cash and those bought on margin) is sufficient to pay off the margin loan. If the cash value of the shares sinks, the investor must sink in more cash.

Technically, your loan is called margin, or a margin loan, because it must be secured with marginable securities and your loan must comply with the SEC and Federal Reserve Board regulations.

The Federal Reserve Board's Regulation T regulates the amount that you can borrow. Currently, this rate is 50 percent of the stock's purchase price (for eligible securities selling at $10 per share or more; the same initial margin is required for selling short). Different securities have different rates. Treasury securities, for example, are marginable up to 90 percent of market value.

A minimum of $2,000 must be maintained in a margin account. In general, such loans must be secured by marginable securities and must conform to the terms defined by the Federal Reserve Board.

Direct purchase programs and dividend reinvestment plans

In recent years, it has become more commonplace to be able to buy stock directly from the company itself. Hundreds of companies let you buy their stock directly by contacting their shareholder services department. The advantage is that usually there are no commission charges (or low service charges).

Buying stock takes place either in a direct purchase plan (for initial investments) or in a dividend reinvestment plan (for existing shareholders).

Direct purchase plans (DPPs)

A direct purchase plan (DPP) allows you to buy stock directly from the company itself, without paying a broker's sales commission. Importantly, you can buy the stock direct even if you are not a current shareholder. This distinguishes DPPs from company-operated dividend reinvestment plans (DRPs), which usually require that you buy at least one share through a broker or other service and then pay a commission.

Watch Out!
Margin trading can backfire if you're not careful. You should definitely use stop-loss orders to minimize downside risk. If the stock falls and triggers the stop loss order, the stock would be automatically sold. The proceeds from the sale would pay off the margin loan.

Moneysaver
One discount bro-
kerage firm that
has reasonable
fees for small
purchases and
that does not
charge to forward
you your stock
certificates is
Mydiscountbroker.
com (1-888-
882-5600).

Of all the ways to invest in the stock market, buying shares through a DPP requires the least amount
of cash. Some companies that offer a direct purchase plan charge a $5 to $20 enrollment fee. As of
June 2000, over 1,500 companies sell their shares
through DPPs, and that number is expected to grow
in the coming years.

Dividend reinvestment plans (DRPs)

DRPs offer a convenient system whereby dividends
on a stock are automatically reinvested in additional
shares of stock, usually without fee and sometimes
even at a discount. DRPs are very popular with
investors because they offer the following advantages:

- Dividends, which are typically paid in cash, can
  easily be used to buy more stock at minimal
  expense.

- Most DRPs provide for optional cash payments
  usually without commissions.

- The power of compounding occurs because
  cash payments and dividends buy stock, which
  in turn generates more dividends.

- All the positives (and negatives) of stock investing are there for the DRP investor, including
  stock splits and dividend increases.

- DRPs are perfect for long-term investing
  because they offer a built-in form of dollar cost
  averaging.

A potential stumbling block to joining a DRP is
that in most programs, you already have to be a
shareholder of the company to enroll.

Brokers offer one avenue for getting that first
share, although the commission to purchase one

share of stock will be quite high in percentage terms of the total investment. However, investors should realize that once the initial investment is made through the broker, they will not need a broker again to purchase stock in that company.

Although DRPs are fairly straightforward investments, investors should be aware of the following:

▪ Although DRPs have historically been free (or a very low cost), recent trends suggest that more DRPs will be charging for a variety of services. Some now charge a fee to set up the account. Public Service Enterprise Group, a utility, has a minimum initial investment of $250 with a $10 set-up fee. Other DRPs charge a fee for subsequent investments with their optional cash payments service. Check with the individual plan administrator regarding all the fees and service charges involved before signing up.

▪ Know the number of shares or minimum initial investment needed to enroll in the DRP. Most plans require only one share. Exxon Mobil, for example, has a minimum initial investment amount of $250. Because it costs money to service DRP investors, it's not surprising that companies are raising their minimums to weed out those individuals whom they feel are not serious investors. Again, check with the DRP administrator.

▪ Some DRPs allow you to purchase stock with optional cash payments once a month, while others do so once a quarter. Some firms suggest that you mail the payment at certain times of the month.

Timesaver
To buy stock directly from hundreds of direct purchase plans, call the Direct Purchase Plan Clearinghouse at 1-800-774-4117, or visit the Web site: www.enrolldirect. com.
Another great Web site to find hundreds of direct purchase plans is www. netstockdirect. com.

Timesaver
Head to your library's reference section and look up either Standard & Poor's or Moody's stock guides. They list companies that have DRPs and tell you how to contact them. The Web site MarketWatch.com also lists companies with DPPs and DRPs.

- Read the plan's prospectus for further details. Direct any questions that you have to the company's shareholder service department. That department will also tell you who the DRP administrator is.

- Keep good records, and make sure that the dividends credited to you match the year-end tax form 1099 that you receive.

DRPs have many attractions for individual investors: Most companies charge no commissions for purchasing stocks through their DRPs, and those that do charge only a nominal fee. More than 100 companies have DRPs that permit participants to purchase stock at discounts to prevailing market prices. These discounts are usually 3 to 5 percent and may be as high as 10 percent.

Most DRPs permit investors to send optional cash payments. Usually you can invest for as little as $25 directly to the company to purchase additional shares. If your investment isn't enough to purchase a whole share, the company will purchase a fractional share, and the fractional share is entitled to that fractional part of the dividend. Optional cash payments are one of the more powerful features of the DRP because it makes stock accumulation affordable for small investors.

For a current list of DPPs and DRPs, visit the following Web sites:

DRIP Investor
www.dripinvestor.com

First Share
www.firstshare.com

The Money Paper
www.moneypaper.com

The following books give more information on DPPs and DRPs:

Directory of Dividend Reinvestment Plans, 2000 Edition

By Charles B. Carlson

A directory that covers more than 1,000 dividend reinvestment plans, including the ones that can be purchased directly from the company. This includes the company's address, phone number, stock symbol, business profile, and plan specifics, including DRP rating, performance rating, and whether any discounts are offered.

No-Load Stocks

By Charles B. Carlson

An expanded directory of more than 145 companies that offer direct purchase plans. Also includes strategies, stock performance, ratings, plan specifics, and contact information.

Buying Stocks Without a Broker, second edition

By Charles B. Carlson

A comprehensive guide to dividend reinvestment plans, which Carlson refers to as DRIPs. These investor-friendly programs provide a safe, proven method for buying stocks directly form issuing companies, often with a discount and always without paying commission fees to brokers.

1,000 Investments You Can Start with as Little as $75

Compiled by Paul Mladjenovic

An extensive list of DPPs and DRPs for only $5.

Web sites for DRPs include these:

DRIP Central
www.dripcentral.com

DRIP Investor
www.dripinvestor.com

First Share
www.firstshare.com

Joining investment clubs

Investment clubs are an excellent way for people to invest money while learning from others. There are thousands of clubs across the country, some of which have gained prominence for their successful stock-picking approach. A good example is the Beardstown Ladies Investment Club, whose members wrote a popular book on investing a few years ago.

For many years, people turned to the National Association of Investment Clubs to learn how to start and succeed as an investment club. This association has since changed its name to the National Association of Investors Corporation (NAIC) to make the public aware that investment clubs are only part of their activities. Visit the Web site www.better-investing.org, or call 810-583-6242 for information.

NAIC has joined the dividend reinvestment plans of a number of corporations. As an individual or club member of NAIC, you can deposit money in any of these plans just by completely filling out and sending in an enrollment form along with your first investment. When your first purchase has been made, your own account will be set up and you will send future payments directly to the corporation's own dividend reinvestment agent.

Unofficially ... Investment clubs have success records that match those of Wall Street analysts. Members of the clubs discuss and debate the purchases made. It's not surprising that this consensus approach works because investments have to be justified. The famed Beardstown Ladies actually used a stock-picking approach based on the Value Line Investment Survey.

NAIC principles for investing are basic and have been producing good results for their participants for more than 45 years. The NAIC has four basic principles of investing:

- Invest regular sums of money once a month in common stock. This helps you obtain a lower average cost on your investments.

- Reinvest all earnings, dividends, and capital gains. Your money grows faster if earnings are reinvested.

- Buy growth stocks—companies whose sales and earnings are increasing at a rate faster than the industry in general. They should have good prospects for continued growth—in other words, they should be stronger, larger companies five years from now.

- Invest in different industries. Diversification helps spread both risk and opportunity.

Successful stock investing involves more than "what" you pick. It also involves being a diligent consumer when choosing what to invest in. Reducing transaction costs means growing your wealth faster over the long term.

Just the facts

- The competition between brokers has provided great consumer benefits to small investors as commissions and initial investment requirements decline.

- Find out about the different types of orders available to you—a market order is not always in your best interest.

- Margin is a powerful leveraging tool to enhance wealth when used properly.

- Direct purchase plans and dividend reinvestment plans are excellent long-term, wealth-building vehicles for small investors

- Investment clubs offer a conducive environment to slowly build wealth and increase your expertise and knowledge.

GET THE SCOOP ON...
Commissions and service fees ▪ Tax
considerations ▪ 401(k)s and IRAs

The Cost of Investing: Taxes and Other Costs

Chapter 11

S ucceeding with stocks is about more than making money. It's also about *keeping* that money. Your gains will continue to shrink as a result of transaction fees, interest expenses, and various taxes unless you take a proactive approach to keeping these costs down.

Considerations at the time of purchase

Although the topic of brokers is treated at length in Chapter 10, "Going It Alone or Using a Broker," it is important to mention them here to remind you that transaction costs and related expenses can eat into your profits. Fortunately, intense competition in the financial industry has kept commissions and fees competitive, but it is still advisable to shop around.

Brokerage fees

So which brokers are cheapest to trade with? The honest answer is, it depends. When you are looking at trading costs, you need to consider the four basic

Unofficially ...
For the latest in
brokerage surveys
and ratings, visit
these Web sites:
Gomez Advisors
www.
gomezadvisors.
com
**Internet
Investing**
www.
internetinvesting.
com
**Smart Money
Magazine**
www.
smartmoney.com
**Super Star
Investor's Broker
Ratings Page**
www.
superstarinvestor.
com/brokers.html

categories of brokerage fees: commissions, ancillary service fees, account minimums, and margin interest.

Commission

What will you be charged to transact an order? Brokers such as Brown & Company will charge you $5 for an online trade (as of April 2000) whether you buy 10 shares, 100 shares, or 500 shares. If you make the trade by telephone, the cost is $12. Ameritrade charges $8, and Scottrade charges $7. Because competition has been heating up in recent years, many brokers offer amazing deals such as no commissions on your first 10 trades, or similar offers. Is there a catch to these great rates? Keep reading.

Keep in mind that once you are with a broker, to get out either you sell your stocks (incurring a commission) or you transfer your stocks to another broker (possibly incurring a service charge). A third option is that you may take physical possession of the stock in the form of a certificate (another charge may apply).

Ancillary service fees

A broker may charge you a cheap rate to trade, but it may have high fees in other services. Some of the charges you may encounter are these:

- Monthly service charges
- Charges for special services, such as sending you a physical stock certificate
- A charge for certain orders, such as a GTC stop order
- A charge to close or transfer an account
- A charge if your account falls below a certain dollar level or activity level

Account minimums

Some brokers have no minimum investment amount; others have a $2,000 minimum. It depends on the broker and the fee structure. Some brokers charge low commissions but require a high account value. The Web site www.freetrade.com, for example, doesn't charge commissions, but customers must maintain at least $5,000 in the account.

Margin interest

When you trade stocks on margin, you will be charged interest. That rate will be a few percentage points above the rate that the broker pays you on your money market account. This interest rate spread is very profitable for brokers, and margin interest is a substantial portion of brokers' earnings. It is important to understand that you should shop around for this as well. When you contact brokers, ask what their margin rates are. Frequently, they can give more favorable rates depending on how much you keep in the account or how well you negotiate.

To find out more, contact the brokers and ask. Refer to Appendix B, "Investing Information Resources," for a list of some of the more popular brokers, their contact information, and their trade fees.

Borrowing to invest

Margin is a form of leverage, but it's not the only kind. In the year 2000, as millions of investors participate in the stock market, using debt to leverage your ability to purchase and profit from stock investing is becoming more common.

Most people readily understand using debt in the world of real estate investing. The same concept can be applied to stock investments as investors turn to mortgages, personal loans, and credit cards for

Moneysaver
Most of the online brokers are competing with price-cutting promotions. As of May 2000, Datek offers new customers the ability to do their first 25 trades free. Ameritrade offered new customers the ability to open an account for as little as a $500 initial deposit, and gives a 50 percent discount from its regular fees (already low at $8 per trade). The bottom line: Keep shopping.

investable funds. The allure is simple. Since 1995, the market has averaged 20 to 25 percent per year in growth. The interest rate over the same time span has been 8 percent (margin loan), 10 percent (home equity line), or 18 percent (credit card account). Why not borrow at rates of 8 to 18 percent and earn 20 to 25 percent? If the growth rates hold, you make some good money. But what if growth rates fall to historical levels of 11 percent? What if your stocks fall in price?

In 1999, investors bought Internet stocks on margin and made a killing. However, in early 2000, those same stocks fell and investors got killed.

Home equity

In early 1999, a couple borrowed against their home to use the proceeds for stock investing. Their house was valued at $200,000 with a first mortgage of $90,000. They took out a second mortgage against the remaining balance of their equity of $110,000 to invest in stocks. They reasoned that the Internet stocks that they would invest in would double in value and that they would then immediately sell the holdings, pay off the debt, and build their wealth.

Bright Idea
If you are going to tap your home equity for investing funds (or any purpose), learn the pros and cons first. Get free information from the National Home Equity Mortgage Association Web site at www.nhema.org.

The result was disastrous. Their stocks fell 80 percent. The couple now had $200,000 in debt to pay off. In addition to both getting full-time jobs, they also got part-time jobs to scrape together the monthly payments on two mortgages.

The point is obvious in this case, but it must be made: Unless you do it with great caution, borrowing to invest in stocks is not advisable. Stocks can go up and down, but debt does not. It must be paid off. The only other option is defaulting on your payments and destroying your credit or worse: bankruptcy.

Consumer credit

Some venturesome investors have borrowed from their credit cards to invest in stocks. If your stocks go up significantly, the strategy works out. You sell your stock and pay off the credit card balance. However, if the stocks go nowhere (or sink), you're stuck with very high-interest debt. Out of all the borrowing you could do, credit card debt is the most burdensome. In 1999, many debt counselors across the country reported a high number of debtors who got into trouble because of a get-rich, speculative impulse.

Margin borrowing

If you are going to borrow to purchase stocks, you might as well borrow from the broker because margin trading is not as dangerous to your financial health as mortgage or consumer debt.

Before getting into a margin loan, here are a few basic points to consider:

- Don't use margin on speculative stocks such as micro-caps or emerging tech stocks.

- Use margin sparingly to acquire large-cap or defensive stocks.

- Consider using margin for high-dividend income stocks. The dividends will help to pay off the loan.

Investors can open a margin account through their broker and borrow from the account to purchase stock. To open the account, investors must secure it with at least $2,000 in cash or eligible securities from their investment portfolio.

Under the Fed's Regulation T, investors may borrow up to 50 percent of the purchase price of stock when buying on margin. For example, an investor who wants to buy 100 shares of a $10 stock could put up $500 of his own money and borrow the remaining $500 through his margin account. Buying stock on margin gives investors leverage and permits them to reap bigger gains than they would using only their own money if the stock price rises.

Only eligible stocks may be purchased on margin. Both the Fed and the broker offering margin credit set the eligibility rules. In general, highly speculative or risky stocks cannot be margined. Borrowers must pay interest on the margin loan but don't have to repay the debt until they sell the margined stock. Margin rates generally range 1 to 2 percentage points above long-term fixed mortgage rates.

Brokerages profit on the spread between the rate they charge customers and the rate they pay to borrow lendable funds in the credit markets. What's the risk? Just as leverage creates opportunities for bigger profits, it also creates the possibility of bigger losses if prices drop for margined stocks. If the value of a margined portfolio falls appreciably, the borrower will face a margin call. The broker will tell the investor to deposit additional funds or stock in his account to make up the decline in the margin stocks' value.

Brokerage firms that are members of the New York Stock Exchange issue margin calls whenever the value of a borrower's investment falls below 75 percent of its original value. If the investor can't meet the call, the brokerage firm can sell his stock to recoup its loan and unpaid interest. The investor takes the loss.

Margin borrowing and margin rules are also features of some derivatives markets. When a lot of people pile up margin debt, the result can be pyramiding and depyramiding. Pyramiding occurs when stock used as collateral appreciates, allowing more borrowing and more stock purchases, which pumps up stock prices further. When prices start to fall, as they always do eventually, the value of the stock-collateral falls, lenders issue margin calls, and forced sales of stock contribute to plummeting prices.

Tax deductions

Whatever expenses you incur to buy, sell, or manage your stock portfolio, there is a strong likelihood that those expenses are tax-deductible. For most investors, stock investment-related expenses are taken as itemized expenses on Schedule A, which accompanies your long-form 1040. There are three categories of itemized expenses: investment interest, contributions, and miscellaneous expenses.

Investment interest

If you have paid any investment interest (such as interest in your brokerage account because you borrowed against your securities), that interest can be tax-deductible. Keep in mind that interest falls into five categories:

1. **Mortgage interest**—If you borrow money against your home's value, using a second mortgage or a home equity line account, the interest is deductible. Many investors have borrowed this way to buy stock.

2. **Consumer interest**—Consumer interest such as auto loans, personal loans, or credit card interest is not deductible.

3. **Student loan interest**—Student loan interest is deductible as an adjustment to your gross income (with some limitations).

4. **Business interest**—Interest on business purchases for your company or an entrepreneurial venture is fully deductible. It is taken on the business portion of your return.

5. **Investment interest**—This is the interest paid when you borrow against your securities. This is the category for stock investors that use margin with their brokers.

Contributions

This category is usually not considered an investment-related category. This would apply to you if you donate any stock from your portfolio.

Your stock investment can provide you with a significant tax benefit. If you have stock that has appreciated and that you have owned for at least one year, you can donate it to an IRS-approved charity and get a tax deduction at full market value.

Say that you bought Scrooge-Meister Inc., common stock in 1995 for $1,000, and the stock in 2000 is worth $5,000. You decide to be charitable with this long-term property by giving it to your favorite (IRS-approved) charity. You donate it to your local church, Our Lady of Perpetual Dividends (the author is Catholic).

Your deduction is valued at market value ($5,000) even though you originally paid only $1,000. If you are in the 30 percent tax bracket, the donation gives you $1,500 in tax savings.

Noncash deductions that exceed $500 are reported on Form 8283, which is an attachment to Schedule A. For further details on donating property, refer to IRS Publication 526, "Charitable Contributions," and Publication 561, "Determining the Value of Donated Property." You can get these forms by calling the IRS publications department at 1-800-829-3676, or you can download them from the Web site www.irs.ustreas.gov.

Miscellaneous expenses
The following are deductible investment expenses subject to the 2 percent (of adjusted gross income) limitation.

- Accounting fees for keeping records of investment income.

- Fees for collecting interest and dividends.

- Investment management or investment advisor's fees. However, fees allocated to advice dealing with tax-exempt obligations are not deductible.

- Safe-deposit box rental fee or home safe to hold your securities, unless used to hold personal effects or tax-exempt securities.

- Subscriptions to investment services.

- Depreciation for computer if used 50 percent or more for investment management.

- Legal costs associated with stockholder issues.

- Travel costs to check investments or to confer with advisers regarding the production of investment income.

You cannot deduct the following expenses:

- Investment or financial-planning seminars

- Costs associated with attending stockholder meetings

- Home office for managing your investments

Tax considerations
Buying and selling investments are transactions that have tax concerns attached to them.

> **"**
> Anyone may so arrange his affairs that his taxes shall be as low as possible; he is not bound to choose that pattern which will best pay the treasury; there is not even a patriotic duty to increase one's taxes.
> —Learned Hand
> **"**

66

I'm proud to be
paying taxes to
the U.S. The
only thing is—
I could be just
as proud for
half the money.
—Arthur Godfrey

99

Capital gains and losses

Before 1997, we had to worry about only two categories of capital gain or loss: short-term and long-term. We still have those two categories, but now long-term gain or loss is broken down into multiple categories. We'll sort them out for you here.

How the categories work

The theory behind these rules is that you gather all the gains and losses within a single category to figure out the overall result for that category before combining the results with another category. For example, if you have both gains and losses in the short-term category, you'll combine them to find the net amount of short-term gain or loss. You can't mix categories until after you've worked out the net amount within each category. After that, if you have gain in one category and loss in another, you combine the two.

Holding period

For the most part, the categories of gain or loss are determined by your holding period for the asset you sold. (There are also some special categories for certain types of assets.) For stocks, your holding period is generally determined by the amount of time that elapses between the trade date of your purchase and the trade date of your sale. But if you acquired your stock other than by purchase, your holding period may relate to some earlier date. For example, if you receive additional stock as a result of a stock split, the new stock has the same holding period as the stock you already held.

Short-term and long-term considerations

The time frame in which you hold your stocks is significant. It breaks down to either short-term or long-term, each with its own tax consequences.

Short-term gain

If the trade date of the sale is one year or less after the trade date of the purchase, you have a short-term capital gain. For example, if you bought on May 12, 1999, and sold on May 12, 2000, you have a short-term gain because you must hold for more than one year to have a long-term gain. Short-term capital gain is taxed at the same rate as ordinary income (such as wages and interest income) unless you have a capital loss that eliminates it. If your gain isn't short-term, it's long-term.

Long-term gain

If the trade date of the sale is more than one year after the trade date of the purchase, you have a long-term capital gain. You pay 10 percent tax on this category of gain if your regular tax bracket is 15 percent; otherwise, you pay 20 percent. If you are in the 15 percent income tax bracket, holdings greater than one year are taxed at 10 percent. Otherwise, long-term capital gains are taxed at 20 percent. The long-term capital gains tax rate could represent a significant savings for all taxpayers. Of course, tax considerations should not be your primary motivation for buying or selling any investment. As long as a stock meets your investment criteria, there is rarely a tax advantage to selling. Conversely, if an investment no longer meets your criteria, there are few good tax-related reasons to hold on to stock.

The goal of tax planning is to minimize short-term capital gains and defer long-term capital gains as long as possible.

Long-term capital gains is a category that provides a benefit at all income levels unless your income is so low that you pay no tax at all. [The 20

percent (or 10 percent) rate went into effect May 7,
1997. For part of that year, it applied only if your
holding period was greater than 18 months. A 28
percent rate applied to capital gains on assets held
more than a year but not more than 18 months.

The IRS Restructuring and Reform Act of 1998,
signed by President Clinton on July 22, 1998, did
away with the 18-month holding period retroactive
to January 1, 1998.]

Additional categories

Additional categories of long-term gain or loss are
summarized later in this chapter. Each of the rates
mentioned is a maximum rate. That means that the
rate will reduce your taxes if you would otherwise
pay a higher rate, but it won't increase your taxes if
your regular tax rate is lower. For example, if you
receive 28 percent gain when your regular rate is 15
percent, your tax on that gain will be 15 percent
unless the gain is large enough to push you up into
the next tax bracket. The following is also true:

- Certain gains from collectibles are treated as
  28 percent gain even if it would otherwise qualify for the 20 percent (or 10 percent) rate.

- Certain gains from sales of real property are
  taxed at a special 25 percent rate.

- The law also includes special rates for property
  held more than five years, but these rules won't
  go into effect until 2001, and Congress will
  probably change them by then.

Strategies for reducing your tax bill

Buy low, sell high. Do that, and you'll be a successful
investor. However, capital gains tax erodes your portfolio's performance. Fortunately, you have some
control over this tax, and tax planning can minimize

the damage. When planning your capital gains tax strategy, you must consider two categories of capital gains: short-term and long-term. Short-term gains are taxed as ordinary income, while long-term gains are taxed at more favorable capital gains rates.

Ordinary income is the general category that includes items such as wages, dividends, and interest that you receive. You have a capital gain when you sell a capital asset for a profit. Any asset that you hold as an investment (stocks, bonds, or real estate, for example) is a capital asset. Capital assets do not include supplies (such as paper and pens) or inventory (anything that you regularly sell in your business). Investment assets such as stocks and bonds are not considered inventory even if you regularly sell them, unless you're a securities dealer.

Of course, you can also lose money when you sell a capital asset: This is a capital loss.

Advantages of capital gains

Capital gains are better than ordinary income for two reasons. First, you don't pay tax on a capital gain until you sell the asset. Normally, you can choose whether to sell sooner or later, so you control the timing of your gain or loss. For example, you can decide to sell late in December or early in January, depending on which year you want to report your gain or loss. Generally speaking, you don't have that kind of choice with ordinary income, such as interest and dividends. The second advantage over ordinary income is that capital gains are taxed at special rates. To qualify for these rates, you must have long-term capital gains. Short-term capital gain is taxed at the same rates as ordinary income.

Special rates for long-term capital gain

The 20 percent (or 10 percent) rate went into effect May 7, 1997. A capital gain or loss is long-term if you held the asset more than one year (at least a year and a day) before you sold it. At that point, you're entitled to a special capital gain rate. In most cases, the rate will be 20 percent (10 percent if the gain falls within the 15 percent bracket). There are exceptions for certain types of assets.

These rates can lower your taxes, but they never increase your taxes. For example, if you are in the 15 percent bracket for ordinary income and you have a long-term capital gain that qualifies for the 28 percent rate, the gain is taxed at your lower 15 percent rate instead of the special capital gain rate.

The 20 percent (or 10 percent) rate should always produce some savings. If your tax bracket for ordinary income is 15 percent, the rate on this category of capital gain is 10 percent; if your ordinary tax bracket is 28 percent or higher, the rate on this category of capital gain is 20 percent. No matter what your tax bracket is, you get some benefit from qualifying for this capital gain rate.

Measuring capital gain

Your capital gain from a sale is measured by the difference between the amount realized in the sale and your basis in the asset that you sold. Roughly speaking, the amount realized is the proceeds received from the sale, usually measured by the sale price minus the brokerage commission. Your basis is based on your cost (usually the purchase price plus the brokerage commission) but may be adjusted as a result of various events. For example, if your stock splits while you own it, the basis splits, too.

To better understand cost basis, assume you made the following stock purchases:

In 1997 you bought 50 shares of Gainsalot Corp., at $10 per share, and in 1998 you bought an additional 50 shares of Gainsalot at $20 per share. Say you sell 75 shares at $30 in 2000. Your cost basis in the shares sold in 2000 is $1,250 (leaving out the commission for simplicity's sake).

The cost basis is the total of 50 shares at $10 (50 × $10 = $500) plus 25 shares at $20 (25 × $20 = $500) or $1000. The capital gain is long-term since all the shares sold were ones purchased more than a year earlier. The capital gain amount is $1,250 (75 shares × $30 = $2,250 less the cost basis of $1,000).

As an example, say that you buy 100 shares of Gainsalot Corp. at $35, paying $3,500 plus a brokerage commission of $40. Your basis is $3,540. Later, you sell when the stock is at $39. You receive $3,900 minus a brokerage commission of $40, so your amount realized is $3,860. Your capital gain is $3,860 minus $3,540, or $320. If your basis is greater than the amount realized, you have a capital loss.

Capital losses

Capital losses reduce your tax and are used first to offset capital gains. If there are no capital gains, or if the capital losses are larger than the capital gains, you can deduct the capital loss against your other income up to a limit of $3,000 in one year. If your overall capital loss is more than $3,000, the excess carries over to the next year. In other words, you treat the extra portion as if it were an additional capital loss in the following year.

As an example, say that in 1998 Bart had a $2,000 capital gain and a $9,500 capital loss. He used $2,000 of the capital loss to offset the capital

Moneysaver
It is better to pay taxes later. Defer capital gains as long as practical. If you can turn a short-term gain into a long-term gain by waiting, then wait. If you must realize a short-term capital gain, try to match that gain with a short-term capital loss. From a tax-savings point-of-view, capital losses are more valuable if used to offset a short-term gain.

gain; that left a net capital loss of $7,500. He claimed $3,000 of the loss on his 1998 return. The effect was to reduce his taxable income by $3,000.

Bart was in the 28 percent bracket, so the loss decreased his 1998 income tax by $840. The remaining $4,500 of capital loss carried over to his 1999 return. In 1999 he had a $1,000 capital gain and no capital losses except for the $4,500 carryover. So, Bart used $500 of the $4,500 carryover to offset the gain, leaving a capital loss of $4,000. Once again, Bart deducts $3,000 of the loss and carries over the remaining $1,000 to 2000. So, if you had a bad year, consider taking advantage of tax-loss selling.

Because every taxpayer has different circumstances, consult with your tax adviser about the specific benefits available to you.

There are also different strategies to which you can apply tax-loss selling, and these need to be verified before action is taken. Specifically, in addition to using the tax-loss strategy to get rid of a poor performer and benefit from the loss, it may also make sense to consider taking a loss as an incentive to taking a profit on another holding.

If Bart has a healthy profit in Gainsalot Corp., he may be reluctant to sell it because he will incur a large tax liability. However, he can reduce his tax liability from the gain if he also sells a stock that has an unrealized loss. If he is holding another investment, EvenWorse Inc., that has been a losing stock, now may be the time to get rid of it and use the loss to offset the profit on Gainsalot Corp.

In planning for tax-loss selling, you need to keep a few rules in mind. Probably the most important caveat is that there is a difference between short-term and long-term losses. If the security has been held for less than a year, the loss is regarded as a short-term loss. If it is held more than a year, it's a long-term loss. This is an important distinction because there is a difference in tax treatment of short-term and long-term gains. Short-term gains are taxed as regular income, whereas long-term gains are taxed at a lower rate.

However, the IRS requires that short-term gains must first be used to offset long-term profits, and only to the extent that they exceed the long-term gains can they be used to offset short-term gains. If the investor has no capital gains against which to offset the loss, the IRS allows for the application of up to $3,000 of the loss against ordinary income. Any excess loss may be carried forward for a period of 15 years with $3,000 per year applicable against income. If the loss exceeds this amount, the investor will not able to take full advantage of the loss.

One other point: When engaging in tax loss selling, a 30-day period must elapse before the shares can be repurchased to take advantage of the loss.

Tax-loss selling is a strategy that investors have available to them in planning portfolio strategies. It is not a cure-all, but, as with stop-loss orders, it is a strategy that can be employed by astute investors to get better performance out of their portfolios—or at least to get some benefit from poor performance.

As stated earlier, though, you should consult a tax specialist for more specific information and explanation of the regulations.

Short sale tax considerations

Note that a short sale is considered short-term regardless of how long the position is held open. This actually makes a kind of sense because the only time you actually held the stock was the time

Watch Out!
The tax law contains rules designed to prevent taxpayers from creating artificial capital losses. One rule you should be familiar with is the wash sale rule. This rule says that you can't claim a loss from sale of a security (such as stock) if you buy the identical security as a replacement within the period beginning 30 days before the sale and ending 30 days after the sale.

between when you bought the stock to cover the position and when you actually delivered that stock to close out the position. This length of time is somewhere from minutes to a few days.

Net capital gains and losses are fully part of adjusted gross income (AGI), with the exception that if your net capital loss exceeds $3,000, you can take only $3,000 of the loss in a tax year and must carry the remainder forward. If you die with carried-over losses, they are lost. Short-term and long-term loss carryovers retain their short- or long-term character when they are carried over.

Tax-advantaged retirement investing: IRAs and 401(k)s

When you buy stocks, minimizing the tax bite is always advisable. To accomplish this, consider using tax shelters for your stocks such as individual retirement accounts (IRAs). The most common are traditional IRAs and Roth IRAs. If you work for a company, there are also 401(k)s, but they are usually meant for mutual funds.

IRAs

Individual retirement accounts (IRAs) allow individual investors to invest up to $2,000 a year tax-deferred. This means that you can deduct the $2,000 from your taxable income and not have to pay income tax on that part of your earnings. (There are income-level restrictions on this option.) You can do this every year that you invest in an IRA until age 70. If you are married, you and your spouse can invest up to $4,000 in an IRA annually. This is an enormous tax benefit that you should definitely take advantage of.

The tax-deferred benefits of IRAs also apply to the capital gains, dividends, and interest that you earn on the IRA-invested dollars. These earnings can compound tax-free until you retire and begin taking distributions. If you were able to invest $4,000 a year for 30 years, and you averaged a solid 12 percent rate of return each year, your account would be worth $965,332!

IRAs allow you to begin withdrawals at age 59 ½. If you are disabled, you can withdraw early, but otherwise early withdrawals are subject to a 10 percent penalty plus regular income tax. Even if you do withdraw funds from an IRA after only five or six years and have to pay penalties, you would still be better off than if you had your money in similar investments with no IRA tax benefits. But like mutual funds, IRAs should be viewed as long-term investment vehicles.

IRAs can be opened at any bank or brokerage firm. The investment options include interest-bearing money market funds, savings accounts, certificates of deposit, mutual funds, and self-directed accounts in common stocks.

The Roth IRA

The Roth IRA was born on January 1, 1998, as a result of the Taxpayer Relief Act of 1997. It's named after Senator William V. Roth, Jr., chairman of the Senate Finance Committee.

The Roth IRA provides no deduction for contributions but instead provides a benefit that isn't available for any other form of retirement savings: If you meet certain requirements, all earnings are tax-free when you or your beneficiary withdraw them. Other benefits include avoiding the early distribution

penalty on certain withdrawals, and avoiding the
need to take minimum distributions after age 70.

Roth IRA pros and cons

The chief advantage of the Roth IRA is obvious: the
ability to have investment earnings completely
escape taxation. The advantage comes at a price,
though: You don't get a deduction when you contribute to the Roth IRA.

So which is more important? It depends on your
personal situation and also on what assumptions you
want to make about the future. How long before you
withdraw money from your IRA? What will your tax
bracket be then? What earnings can you anticipate
in the interim?

You can do lots of fancy analysis, but the bottom
line is that most people are better off in the Roth
IRA. The chief reason is that the Roth IRA is effectively bigger than a regular IRA because it holds
after-tax dollars. If you can take advantage of this
feature of the Roth IRA by maximizing your contributions, you'll add greater tax leverage to your
retirement savings.

There are two other significant advantages to the
Roth IRA. One is that the minimum distribution
rules don't apply. If you're able to live on other
resources after retirement, you don't have to draw
on your Roth IRA at age 70. That means that your
earnings continue to grow tax-free. The other
advantage is the ability to take certain early distributions without paying the early distribution penalty.
In short, the Roth IRA makes it easier to keep your
money in and easier to take your money out.

You can establish a Roth IRA if you're eligible for
a regular contribution to a Roth IRA or a rollover
(or conversion) to a Roth IRA.

You're eligible to make a regular contribution of up to $2,000 per year to a Roth IRA even if you participate in a retirement plan maintained by your employer. There are two requirements. First, you or your spouse must have compensation or alimony income equal to the amount contributed. Second, your modified adjusted gross income can't exceed certain limits. For a full $2,000 contribution, the limits are $95,000 for single individuals and $150,000 for married individuals filing joint returns. The amount you can contribute is reduced gradually and then completely eliminated when your modified adjusted gross income exceeds $110,000 (single) or $160,000 (married filing jointly).

You can convert your regular IRA to a Roth IRA (in other words, make a rollover to a Roth IRA) if you meet the following criteria:

1. Your modified adjusted gross income is $100,000 or less.

2. You're single or file jointly with your spouse. You'll have to pay tax in the year of the conversion (or spread the tax over four years if you convert in 1998), but for many people the long-term savings greatly outweigh the conversion tax.

Distributions

Distributions from Roth IRAs are tax-free until you've withdrawn all your regular contributions. After that, you'll withdraw your rollover (conversion) contributions, if any. Special rules apply when you withdraw your rollover contributions. When you've withdrawn all your contributions (regular and rollover), any subsequent withdrawals come

Bright Idea
Visit some excellent Web sites on the topic of taxes: For general information on tax planning, go to Fairmark at www.fairmark. com and at Tax Web www.taxweb. com. Get estate tax information at Nolo Press, at www.nolo.com. For IRA information, go to www.iradoctor. com. For information on retirement plans, go to Pension Place at www. pensionplace. com.

from earnings. The withdrawals are tax-free if you're over age 59 and if at least five years have expired since you established your Roth IRA. Otherwise (with limited exceptions), they're taxable and potentially subject to the early withdrawal penalty.

For more information on the Roth IRA ...

One whole site is devoted to nothing but the Roth IRA: www.rothira.com. This site has original articles as well as links to many other sources. Companies that actually sell IRAs are offering educational information on their Web sites as well. Here are some you might try:

Strong Funds
www.strongfunds.com

T. Rowe Price
www.troweprice.com

The Vanguard Group
www.vanguard.com

Remember that with all calculators and numerical examples, you need to be clear about two key assumptions that are being made:

- Are new contributions measured in pre-tax or post-tax dollars?

- On a rollover, are the taxes due being paid from the IRA itself or from outside funds?

Some IRA strategies

Stock investors can use IRAs in several ways.

- If you are an active stock investor, consider opening a self-directed IRA with a brokerage. In this type of account, you have discretion regarding your stock transactions. Because the IRA is a tax shelter until you start taking money out in your retirement years, there are no capital gains tax consequences while the stock transactions are in the IRA.

▪ If you open a direct purchase plan with a particular company and then enter into the dividend reinvestment plan, you can do this in an IRA as well. Speak to the shareholder service department of your chosen company for further details.

Keogh

A Keogh plan works like the typical corporate-defined benefit or profit-sharing plans, but it is specifically for nonincorporated businesses. Basically, you can sock away up to $30,000 from your self-employment income per year, with some percentage limitations.

However, there are a few drawbacks. First, if you have employees, the percentage that you elect for yourself must be used for all other employees who qualify. Second, as the employer, you make all the contributions and you make all the investment decisions. The good news is that just as with corporate plans, deferred vesting is allowed so that you can require employees to work for up to three years before they are covered. Perhaps even better news is that even if you are participating in another retirement plan, you can still set up a Keogh.

For more information on Keogh plans and other IRS-approved pension plans, get Publication 560 from the IRS at 1-800-829-3676, or download the publication from the Web site www.irs.ustreas.gov.

401(k)s

401(k) plans mainly deal with mutual fund investments and have little impact for investors in

Timesaver
How do you figure the benefits of a Roth IRA versus a traditional IRA? How do you figure the amount that you will need to retire with? Use some of the great, free financial calculators available online. There are many to help you with your investing and financial planning at www.ifigure.com.

individual stocks. If your company has a 401(k) plan, take advantage of it. The ability to defer taxes on up to $10,000 year after year is a powerful wealth-building tool.

Many companies offer 401(k) savings plans that allow you to invest some of your income on a tax-deferred basis and many companies will match a percentage if not all of the contribution that you make. 401(k)s allow you to invest much more than the $2,000 per year that you can invest in an IRA, but they are subject to different tax restrictions. In the past few years, much of the money invested in the market by mutual funds has come from corporate 401(k) investors. If your company offers a 401(k) plan, you should definitely consider participating. It's another way of keeping more of your money!

Just the facts

- Be more than a smart investor; be a smart consumer and shop around for the best rates and services.

- Keep borrowing to a minimum, and control any debt that you use for stock investing.

- Track all your expenses so that you can take all your allowable deductions.

- Seek long-term capital gains with your winning stocks while ridding your portfolio of losers through tax-loss selling for maximum tax benefit.

- Use tax shelters such as IRAs to minimize the tax bite from your long-term stock investing.

Managing Your Portfolio

GET THE SCOOP ON...
Diversification ▪ Stock and market analysis
services ▪ What affects a company's prospects
▪ Reading the stock pages

PART V

Monitoring Your Investments

Chapter 12

You've done your homework: researched the stock market and chosen a stock. But it doesn't end there. Successful stock investing means staying informed about your portfolio of stocks. The first step is to make sure that you are adequately diversified.

Diversification

Diversification is an investing strategy that seeks to minimize risk by having your wealth in many types of investments. Diversification is a concept directly related to risk because the more you are diversified, the less risk you are exposed to.

To have all your money in one stock is financially dangerous for several reasons:

- If the entire stock market falls, this would have a negative impact on your stock. You could have been invested in the finest companies in the market in 1972, but your wealth would have still been decimated in the 1973–1974 bear market when the market fell by 45 percent.

■ If the stock market is doing well but your company's industry is not, your stock will decline. You could have owned stock in an excellent oil and gas company in 1981, but you would have still seen it drop by 60 percent or more as the worldwide oil glut hit America's energy sector.

■ If both the general market and the industry are doing well, your stock could still fall if problems are affecting the company itself. You'll read a classic example in "Owning Stock in Your Own Company" on the following page.

The way to avoid these pitfalls is to diversify. Of course, you know you were admonished in your youth to "never put all your eggs in one basket" anyway. If you instead had some of your money in several stocks (minimally 3 to 4, and preferably 5 to 10) and the remainder of your wealth in mutual funds, real estate, bonds, and bank accounts, you would be greatly reducing risk while maintaining growth.

Diversification does not have to be a complicated science or involved economic theory. At the very least, you should ask yourself the following questions and answer them as completely and as accurately as possible:

■ Would you experience financial hardship if any one of your assets became worthless? This may sound like a harsh question, but it is a necessary one. If half your wealth was tied up in Crazy Tech Corporation, you would suffer if their stock takes a sudden plunge. A bear market would wipe you out.

■ If hardship does not apply, would your financial goals or aspirations change radically if any one of your assets became worthless? In 1972, many people on the verge of retirement had their money tied up in a couple blue-chip stocks and had to postpone retirement because these stocks were hit by a savage bear market. The stock portfolio's decline may not have caused them financial hardship, but it did force an abrupt and unwelcome change in their lifestyles.

■ How secure is your largest asset? In 1999, many people were invested in Microsoft. The antitrust lawsuit brought against them by the Federal Department of Justice caused a major decline in the stock. The company was a solid enterprise, but it was vulnerable to government intervention. Having too much of your portfolio in one stock can be hazardous to your wealth, even if it's a company that you are very comfortable with, such as your employer.

Owning stock in your own company

Diversification is important even when you are an employee of the company. Owning stock in the company that you are working for has been a very profitable strategy for many people over many years. Corporate stock purchase programs have helped even employees with modest incomes to accrue a six-figure stock portfolio. This is great if the company is doing well. People who are not comfortable investing in the general stock market are quite comfortable investing in their own company because this is something they know about. When you work for the company, your knowledge as an employee

Bright Idea
You can discuss stock investing with others who invest in the same stocks at the Stock Club Web site. There is no charge to become a member, which gives you the opportunity to read and post responses to hundreds of forums on individual stocks. For more information, go to the Web site www.stockclub.com.

can be a benign form of "insider knowledge" that you can use to build your wealth. But are there dangers in buying your own company's stock?

In March 2000, Procter and Gamble (PG) stockholders were stunned when PG's stock nose-dived to 52 from a high of 118 in January 2000. Many of these stockholders were employees and retirees that had PG as the bulk of their portfolio and had held it for many years. Many saw their holdings shrink by a six-figure amount. One stockholder, who retired after a long career with PG, saw his portfolio lose $900,000 in value. Everyone (including the analysts who issued "buy" orders on PG in January) was surprised as this huge, Fortune 500 industry giant fell 55 percent in market value in such a short period. It was a lesson to all about the dangers of being overinvested in a single company.

When you have a large percentage of your wealth tied to one company, your fortunes rise and fall with the company's performance. As we have discussed in past chapters, how you invest can be as important as what you invest in. In a mature bull market, PG stockholders (like any stockholders) should have had trailing stops on their holdings to protect that from downside risk.

PG was not alone in falling so hard. In 2000, many companies, especially Internet stocks, fell by 80 percent or more. Diversification should obviously be a concern for stockholders who have too much at stake by owning one stock (or having too much money tied to one stock). However, diversification is a concern even when you don't yet own a particular stock. Many employees will own stock in their company through stock options. Because of the popularity of stock options, this deserves some attention.

Stock options

In recent years, stock options have become a widely used form of compensation. As the market rose during 1995–1999, more employees were very happy to be paid with stock options.

Although there are different variations on the theme, the basic employee stock option gives the employee an opportunity to buy the company's stock at a favorable price. There are usually limitations on when you can exercise your option and for how many shares.

Let's describe a typical situation. Say that you just became an employee with stock options at Crazy Tech Corporation (CTC) in February 1999. As part of your compensation, you can buy 1,000 shares of CTC at $40 at any time after being with them two years. In other words, you can buy CTC for $40 in February 2001 or later. If you leave any time between now and then, your stock option expires. If the stock of CTC is at $70 per share, you stand to pick them up at a great discount to the market price. In February 2001, you could easily buy them at $40 and immediately resell them at $70 to bag a nice profit.

Imagine that it is a bull market and the stock goes to $100 per share. Late at night, you lie in bed pondering the possibilities. Do you get a BMW or take that trip to Hawaii? Not so fast—February 2001 is not here yet, and anything could happen. What happens if the market turns against you?

In early 2000, the Nasdaq Composite suffered a heavy hit; during March and April 2000, the Nasdaq fell 35 percent. Many tech and Internet stocks plunged big-time. The average Internet stock drop ranged from 60 to 80 percent. Tech stocks fell 30 to

50 percent. CTC fell 75 percent; it went from $100 per share to $25. If it stays at $25, would it make sense for you to exercise the option and buy it at $40? No way! You might as well buy on the market at $25. Suddenly the generous stock option isn't so lucrative anymore.

Keep in mind that employee stock option plans or discount purchase plans are excellent vehicles for you to buy stock. But just because you work for the company doesn't mean that you can stop looking at the stock through an analytical eye. You analyze it like you would any other stock. Actually, because you work for the company, you should analyze it even more. After all, this is also the source of your livelihood. Read the company's annual report as well as analysts' reports to get a balanced perspective. Don't get blindsided the way that PG employees did (as well as stockholders of many other companies).

If you have stock options, what can you do with them? When the time comes for the options to be exercised, most people are not sure what to do. They don't know whether to take the money in cash or to exercise the options and hold the company's stock. Three options are available.

A person can take the options, convert them to stock, and sell all the stock immediately. Or, that person can convert the options to stock and sell part of the stock and hold part of the stock to sell at a later date. The third option is to convert the options to stock and hold all the stock to sell at a later date. The choice is entirely up to that individual and her or his own unique circumstances.

In any case, the options need to be converted to stock. Many companies will help their employees convert their options to stock without having to put up any money. Other people have to go to a bro-kerage firm to convert their options to stock. Furthermore, if employees want the cash instead of the stock, they then have to sell the stock. This involves transaction costs. And the brokerage firm has to lay out its own money for the initial purchase of the stock if employees want to convert it to cash and don't want to put up any money. So, there is also a loan involved in which the firm is entitled to interest. For this service, the broker will charge a fee; it is advisable to shop around for brokers and negotiate the fees.

Another concern is that at many companies, large numbers of employees may vest at about the same time. If a large number of employees do this and subsequently sell the stock, it would cause the stock's price to drop significantly.

You need to judge your individual situation to see if your portfolio is over-represented by a single stock. If you can sell a portion of your stock and use the cash to diversify into other securities, you will be better off in the long run.

If you do have all your eggs in one basket, watch that basket like a hawk. Never stop monitoring your investment's progress. Make it a habit to read the financial news and scan financial news Web sites for any stories about your stock.

Monitoring and reassessing your portfolio

Diversification is not really a goal, it's a process. The responsible investor does continuous assessment and reassessment of risk. If you don't have confidence in your choices, you may be too eager to trade if your stocks are not doing well immediately. If you sell your stock too quickly, you risk missing out on great opportunities due to lack of patience.

Watch Out!
Although company stock options give you the opportunity to buy the company's stock at a favorable price at a future date, don't treat them as if you already owned the stock. A stock option is only a claim to stock, not the stock itself. You may be a potential millionaire but the risk is that you could lose this "wealth" just as easily.

If you do not reassess frequently, you risk being stuck with a bad investment too long and watching what was once an excellent investment turn around to your detriment.

On a regular basis (at least two or three times a year), ask yourself questions regarding your stock investment. The investment should continue to justify its place in your portfolio.

- Has the market for the company's product developed as you thought it would? Is it better or worse?

- Has the management of this company performed as you thought it would?

- Have the profit margins and financial ratios you examined remained strong? Do they show signs of future improvement or decline?

- Have new facts, products, or competitors entered the market that make this product or service more difficult to market?

- Does an alternate investment interest you more?

The answer to these and other questions will dictate your investment decisions. Your ability to answer these questions in a logical manner will help make you a more savvy investor. You don't have to do it alone, either—there are many great resources to help you monitor your current and future investments. One of them is Value Line.

Stock and market analysis services: Value Line

There are many places to turn to for stock analysis. One of the best is Value Line.

Value Line is a highly respected stock and market analysis service that has served investors for nearly

> 66
> Knowledge is of two kinds. We know a subject ourselves, or we know where we can find information upon it.
> —Johnson
> 99

35 years. Its proprietary stock selection system is a blend of fundamental and technical analysis, and it is widely regarded as a reliable guide for selecting high-performing stocks.

Investment survey

The *Value Line Investment Survey* is a three-part publication available to subscribers in print and on CD. Value Line's Web site, www.valueline.com, contains a Value Line University area that introduces you to the information. The survey provides timely stock information and tells how you can benefit from it.

"Ratings & Reports" is the core of the survey. This section provides regularly updated information and analysis on each of 1,700 major stocks in more than 90 different industries. The survey reports on stocks and industries in a distinctive one-page format. Information on each page is updated every 13 weeks.

"Summary & Index" is a weekly guide to the contents of the *Value Line Investment Survey*. It lists the page numbers for all the companies analyzed and also lists the industries that are covered. This section also provides a capsule summary of essential statistics for each stock in the survey, along with other current information.

The "Selection & Opinion" section presents Value Line's latest economic and stock market commentary, plus analysts' advice on current investment strategies, one or more interesting stock selections, and a variety of timely economic and stock market statistics. It also includes three hypothetical stock portfolios, each designed to meet a different investment objective. Stocks are ranked in categories of timeliness, safety, and technical factors.

Timeliness ranking

The timeliness ranking is simply Value Line's method for judging the relative strength of a stock. Value Line ranks stocks by their expected price performance relative to all the other approximately 1,700 stocks Value Line follows over the coming 6 to 12 months. The timeliness ranking identifies those stocks followed in the investment survey that are likely to have the best relative performance.

All the 1,700 stocks Value Line tracks in its investment survey are ranked in relationship to each other, from 1 (the highest rank) to 5 (the lowest rank). Stocks ranked 1 and 2 are expected to show stronger price performance than the remaining stocks, and those ranked 4 and 5 are likely to underperform or have weaker price performance.

At any given time, the following is true:

- 100 stocks are ranked 1
- 300 stocks are ranked 2
- 900 stocks are ranked 3
- 300 stocks are ranked 4
- 100 stocks are ranked 5

Although the rankings are not always an accurate barometer of the stock's success as compared to the group, it is a sound basis for further investigation.

Relative earnings and price growth over the past 10 years is the major factor in determining timeliness. Companies whose earnings growth over the past 10 years has been greater than the increase in their stocks' prices tend to be ranked 1 or 2. Other factors that influence the timeliness rankings include stock price momentum, quarterly earnings performance, and earnings surprises.

Stocks ranked 1 and 2 for timeliness can be more volatile than the market in general and frequently are stocks of smaller companies.

Safety ranking

Value Line also looks at the fundamentals of the stock by ranking them by safety. In other words, it looks at the financial strength of the company—the company's risk—compared to others in the survey.

Each of the 1,700 stocks tracked in the investment survey is ranked in relation to each other, from 1 (the highest rank) to 5 (the lowest rank). Stocks ranked 1 and 2 are most suitable for conservative investors; those ranked 4 and 5 will be more volatile. Volatility means that prices can move dramatically and often unpredictably, either down or up.

The major influences on a stock's safety ranking are the company's financial strength—measured by the balance sheet and financial ratios—and how stable its price has been over the past five years.

Technical ranking

Value Line provides a technical ranking for each stock as a predictor of short-term (three to six months) price changes. Like the other Value Line rankings, this one is relative, assigning scores to each stock tracked in the investment survey in relation to the others, from 1 (the highest rank) to 5 (the lowest rank). The ranking itself is based on a proprietary model that evaluates 10 price trends over the past year. For a sample Value Line single-page analysis, see Figure 12.1.

The easiest way to get the rankings is to subscribe to the service; however, many public libraries also carry the Value Line surveys in their reference areas.

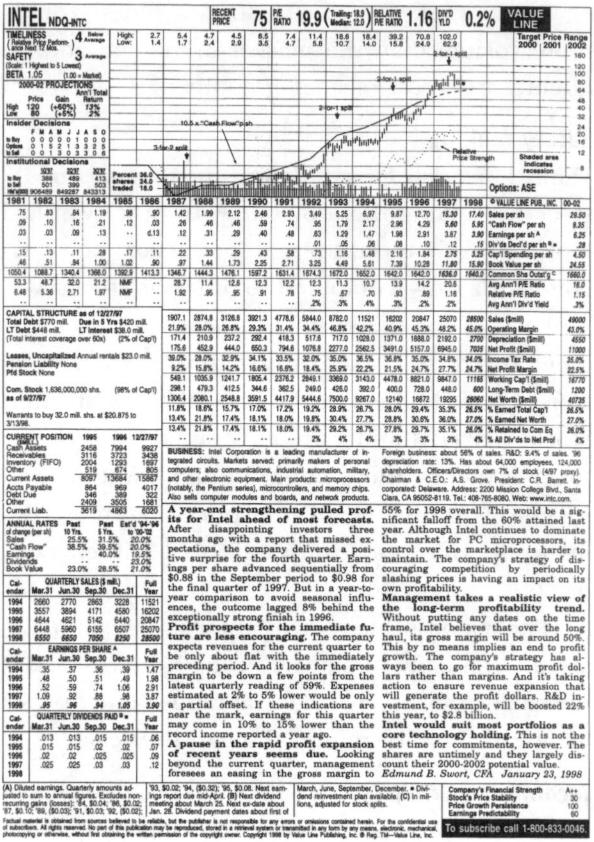

BUSINESS: Intel Corporation is a leading manufacturer of integrated circuits. Markets served: primarily makers of personal computers; also communications, industrial automation, military, and other electronic equipment. Main products: microprocessors (notably, the Pentium series), microcontrollers, and memory chips. Also sells computer modules and boards, and network products. Foreign business: about 56% of sales. R&D: 9.4% of sales. '96 depreciation rate: 13%. Has about 64,000 employees, 124,000 shareholders. Officers/Directors own 7% of stock (4/97 proxy). Chairman & C.E.O.: A.S. Grove. President: C.R. Barrett. Incorporated: Delaware. Address: 2200 Mission College Blvd., Santa Clara, CA 95052-8119. Tel.: 408-765-8080. Web: www.intc.com.

A year-end strengthening pulled profits for Intel ahead of most forecasts. After disappointing investors three months ago with a report that missed expectations, the company delivered a positive surprise for the fourth quarter. Earnings per share advanced sequentially from $0.88 in the September period to $0.98 for the final quarter of 1997. But in a year-to-year comparison to avoid seasonal influences, the outcome lagged 8% behind the exceptionally strong finish in 1996.

Profit prospects for the immediate future are less encouraging. The company expects revenues for the current quarter to be only about flat with the immediately preceding period. And it looks for the gross margin to be down a few points from the latest quarterly reading of 59%. Expenses estimated at 2% to 5% lower would be only a partial offset. If these indications are near the mark, earnings for this quarter may come in 10% to 15% lower than the record income reported a year ago.

A pause in the rapid profit expansion of recent years seems due. Looking beyond the current quarter, management foresees an easing in the gross margin to 55% for 1998 overall. This would be a significant falloff from the 60% attained last year. Although Intel continues to dominate the market for PC microprocessors, its control over the marketplace is harder to maintain. The company's strategy of discouraging competition by periodically slashing prices is having an impact on its own profitability.

Management takes a realistic view of the long-term profitability trend. Without putting any dates on the time frame, Intel believes that over the long haul, its gross margin will be around 50%. This by no means implies an end to profit growth. The company's strategy has always been to go for maximum profit dollars rather than margins. And it's taking action to ensure revenue expansion that will generate the profit dollars. R&D investment, for example, will be boosted 22% this year, to $2.8 billion.

Intel would suit most portfolios as a core technology holding. This is not the best time for commitments, however. The shares are untimely and they largely discount their 2000-2002 potential value.

Edmund B. Swort, CFA January 23, 1998

Company's Financial Strength	A++
Stock's Price Stability	30
Price Growth Persistence	100
Earnings Predictability	60

To subscribe call 1-800-833-0046.

Figure 12.1: Sample Value Line analysis.

News and events that affect a company's prospects

Being alert to what is going on with the company is important to the serious investor. The news could affect the company and its stock from either an external or an internal point of view. External news refers to events and developments that will have a significant effect on company operations, such as labor strikes, hurricanes, government litigation, new taxes, and so on. Internal news refers to what is going on inside the company, such as insider trading or new product announcements.

A good example of how seemingly unrelated events can be tied together is Dell Computers. A major headline in 1999 was the earthquake in Taiwan. How did it affect Dell in the United States? The earthquake harmed many companies in Taiwan, including manufacturers that served Dell. This caused a problem for Dell's inventory needs and its distribution network. Some analysts downgraded Dell's stock because the earthquake would have an adverse impact on earnings.

Is your company in the news? Is the news good or bad? What are the latest developments? Products, services, markets, changes?

The local or city newspaper for the company's corporate headquarters serves as a great starting point. This resource will likely have numerous articles on your company. For example, the 39 local business journals across the country are important resources for many professionals. You can search all 39 journals simultaneously at the American City Business Journals Web site, www.amcity.com.

A number of Web sites provide links to online newspapers throughout the world. For starters, you might try these news Web sites:

Electric Library
www.elibrary.com

E&P MediaInfo Links
www.mediainfo.com/emedia

NewsPaperLinks
www.newspaperlinks.com
When you find the local newspaper for your company, scan the main page for the terms

Timesaver
Standard & Poor's stock guides give a succinct two-page synopsis on public companies. They publish these guides several times a year for timeliness and cover stocks from the NYSE, AMEX, and the major issues on Nasdaq. Check with your local reference librarian for further information. Moody's Investment Services publishes a similar line of stock guides.

"Archives" or "Search" or "Back Issues" to research past articles.

Yahoo! Finance
http://finance.yahoo.com

These are other key sites for locating company news articles and press releases:

American Journalism Review Newslink
http://ajr.newslink.org/mag.html
Provides links to a large number of online magazines.

Excite's Newstracker
www.excite.com
Searches the Internet for recent news articles on your company.

Fortune Magazine
http://cgi.pathfinder.com/time/search/index.html
Mirrors the magazine in business content.

News Alert
www.newsalert.com
Offers stock quotes; news articles from Reuters, PR Newswire, and Businesswire; and a wide variety of other financial information.

NewsCentral
www.all-links.com/newscentral
Provides company information, press releases, and periodical articles with valuable company information.

News Directory
www.NewsDirectory.com
Excellent search engine for newspapers and publications. You can register for free to get email alerts on stories covering your topic or company.

Timesaver
More financial news Web sites now have free services to help you stay on top of the news for your chosen company. Register your e-mail address with them, and they will periodically send you messages regarding your company's activities.

Northern Light
www.northernlight.com
Searches a variety of newspapers, newswires, and magazines and provides abstracts and citations of all articles for free. Full-text documents can be purchased for a nominal fee.

TIME.com
www.time.com
Enables you to search Time Warner publications including *Fortune, Time,* and *Money.*

Transium's Business Search Engine
http://databox.transium.com
Provides a rich mix of articles from mainstream and specialty periodicals, and categorizes the material to reveal relationships. Abstracts are available for free, and full-text articles can be purchased for a nominal charge.

After researching a company, you may want to stay current on news articles, analysts' reports, patents, trademarks, and other business activities. You can register (free) at Company Sleuth, at www.companysleuth.com, to receive daily e-mail reports on up to 10 U.S. public companies.

The business press and the mass media will tell you what public things are happening with your company. It is also a good idea to look at what's going on inside the corporate entity. Fortunately, you can tell because of the mandatory reporting requirements of insiders.

Insider trading
Maybe you can't read the mind of the CEO or the corporate treasurer, but what they do is more important to you than what they are saying. Make it a habit

Moneysaver
If you have a large amount of your money in a particular stock, access some of the independent services available for a second opinion. Although they specialize in rating the financial strength of insurance companies and banks, Weiss Ratings also offers safety ratings reports on many public companies. You can call Weiss at 1-800-289-9222 ($15 per rating) or visit the Web site www.martinweiss.com.

Bright Idea
If corporate insiders own 10 percent or more of the company's stock, that is generally a positive sign. The more stock that management owns, the greater their commitment to the company's success.

to see the SEC reports on what insiders are doing with their stock. When people in the know are buying or selling their stock, this gives you valuable clues about what is really going on.

It is not significant if a few insiders buy or sell the stock. It is more important to know if many insiders are buying or selling the stock.

If many insiders are buying

When an insider makes a stock purchase, this is an unequivocally positive sign for investors. The more insiders who buy company stock, the better. More times than not, when there is significant buying by a large number of insiders, the stock price rises significantly soon thereafter.

Insider selling is not as clear a signal as insider buying. There can actually be many reasons why an insider is selling stock that have nothing to do with the company's prospects. Perhaps the insider is cashing in stock to buy a house or to finance college. Perhaps that person's adviser warned about becoming more diversified by shifting money out of company stock and into mutual funds. If the occasional insider sells stock, it shouldn't raise eyebrows. The real signal is if many insiders sell their stock. A good example is General Motors. In January 1999, the stock hit a 52-week high of $95. SEC reports show that 21 company executives sold a total of $20 million worth of GM stock that month. Within a matter of weeks, the stock lost over a third if its value.

Keep in mind that insider selling (or buying) doesn't cause the stock to fall (or rise). It is merely a short-term gauge for what may be happening at the company. If the insiders expect good things, it is generally a buy signal, and vice versa.

These are some of the Web sites that track insider trading:

Insider Scores
www.insiderscores.com

Insider Trader
www.insidertrader.com

Ten K Wizard
www.tenkwizard.com

Sometimes the insider buying the company's stock is not an individual; sometimes it is the company itself through its management.

Corporate buybacks

Another form of insider activity is when management decides to buy the company's stock. A company might want to do this for several reasons, but these are the most common:

■ To defend against the potential of unwelcome takeover bids

■ To buy stock for employee compensation programs such as stock option plans

■ To increase the company's equity by diminishing the supply of shares available in the market

■ To boost the company's earnings per share (EPS) without actually generating more profit

Here's how it works: Say that Porcupine Balloon Corporation (PBC) has five million shares outstanding and expects to earn $10 million during 2000. According to these figures, the EPS would be $2.

Suppose that PBC buys 250,000 shares, or 5 percent, of shares outstanding, leaving 4.75 million shares remaining in circulation. This would inflate the EPS to $2.11 ($10 million in earnings divided by 4,750,000 shares) That's somewhat misleading

Watch Out!
When a company announces a secondary public stock offering, check the company's financial condition. Frequently, if the company is in trouble, it will sell new stock to the public, which is really a disguised opportunity for insiders to bail out of the company by selling their shares to unwitting investors.

Unofficially ...
If a would-be acquirer has already acquired some of its target's shares, the target can offer to buy those shares back, generally at a premium, to appease the acquirer and thwart the offer. This type of transaction is called greenmail.

because the company didn't generate any added revenue from corporate operations. Because earnings are scrutinized by the market and the business media, it can put undue pressure on the company's management to make the numbers look good.

A corporate buyback of stock is acceptable if the buyback is being financed by profits or from cash accounts. The problem occurs when the money comes by increasing debt. Borrowing can result in added interest expense that can significantly dilute earnings in a subsequent period. Borrowing for a stock buyback should always be questioned because getting into debt is better left for purposes that can increase the company's value, such as modernizing equipment or buying income-producing assets. However, there are occasions when using debt to buy back equity can be a wise move on the part of the company if it is simply trying to reach what it considers an ideal debt-to-equity ratio.

Very often, when buybacks are announced, the share price of the company moves higher to reflect the increased demand in the market, which certainly benefits stockholders. Also, because price appreciation is based in part on earnings growth, the market may reward the stock for its higher EPS after a buyback.

Buybacks reduce the total shares outstanding, which could be a problem in micro-cap stocks because it affects the stock's trading liquidity. Investors could be negatively affected as the ability to move in and out of a stock quickly is diminished, which may prevent them from getting the best price.

To find out more about corporate buybacks and insider trading, use the news sources and Web sites referenced in the prior section and in Appendix B, "Investing Information Resources."

When you know what is happening with the company, you should see what is happening with its stock. To do this, you need to become proficient at reading the stock quotes in the financial pages.

Reading the stock pages

The stock pages aren't the first place you look when you start investing in stocks. They're really the last place. These pages are meant for people who already own stock or who know what stocks they will be acquiring.

It's not the first place to look because it can be confusing and overwhelming if you don't know what you are looking for. You see thousands of numbers and figures in small print. How do you make sense of it?

The tables make sense once you know what stock you are interested in. If you own Home Depot, for example, you can go straight to that entry and see exactly what happened to the stock on that day's trading.

Stock prices from the previous day's trading are printed in tables in most newspapers Tuesday through Saturday, and the week's activity is commonly summarized on Sunday. These tables use an extremely abbreviated format, including footnotes to indicate various situations. The tables are distributed by the Associated Press. This section lists the most commonly used footnotes about stock prices, the stock itself, and dividends, so if your newspaper doesn't explain its tables, this might help.

The Wall Street Journal

The Wall Street Journal is the granddaddy of stock reporting publications. Its stock table format is generally duplicated by other major dailies, with minor differences. To give you a sense of what the actual tables look like, refer to Figure 12.2.

Figure 12.2: Sample *Wall Street Journal* stock table.

	52 Weeks					Yld		Vol				Net
	Hi	Lo	Stock	Sym	Div	%	PE	100s	Hi	Lo	Close	Chg
			-A-A-A-									
	28 1/2	14 7/8	AAR	AIR	.34	2.2	10	305	15 7/8	15 11/32	15 9/16	+ 1/4
	30 15/16	19 1/4	ABM Indus	ABM	.62	2.5	15	409	25 3/16	25 1/16	25 3/16	...
	25 13/16	19 15/16	ABN Am ADR	ABN	.73	3.6	...	565	20 1/4	19 15/16	20 1/16	– 1/16
	25 3/4	19 3/16	ABN Am pfA		1.88	9.1	...	559	21	20 3/4	20 3/4	– 1/16
	25 1/2	18 7/8	ABN Am pfB		1.78	8.9	...	914	19 15/16	19 5/8	19 15/16	...
n	24	20 1/4	ACE CapTr		.62	2.8	...	408	23	22 7/16	22 1/2	+ 3/8
	35 1/4	14 1/16	♣ ACE Ltd	ACL	.44	1.7	9	5216	25 7/16	24 9/16	25 3/8	+ 11/16
n	58 1/8	47 11/16	ACE LtdPRIDES			...	...	127	55 15/16	55	55 5/8	+ 5/8
	8 3/4	6 5/16	ACM GvtFd	ACG	.78	11.3	...	630	6 7/8	6 13/16	6 7/8	– 1/16
	8	6 1/4	ACM OppFd	AOF	.72a	9.8	...	158	7 5/16	7 5/16	7 5/16	...
	8 1/4	6 3/16	ACM SecFd	GSF	.78	11.7	...	883	6 3/4	6 5/8	6 11/16	...
	6 1/16	5 1/8	ACM SpctmFd	SI	.60	10.4	...	847	5 13/16	5 11/16	5 3/4	+ 1/16
▼	11 1/2	8 1/4	ACM MgdDlr	ADF	1.20	14.5	...	565	8 5/16	8 1/8	8 1/4	– 1/16
	8 15/16	5 1/2	ACM MgdInco	AMF	.84	14.0	...	307	6 1/16	5 15/16	6	...
	13 15/16	10 1/8	ACM MuniSec	AMU	.87	8.0	...	107	10 7/8	10 3/4	10 7/8	+ 1/8
s	9 1/8	2 3/8	ACX Tch A	GPK		...	7	1439	3 11/16	3 1/2	3 1/2	– 1/16
	92 1/2	48 3/8	♣ AES Cp	AES		...	41	9716	87 9/16	83 1/2	85 1/8	– 7/16
nl	42 1/2	41	AES Cp wi			...	...	367	43 1/4	41 5/8	42	– 1/2
n	72	47 1/4	AES Tr		1.71e	2.5	...	120	69 1/2	68	69 1/4	+ 3/8
	54 5/16	33 9/16	AFLAC	AFL	.34f	.7	24	5339	45 15/16	45 5/16	45 9/16	– 1/4
	14 7/16	8 1/4	AGCO Cp	AG	.04	.3	dd	1322	12 1/16	11 3/4	11 15/16	+ 1/8
	20 3/4	15 9/16	AGL Res	ATG	1.08	6.0	14	1968	18 1/4	17 3/4	18 1/8	+ 7/16
	31 9/16	13 7/8	AgSvcAm	ASV		...	15	138	20 1/2	20	20 1/2	– 1/8
	24	9 3/4	AICI CapTr pf		2.25	19.5	...	146	12	11 3/8	11 9/16	– 7/16
	31 5/8	16 11/16	AIPC	PLB		...	18	330	25 1/2	24 1/2	25 5/16	+ 9/16
	28 1/2	7 7/8	♣ AK Steel	AKS	.50	4.4	24	4753	11 1/2	11 1/8	11 3/8	– 1/8
	23 1/2	18	♣ AMB Prop	AMB	1.48f	6.4	11	4070	23 1/16	22 3/4	23	+ 1/8
	25 1/2	19 1/8	♣ AMB Prop pfA		2.13	9.9	...	15	21 1/2	21 7/16	21 1/2	– 1/16

The first table to get familiar with is the New York Stock Exchange Composite Transactions (Figure 12.2). We'll read the columns from left to right and then explain the footnotes that dot the black-and-white newsprint landscape. (We'll use ABM Industries Incorporated [ABM] as a representative company.)

The first two columns show the stock's most recent 52-week high and low prices. In other words, they indicate the highest price and the lowest price that the stock hit in the most recent 52 weeks. ABM had a high of 30 15/16 and a low of 19 1/4. These two columns are there to give you a some perspective on the stock's price. Is today's price near its 52-week high or not? What if it is close to its 52-week low?

Has the stock "bottomed out" and is now ready to move up? Keep in mind that the 52 weeks in question is not a fixed period. As each day passes, those 52 weeks keep following like a long, trailing tail to keep the perspective updated.

To the left of these columns, you may see *n*, *s*, or *x*. The *n* indicates that the company has been listed only within the past 52 weeks; it doesn't have a full 52 weeks from which to give an adequate historical perspective. If the stock has been listed for only two weeks, it would be misleading to judge it the same way as a company that has been there for 52 or more weeks.

The *s* indicates that a stock split occurred within the most recent 52 weeks. This is to warn you against misleading quotes. Imagine if you bought a stock at $180 per share six months ago. What if that stock had a 2-for-1 stock split three months ago? If the price remained stable, you would see the price as $90. It would confuse you to see a stock you bought at $180 having a high of 139 and a low of 81. The *s* warns you that the stock table reflects the new post-split price.

The *x* indicates that the stock is ex-dividend. Ex-dividend means the company has entered a three-day period during which a buyer of the stock will not qualify for the quarterly dividend that is coming due. Companies pay dividends to stockholders of record. However, on the day that stock is bought (the "day of execution"), the buyer is not officially a stockholder until the day of settlement, which is three days later. Say that you bought the stock of Public Service Enterprise Group, a public utility, to immediately qualify for its pending quarterly dividend of 54 cents per share. Assume that the

> 66
> The saying that knowledge is power is not quite true. Used knowledge is power, and more than power. It is money, and service, and better living for our fellowmen, and a hundred other good things. But mere knowledge, left unused, has not power in it.
> —Edward E. Free
> 99

company pays this dividend to stockholders of record as of May 10. The ex-dividend date would be May 7. If you bought the stock on May 8, you would not be on record as a stockholder until May 11. Therefore, you wouldn't receive the quarterly dividend. A small consolation is that during the ex-dividend period, the stock trades slightly lower (in this case by approximately 54 cents).

Additionally, you may also see a triangle, pointing up or down. An upward-pointing triangle means that the stock just reached a new 52-week high. The downward-pointing triangle means that the stock just hit a new 52-week low.

The third column is the company's name in abbreviated form. This column also shows you a lowercase *pf* to denote that it is a preferred stock.

The fourth column shows the stock's ticker symbol. In this example, it is ABM.

The fifth column indicates the stock's dividend, if any. ABM's dividend is 62 cents per share.

The sixth column indicates the stock's dividend yield (or just "yield"), which is calculated by dividing the annual dividend by the most recent stock price. ABM's dividend yield is 2.5 percent (62 cents divided by the closing share price of 25^3/_{16}$).

If the dividend was $2 and the stock price was $25, the dividend yield would be 8 percent. The yield lets you compare the income from this investment to any other investment. This is important for income investors because they want to see how the dividend stacks up against the dividend from another stock. You can also compare with nonstock investments such as bank accounts or bonds. A stock with an 8 percent dividend yield compares favorably with bank certificates of deposit that may yield 8 percent or less.

The seventh column is the P/E ratio. This ratio is derived by dividing the stock's most recent price with the company's earnings on a per share (EPS) basis. ABM's P/E ratio is 15, which is generally considered to be a reasonable level.

If the stock price was $40 and the EPS $2, the P/E ratio would be 20. Generally, the lower the P/E ratio, the less expensive the stock is. Conversely, the higher the P/E ratio, the more expensive the stock is (based on a multiple of the company's earnings). The P/E ratio effectively sets a relationship between the stock price and the company's operations. (This topic is given more detailed treatment in Chapter 7, "Value Investing.")

Sometimes in this column you will see *dd* or *cc*. The symbol *cc* indicates that the company has a P/E ratio of 100 or more. A P/E ratio of 100 or more means that you are paying a very high price for the company's earnings. The symbol *dd* means that there is no P/E ratio because the company has no earnings.

The eighth column gives the trading volume for the stock; ABM's volume is 40,900 shares. This indicates how many shares changed hands that day. Stocks typically trade in a regular range unless something unusual has occurred with the company or market that day. If a stock normally trades 10,000 to 15,000 shares per day day-in and day-out and the volume suddenly jumps to 50,000 shares, you'd better check it out!

A large jump in volume is not necessarily good or bad; it is just a signal to investigate why trading has increased so significantly. Maybe the increased volume occurred because the company reported better-than-expected earnings, or it's coming out

Moneysaver
Because *The Wall Street Journal* is published by Dow Jones & Co., subscribers to the paper can also sign on to *The Wall Street Journal* interactive edition at lower rates at the Web site www.wsj.com. This Web site also gives you access to *Barron's* and other proprietary publications at no additional cost.

with a great new product or invention. Maybe the increased volume occurred because of a negative development. Perhaps the SEC penalized the company, or the company reported lower-than-expected earnings.

The last four columns indicate how trading went for the stock on that day. The columns are labeled High, Low, Close, and Net Change. They tell you the stock's high and low price for that trading day, as well as the price at which the stock closed.

ABM's stock traded that day from a high of $25^3/_{16}$ to a low of $25^1/_{16}$, and it closed for the day at $25^3/_{16}$. Because there is no number for ABM in the Net Change column, this indicates that the stock's price changed at the same price as the previous day's close.

If a stock closed at 55 at the end of the trading day, and the net change shows "$+^1/_2$," this indicates that the stock closed a half-point higher than it did the previous day. In this case, the previous day the stock had closed at $54^1/_2$.

There are other symbols to be aware of as well. These are covered in *The Wall Street Journal's* stock table explanatory notes:

y	Ex-dividend and sales in full
z	Sales in full
g	Dividend or earnings in Canadian currency
n	New issue in the past 52 weeks (that is, the high/low aren't true 52-week figures)
pp	Holder owes installments of purchase price
rt	Rights
s	Split or stock dividend of more than 25 percent in the past 52 weeks
un	Units
v	Trading was halted on the primary market

vj	Bankrupt, reorganizing, or some similar condition
wd	When distributed
wi	When issued
wt	Warrants
ww	With warrants
xw	Without warrants
a	Also extra(s)
b	Annual rate plus stock dividend
c	Liquidating dividend
e	Declared or paid in preceding 12 months
f	Annual dividend rate increased
i	Declared or paid after stock dividend or split-up
j	Paid this year, dividend omitted, deferred, or no action taken at the last dividend meeting
k	Declared or paid this year, an accumulative issue with dividends in arrears
r	Declared or paid in preceding 12 months plus stock dividends
t	Paid in stock in preceding 12 months, established cash value on ex-dividend or ex-distribution date
boldface	Stock's price changed 5 percent or more from previous day
<u>underline</u>	Stock's trading volume equaled or exceeded 2 percent of the total number of shares outstanding

Investors Business Daily

Investors Business Daily is considered the leading competitor to *The Wall Street Journal*. However, it is better to consider them papers that complement each other rather than as adversaries. Each adds information and perspectives to the benefit of the investor.

Investors Business Daily embodies the data necessary to employ the essential investing philosophy of its founder, William O'Neill. His popular CANSLIM (see Chapter 4, "Analyzing Past Winners") method is evident throughout the paper's section.

Whether you are a novice or a experienced investor, *Investors Business Daily* gives you vital data to help you improve your investment decisions. This newspaper is the only source of financial information based on an ongoing 45-year study of the greatest stock market winners (stocks that doubled or tripled or more in price within any one-year period).

A close analysis of all fundamental and technical factors has revealed certain critical characteristics that have appeared again and again since 1954. These common characteristics are the basis for the proprietary ratings found in *Investors Business Daily*. Most financial papers don't provide this service.

For stock investors, *Investors Business Daily* is different from *The Wall Street Journal* in several ways. First, *Investors Business Daily* takes technical analysis more seriously than *The Wall Street Journal*. It offers more charts of stocks in the news and also presents a feature called SmartSelect Corporate Ratings with the features detailed in the next sections. For an actual table, see Figure 12.3.

EPS rating

The earnings per share (EPS) rating looks at the growth rate because it is one of the most important components affecting the stock's price. The EPS rating helps you identify companies with excellent earnings records. It measures each company's short- and long-term earnings growth rate and compares it to the market.

The results are rated on a percentage scale from 1 to 99, with 99 being the top score. For example, a stock with an EPS rating of 85 percent outperformed 85 percent of all other stocks in earnings growth. Investors should look for companies with EPS ratings of 75 or more.

Bright Idea
For best results, use all five of the *Investors Business Daily* SmartSelect Corporate Ratings. Usually, companies with SmartSelect ratings of 80-80-B-B-B or higher are a good consideration for closer investigation. Those companies that rate 90-90-A-A-A probably have even greater potential.

IBD *SmartSelect*™ CORPORATE RATINGS
Earnings Per Share
Relative Price Strength
Industry Group Relative Strength
Sales+Profit Margins+R.O.E.
Accumulation/Distribution

Earnings Per Share	Relative Price Strength	Industry Group Relative Strength	Sales+Profit Margins+R.O.E.	Accumulation/Distribution	52-Week High	Stock	Symbol	Closing Price	Price Chg	Vol.% Chg	Vol. 100s	Dvd Yld	Day's High	Low	
44	38	D	B	C	75 7/16	AMR	cr5 AMR	56 7/16	+1 3/16	+71	1.7m	..	57 1/8	54 1/8	o
3	97	B	.	A	14 1/2	AOTatneft	TNT	10 5/8	− 3/16	−75	529	0.2	10 3/4	10 9/16	
3	84	A	D	B	8 7/16	APTSatellite	ATS	7 5/16	+ 3/8	−54	1025	..	7 5/16	6 11/16	
	42	B	.	B	24	ASALtd	ASA	17 7/16	+ 1/8	+66	859	3.4	17 5/8	17 3/8	k o
28	46	A	B	B	63 13/32	AT&T	5 T	51	−1 1/2	−22	8.8m	1.7	53	50 1/2	o
14	81	A	D	B	58 15/16	LMGA	r LMGA	52 7/8	− 3/8	−5	2.4m	..	54 3/8	52 7/8	o
14	84	A	D	G	73 1/8	LMGB	r LMGB	60 1/8	−1 5/8	+83	196	..	61 15/16	60	
77	92	A	C	A	65 11/16	AVX	r AVX	63 11/16	+1 13/16	+20	2210	0.4	64 1/2	61 5/8	o
88	54	C	C	B	73 5/8	AXAAds	AXA	66 5/16	+1 1/8	+119	1473	1.1	67	63 7/8	
95	56	C	C	D	38 3/4	AXAFncl	AXF	33	−1	−22	5215	0.3	34 1/16	33	k o
90	30	E	B	C	22 1/4	AaronRents	r RNT	14 15/16	....	−41	134	0.3	15 1/16	14 11/16	
61	17	D	A	E	53 5/16	AbbottLabs	c5 ABT	33 1/16	+ 3/16	−16	4.6m	2.1	33 1/4	32 3/4	o
99	6	C	A	D	50 3/4	Abercrmbie	ANF	21 1/8	+ 5/16	+22	1.7m	..	21 5/16	20 9/16	k o
46	58	C	D	B	13 13/16	AbitibiCons	c ABY	12 1/4	− 1/16	−19	1432	2.2	12 7/16	11 15/16	o
52	49	A	.	B	20	AckerleyGp	AK	16 3/8	+ 5/16	−41	132	0.1	16 3/8	15 5/16	k
96	17	E	C	E	32 3/4	ACNielsen	ART	20 9/16	+ 5/16	+85	3962	..	21 3/16	20 5/16	k o
29	65	A	C	A	18 1/16	Acuson	ACN	14 7/16	+1 1/8	+304	2629	..	14 1/2	13 3/8	k o
	64	B	.	B	34 1/8	AdamsExprs	r ADX	33	− 3/16	−31	296	0.6	33 1/4	32 7/8	
80	62	B	A	B	24 7/16	Provida ADS	PVD	20 5/16	+ 5/16	+129	362	4.6	20 5/16	20	
69	80	B	C	B	31	Administaff	r ASF	25	− 1/4	−42	490	..	25 1/4	24 1/2	k o
12	83	A	.	A	14 3/4	AdvCmmtyGr	ADG	11 1/4	− 3/16	+78	3214	..	12	10 1/16	k o
51	86	A	E	A	45 1/8	AdvMicroDv	5 AMD	36 1/16	− 1/2	−46	2.0m	..	36 1/2	35 9/16	o
72	34	B	C	A	25 1/4	AdvestGrp	cr ADV	18 5/16	− 1/8	−96	9	1.1	18 5/16	18 5/16	
80	74	B	.	A	27 5/8	Advo	cr AD	26 7/16	+ 3/16	−57	385	..	26 1/2	26	o
79	21	E	B	D	113	AegonNV	AEG	74 11/16	+2 5/8	+62	1831	1.3	74 7/8	72 1/2	o
78	73	A	A	A	22 3/8	Aeroflex	r ARX	13	+ 7/8	+23	2171	..	13 5/16	11 7/8	k o

Figure 12.3: Sample *Investors Business Daily* stock table.

RS rating

The relative price strength (RS) rating helps you identify stocks that have shown better price performance compared to other companies. The RS rating tracks the stock's price movement over the most recent 12 months and compares it to the market. The results are plotted on a percentage scale from 1 to 99, with 99 indicating the best price performers. If a stock has a RS rating of 95, it bested 95 percent of all other stocks in the most recent 12 months.

Generally, stocks of about a 70 rating are superior performers; of course, higher is better.

Industry rating

Investors Business Daily's industry group relative strength rating compares the stock's industry group price performance over the most recent six months with other industry groups. The newspaper tracks 196 industry groups and breaks down the ratings into quintiles. The top 20 percent get an A, the next 20 percent get a B, and so on.

Combination rating

The combination rating is a smorgasbord of fundamentals. It combines the company's sales, profit margins (both pretax an after-tax figures), and return on equity into a single rating. The rating ranges from A to E, with A meaning that the company is in the top 20 percent of all stocks.

A/D rating

The accumulation/distribution (A/D) rating helps you to interpret the buying and selling activity of the stock. It uses a proprietary formula to analyze each stock's daily price and volume changes. It uses a rating range of A to E, with A indicating signifying heavy buying for the stock, B indicating signifying moderate buying, and so on.

Vol percent Chg

Investors Business Daily's "Vol percent Chg" (volume percent change) helps you identify stocks with unusual changes in daily trading volume. Vol percent Chg attempts to help you spot stocks with increased trading volume and compare it with the stock's average daily trading volume for the past 50 trading days. Stocks with increased volume tend to show greater price movement.

Stocks at a new price high or up 1 point or more are boldfaced. A quick scan of boldfaced stocks will identify the day's relevant market performers. Stocks at new price lows or down 1 point or more are underlined. Boldfaced italicized stocks have 80 or higher EPS and relative price strength ratings and were new issues (IPOs) in the past eight years. Research has shown that the majority of past big-winning companies were IPOs at some point within the last eight years. The following paragraphs discuss special codes that *Investors Business Daily* uses to alert the investor to relevant points about that individual stock:

A small bold **5** after a company's name indicates that it is in the S&P 500. A small bold *c* means the company has had a new CEO in the last two years. A bold *r* means that the company has been repurchasing its own stock in the open market in the last 12 months.

In a daily rotating column, IBD gives you the P/E ratio on Monday, Wednesday, and Friday. On Tuesday, you get an institutional sponsorship rating, which averages the three-year performance rating of mutual funds owning that stock, plus the stock's trend in recent quarters. Again, the ratings range is A to E, with A being best. On Thursday, you get the dividend yield percent.

Where the big money is flowing

Because institutional investors have a big impact on stock prices, *Investors Business Daily* tracks their stock-investing habits. The paper's "Where the Big Money's Flowing" section helps you isolate stocks with significant increases over their average trading volume. Big increases in volume (both total shares and as a percentage) often indicate buying activity generated by institutional investors, which could mean a higher share price.

Investors Business Daily also uses the following codes in its stock tables:

(x)	ex-dividends or ex-rights
(k)	earnings due to be reported in the next four weeks
(-)	earnings report appears in today's *Investors Business Daily*
(o)	stock has listed options
(s)	stock split
(b)	company is bankrupt, in receivership or in reorganization
(d)	distribution

Barron's

Barron's is one of the premier financial papers covering the U.S. economy and financial markets. It is a very influential publication put out by Dow Jones that comes out every Monday.

Looking through its pages for incisive commentary, analysis, and comprehensive reportage will serve you well. The following sections in *Barron's* contain especially relevant information for investors.

- **"Up & Down Wall Street"**—This column is usually written by Alan Abelson and highlights his respected and pointed commentary on the financial events and issues of the week.

- **"Review & Preview"**—This section highlights the relevant events from the past week and the coming week. Here they mention what economic reports are scheduled to be released, corporate news, mergers, Federal Reserve meetings and announcements, and so on.

- **"Market Week"**—This pull-out section gives you the latest information, in comprehensive detail, on the markets, economic indicators, and the indexes. Stock investors can read a week's worth of data on companies' stock price movements.

Barron's puts a great deal of emphasis on fundamentals and value investing, which is something no investor should ignore. Its feature stories are among the best in the financial reporting industry.

Just the facts

- Diversification is the widely advised and easiest way to minimize risk in your portfolio.

- If you have a large portion of your assets in a single company, either sell a portion or use trailing stops to protect yourself from the downside risk.

- Be an avid news reader; use the Internet to monitor your company's activity.

- Track insiders because their actual buy or sell transactions give you clues about the stock's short-term prospects.

- Get familiar with the major financial publications that track the market so that you can get informed—and stay informed—about the stock's performance.

Unofficially ...
A good example of how *Barron's* can influence markets is its March 20, 2000 issue. The cover story, "Burning Fast," was an investigative piece that pointed out that more than 200 Internet companies would run out of money and risk bankruptcy. The article sent shock waves through the investment community, and the dotcoms' stock started their descent. By May 2000, most Internet companies were down, on average, 80 percent.

GET THE SCOOP ON...
Avoiding fraud ▪ Investment newsletters:
analysis or advertising? ▪ Classic scams
▪ Where to turn for assistance

Protecting Your Investments

Avoiding fraud

It's tough enough to gain a good return on your investments. You guard against risk every day, and you worry about encroachment on your money from greedy relatives, overpriced advisers, and, of course, the IRS. But the world is not finished throwing the kitchen sink at you; money-hungry fraudulent operators lurk everywhere. Their acts of fraud come is various forms:

- **"Shell" companies**—These are companies that don't really exist except as a conduit to pry you free of your hard-earned money.

- **Microcap fraud**—Con games are frequently involved with small companies that offer little information to investors.

- **Brokers and advisers**—First they seek your confidence; then they seek your nest egg.

403

66

It is not the
return on my
investment that
I am concerned
about; it is the
return of my
investment.
—Will Rogers

99

- **Outright thievery**—In electronic trading, thieves can take your money by "hacking" or illegally accessing your account without your knowledge or agreement.

- **Information schemes**—You pay good money for bad advice in the form of information products.

- **Buried overcharges**—Legitimate investment products and services can have hidden charges or excessive sales charges or "loads."

The schemes to take your money can be simple and brazen or elaborate and seductive. Although new types of fraud continually arrive on the scene, classic con games keep returning. To paraphrase a cliché, "There are no old con games, only new victims."

In a mature bull market, the public is more susceptible to con games and deceptive practices. When people see that their neighbors seem to be getting rich and market fortunes are passing them by, it's easy to feel envious and want a piece of the action.

To be certain, there are many schemes in bear markets, too. If the economy is not doing well and your portfolio is floundering, the temptations are there as well. Investors must always be vigilant for those who want the fruits of their labor, be it the tax man or the con man. However, in a bear market, people are usually more wary of money-making schemes, especially if they lost their money because of the bear market.

Microcap fraud

Information is the investor's best tool when it comes to investing wisely. But accurate information about microcap stocks (low-priced stocks issued by the smallest of public companies) may be difficult to find. Many microcap companies do not file financial reports with the SEC, so it's hard for investors to get the facts about the company's management, products, services, and finances. When reliable information is scarce, fraudulent operators can easily spread false information about microcap companies, making profits while creating losses for unsuspecting investors.

In the battle against microcap fraud, the SEC has toughened its rules and taken actions against criminals, but it can't stop every microcap fraud. You need to be vigilant as well.

What is a microcap stock?

The term *microcap stock* applies to companies with low or "micro" capitalizations, meaning the total value of the company's stock. Microcap companies typically have limited assets. For example, in recent cases in which the SEC suspended trading in microcap stocks, the average company had only $6 million in net tangible assets, and nearly half had less than $1.25 million. Microcap stocks tend to be low-priced and trade in low volumes.

Where do microcap stocks trade?

Many microcap stocks trade in the over-the-counter (OTC) market and are quoted on OTC systems, such as the OTC Bulletin Board (OTCBB) or the pink sheets.

The OTCBB is an electronic quotation system that displays real-time quotes, last-sale prices, and volume information for many OTC securities not listed on the Nasdaq Stock Market or a national securities exchange. Brokers who subscribe to the

Moneysaver
The adage goes, "An ounce of prevention is worth a pound of cure." Check out the agencies and Web sites that alert investors and consumers to fraud. The National Fraud Information Center regularly monitors the scams that are making the rounds. Check them out at www.fraud.org.

system can use the OTCBB to look up prices or enter quotes for OTC securities.

Although the NASD oversees the OTCBB, the OTCBB is not part of the Nasdaq Stock Market. Fraudsters often claim that an OTCBB company is a Nasdaq company to mislead investors into thinking that the company is bigger than it is.

The pink sheets, named for the color of paper they've historically been printed on, are a weekly publication of a company called the National Quotation Bureau. They are updated electronically on a daily basis. Brokers who subscribe to the pink sheets can find out the names and telephone numbers of the "market makers" in various OTC stocks, meaning the brokers who commit to buying and selling those OTC securities. Unless your broker has the pink sheets or you contact the market makers directly, you'll have a difficult time finding price information for most stocks that are quoted in the pink sheets.

How are microcap stocks different from other stocks?

The biggest difference between a microcap stock and other stocks is the amount of reliable, publicly available information about the company. Larger public companies file reports with the SEC that any investor can get for free from the SEC's Web site. Professional stock analysts regularly research and write about larger public companies, and it's easy to find their stock prices in the newspaper. In contrast, information about microcap companies can be extremely difficult to find, making them more vulnerable to investment fraud schemes. The SEC has proposed new rule changes that will increase the amount of information that brokers must gather about microcap companies before quoting prices for their stocks in the OTC market.

No minimum listing standards

Companies that trade their stocks on major exchanges and in the Nasdaq Stock Market must meet minimum listing standards. For example, they must have minimum amounts of net assets and minimum numbers of shareholders. In contrast, companies on the OTCBB or the pink sheets do not have to meet any minimum standards.

Risk

Although all investments involve risk, microcap stocks are among the most risky. Many microcap companies tend to be new and have no proven track record. Some of these companies have no assets or operations. Others have products and services that are still in development or that have yet to be tested in the market.

Which companies file reports with the SEC?

In general, the federal securities laws require all but the smallest of public companies to file reports with the SEC. A company can become "public" in one of two ways: by issuing securities in an offering or transaction that's registered with the SEC, or by registering the company and its outstanding securities with the SEC. Both types of registration trigger ongoing reporting obligations, meaning that the company must file periodic reports that disclose important information to investors about its business, financial condition, and management.

This information is a treasure trove for investors: It tells you whether a company is making or losing money and why. You'll find this information in the company's quarterly reports on Form 10-Q, annual

Unofficially ...
As a simple rule of thumb, if the investment is not regularly tracked in the stock tables of *The Wall Street Journal* or *Investors Business Daily,* avoid it altogether.

reports (with audited financial statements) on Form 10-K, and periodic reports of significant events on Form 8-K.

A company must file reports with the SEC if it has 500 or more investors and $10 million or more in assets, or if it lists its securities on a major stock exchange.

If you'd like to learn more about the SEC's registration and reporting requirements, read the SEC's pamphlet "Q&A: Small Business and the SEC." Currently, only about half of the 6,500 companies whose securities are quoted on the OTCBB file reports with the SEC. In January 1999, the SEC approved a new NASD rule allowing the NASD to require that all OTCBB companies file updated financial reports with the SEC or with their banking or insurance regulators. The new rule applies immediately to companies that first appear on the OTCBB after January 4, 1999. For those companies that were on the OTCBB as of January 4, 1999, the new rule was phased in over a 12-month period beginning in July 1999. The new rule applies to all companies on the OTCBB. Companies refusing to file with the SEC or their banking or insurance regulators cannot remain on the OTCBB.

With few exceptions, companies that file reports with the SEC must do so electronically, using the SEC's EDGAR system. (EDGAR stands for electronic data gathering and retrieval.) The EDGAR database is available on the SEC's Web site at www.sec.gov. You'll find many corporate filings in the EDGAR database, including annual and quarterly reports and registration statements. Any investor can access and download this information free of charge from the SEC's Web site.

By law, the reports that companies file with the SEC must be truthful and complete, presenting the facts that investors find important in making decisions to buy, hold, or sell a security. However, the SEC cannot guarantee the accuracy of the reports that companies file. Some dishonest companies break the law and file false reports. Every year, the SEC brings enforcement actions against companies who have "cooked their books" or failed to provide important information to investors. Read SEC filings—and all other information—with a questioning and critical mind.

Smaller companies (those with less than $10 million in assets) generally do not have to file reports with the SEC. But some smaller companies, including microcap companies, may voluntarily choose to register their securities with the SEC. As described previously, companies that register with the SEC must also file quarterly, annual, and other reports.

Any company that wants to offer or sell securities to the public must either register with the SEC or meet an exemption. Here are two of the most common exemptions that many microcap companies use:

- **"Reg A" offerings**—Companies raising less than $5 million in a 12-month period may be exempt from registering their securities under a rule known as Regulation A. Instead of filing a registration statement through EDGAR, these companies need only file a printed copy of an "offering circular" with the SEC containing financial statements and other information.

- **"Reg D" offerings**—Some smaller companies offer and sell securities without registering the transaction, under an exemption known as

Regulation D. Reg D exempts from registration companies that raise less than $1 million dollars in a 12-month period. This also includes companies seeking to raise up to $5 million, as long as the companies sell only to 35 or fewer individuals or any number of "accredited investors" who must meet high net worth or income standards.

In addition, Reg D exempts some larger private offerings of securities. Although companies claiming an exemption under Reg D don't have to register or file reports with the SEC, they must still file what's known as a Form D within a few days after they first sell their securities. Form D is a brief notice that includes the names and addresses of owners and stock promoters, but little other information about the company. You may be able to find out more about Reg D companies by contacting your state securities regulator. Unless they otherwise file reports with the SEC, companies that are exempt from registration under Reg A, Reg D, or another offering exemption do not have to file reports with the SEC.

Many of the microcap companies that don't file reports with the SEC are legitimate businesses with real products or services. But the lack of reliable, readily available information about some microcap companies can open the door to fraud. It's easier for fraudsters to manipulate a stock when there's little or no information available about the company. Microcap fraud depends on spreading false information. Here's how some shady types carry out their scams:

- **Questionable press releases**—Fraudsters often issue press releases that contain exaggerations or lies about the microcap company's sales, acquisitions, revenue projections, or new products or services.

▪ **Paid promoters**—Some microcap companies pay stock promoters to recommend or "tout" the microcap stock in supposedly independent and unbiased investment newsletters, research reports, or radio and television shows. The federal securities laws require the newsletters to disclose who paid them, the amount, and the type of payment. But many fraudsters fail to do so and mislead investors into believing that they are receiving independent advice.

▪ **Internet fraud**—Fraudsters often distribute junk e-mail or "spam" over the Internet to spread false information quickly and cheaply about a microcap company to thousands of potential investors. They also use aliases on Internet bulletin boards and chat rooms to hide their identities and post messages urging investors to buy stock in microcap companies based on supposedly "inside" information about impending developments at the companies. For more information about Internet fraud and online investing, read the regular bulletins on fraud posted at the Web site www.fraud.org.

▪ **"Boiler rooms"**—Dishonest brokers set up "boiler rooms" in which a small army of high-pressure salespeople use banks of telephones to make cold calls to as many potential investors as possible. These strangers hound investors to buy "house stocks," stocks that the firm buys or sells as a market maker or has in its inventory.

Watch Out!
As the world gets smaller and national boundaries break down, more fraud is being perpetuated by international sources. Check to see if the company or organization has registered with the SEC. Also, find out what agency has enforcement authority in case there is a problem. If you can't find an agency that oversees the company or its industry, simply avoid it.

▪ **The off-shore scam**—Under a rule known as Regulation S, companies do not have to register stock they sell outside the United States to foreign or "off-shore" investors. In the typical off-shore scam, an unscrupulous microcap company sells unregistered Reg S stock at a deep discount to fraudsters posing as foreign investors. These fraudsters then sell the stock to U.S. investors at inflated prices, pocketing huge profits that they share with the microcap company insiders. The flood of unregistered stock into the United States eventually causes the price to plummet, leaving unsuspecting U.S. investors with enormous losses. The SEC recently strengthened Reg S to make these frauds harder to conduct.

If you've been asked to invest in a company but you can't find any record that the company has registered its securities with the SEC or your state, or you can't determine that it's exempt from registration, call or write your state's securities regulator or the SEC immediately with all the details. You may have come face to face with a scam.

To invest wisely and avoid investment scams, research each investment opportunity thoroughly and ask questions. These simple steps can make the difference between profits and losses:

1. Find out whether the company has registered its securities with the SEC or your state's securities regulators.

2. Make sure that you understand the company's business and its products or services.

3. Carefully read the most recent reports that the company has filed with its regulators, and

pay attention to the company's financial statements, particularly if they are not audited or not certified by an accountant. If the company does not file reports with the SEC, be sure to ask your broker for what's called the "Rule 15c2-11 file" on the company. That file will contain important information about the company.

4. Check out the people running the company with your state securities regulator, and find out if they've ever made money for investors before. Also ask whether the people running the company have had run-ins with the regulators or other investors.

5. Make sure that the broker and his or her firm are registered with the SEC and are licensed to do business in your state. Also ask your state securities regulator whether the broker and the firm have ever been disciplined or have complaints against them.

6. The SEC has the power to suspend trading in any stock for up to 10 days when it believes that information about the company is inaccurate or unreliable. Think twice before investing in a company that has been the subject of an SEC trading suspension. You'll find information about trading suspensions on the SEC's Web site.

7. Beware of brokers who pressure you to buy before you have a chance to think about and investigate the "opportunity." Dishonest brokers may try to tell you about a "once-in-a-lifetime" opportunity or one that's based on "inside" or "confidential" information. Don't

Moneysaver
Get the publication "Internet Fraud and Questions to Ask" from the SEC. You'll find these and other useful publications on the "Investor Assistance and Complaints" section of the SEC's Web site or from its toll-free publications line at 1-800-732-0330.

fall for brokers who promise spectacular profits or "guaranteed" returns. These are the hallmarks of fraud. If the deal sounds too good to be true, it probably is.

8. Many fraud schemes involve unusual transactions among individuals connected to the company. These can be unusual loans or the exchange of questionable assets for company stock that may be discussed in the footnotes of the company's annual report.

9. Be wary when a company's auditors have refused to certify the company's financial statements or if they've stated that the company may not have enough money to continue operating. Also question any change of accountants.

10. In many microcap fraud cases (especially "pump and dump" schemes), the company's officers and promoters own significant amounts of the stock. When one person or group controls most of the stock, they can more easily manipulate the stock's price at your expense. You can ask your broker or the company whether one person or group controls most of the company's stock, but if the company is the subject of a scam, you may not get an honest answer.

11. Don't deal with brokers who refuse to provide you with written information about the investments they're promoting. Never tell a cold-caller your social security number or numbers for your banking and securities accounts. And be extra wary if someone you don't know and trust recommends foreign investments.

Making sure that the companies you invest in are registered with the SEC will help you when problems do arise.

What if you run into trouble?

With public companies and brokers, investors have recourse if there are problems.

The SEC and the NASD have procedures to address the trouble that may occur. If you run into trouble—if you see unauthorized charges or trades, or other unusual transactions—act immediately. By law, you have only a limited time to take legal action.

Follow these steps to solve your problem:

1. Talk to your broker and explain the problem. What happened? Who said what, and when? Were communications clear? What did the broker tell you? Did you take notes about what your broker said at the time? If so, what do your notes say?

2. If your broker can't resolve your problem, talk to the broker's branch manager.

3. If the problem is still not resolved, put your complaint in writing and send it to the compliance department at the firm's main office. Explain your problem clearly and tell the firm how you want it resolved. Ask the compliance office to respond to you in writing within 30 days.

4. If you're still not satisfied, send a letter to your state securities regulator or to the Office of Investor Education and Assistance at the SEC along with copies of the letters you've sent already to the firm.

The address for the SEC's Office of Investor Education and Assistance is:

❝
When a man with
money meets a
man with experi-
ence, the man
with experience
gets the money,
while the man
with money
gets experience.
—Anonymous
❞

Office of Investor Education and Assistance

U.S. Securities and Exchange Commission

450 Fifth St. NW

Washington, D.C. 20549-0213

Phone: 800-SEC-0330

Fax: 202-942-9634

E-mail: help@sec.gov

Web site:

www.sec.gov/consumer/microbro.htm

Investment newsletters: analysis or advertising?

Investors may use one or more of the many excellent newsletters available to help navigate the investing world. Appendix B, "Investing Information
Resources," has an extensive listing of the better
ones out there. However, there are newsletter practices that you should be aware of.

Many investors are attracted to investing because
of the opportunity of making a large, quick profit.
With big profits comes tremendous risk. In trying to
reduce the amount of risk with any investment,
investors seek out and rely on research, information,
and professional reports. With the advent of the
information age, investors now have access to
research from across the investment world.

However, among the available information is
information that falls under the category of promotion in the form of investment letters and analysis.
The unsophisticated and even more experienced
investor will sometimes be fooled by what appears to
be a professional report, but what is in fact unadul-
terated advertisement. The wolf dressed in sheep's
clothing is none other than a paid promoter

pushing a stock under the guise of independent research called the investment newsletter.

Many investment newsletter writers are being paid to write positive reports for the companies that have paid them. In a world where many investors have to rely on professional reports to make important investment decisions, such biased and paid newsletters can lead the unwary down a path of misfortune.

Section 17(b) of the Securities Act of 1993 makes it unlawful for any person to publish or circulate any letter, investment service, or communication that describes a security without disclosing that the publisher is receiving compensation and the amount of such compensation. The disclosure is required not only when the publisher is promoting the stock positively, but also when he or she is merely describing or discussing the stock.

You as the investor should be on the lookout for statements in newsletters that fail to fully disclose any compensation or disclose compensation paid to the publisher by the company that he or she is recommending.

Where can you find the publisher's disclosure?

You will find the publisher's disclosure in the disclaimer section of the newsletter. When reading any disclaimer, be mindful that compensation is given in different ways. Compensation doesn't only mean the payment of money, but can include the following:

- The issuance of shares to the publisher or any other compensation that ultimately benefits the publisher for publishing the newsletter recommendation

- The hiring of the publisher as consultants or advisers

- The publisher purchasing shares of the company before its recommendation and the sale of such stock immediately after the stock recommendation

Don't believe everything you read in investment newsletters. Writers of many newsletters are paid by the companies they are writing about. Check the disclaimers at the end of the newsletters to determine whether they are being paid by the company they are recommending.

Investment newsletter red flags

The following statements and phrases should be red flags when reading investment newsletters. You must be vigilant for conflicts of interest whenever a newsletter publisher is overly positive about a specific company's stock.

> "The publisher may from time to time have a position in the securities mentioned."

> "The publisher has been retained as an adviser."

> "The publisher has been retained to provide consulting services."

> "The publisher will therefore benefit from any increase in share price as to the stock of any company advertising herein which is held by the publisher."

> "Members of the organization, its officers, directors, employees, and associated individuals may have positions in investments referred to in this newsletter and may add or dispose of the same."

"The publisher may provide investment banking services."

"The publisher reserves the right to buy or sell stock in any featured company."

"The publisher may receive compensation for the efforts in presentation and dissemination of information on companies featured on our Web site and within our newsletters."

"We receive fees from the companies we write about in our newsletter."

"The publisher will trade in these positions prior to stock pick announcement, and its administrators, representatives, or employees reserve the right to liquidate or sell all or portions of these positions immediately after the stock pick announcement in our newsletter."

"We may be paid a fee by the company referred to in this newsletter."

The problem with all these disclaimers is that they hint at the fact that they have received compensation directly or indirectly, but they never indicate the amount of the compensation, which is unlawful. If you come across any such statements, be aware that the publisher is not giving an impartial professional analysis of the company that he or she is recommending. The publisher is being compensated to promote the stock.

What to do? When you see an investment newsletter remember these helpful hints:

▪ Read the investment newsletter carefully, and try to locate the disclaimer or the publisher's disclosure statement, which might not be in its disclaimer page. Some publishers will give blanket disclosures that are not connected to any one feature in a newsletter but that apply on the whole or to some of the features.

- Be leery of any newsletter that hides the required disclosure in small print.

- Be wary of any disclosure that is vague or confusing.

- Be suspicious of any newsletter or recommendation that you find in your e-mail box.

- Be cautious of any small-cap company that is talked about in message boards or chat rooms. Promoters will try to entice inexperienced investors to buy worthless microcap stocks by talking to each other on message boards, giving the impression that they don't know each other when in fact that are conspiring to excite the market.

- Always do your own research.

- Always check the SEC filings to determine whether there have been any enforcement actions or complaints against the company.

- Check out whether the publisher has been in trouble with the SEC or a state regulator or with NASD regulation.

Other information sources: buying money-making secrets

There will always be opportunities to make money, no matter how good or bad the economy is. But as long as there are people who want to gain easy money, there will be fraud.

Sometimes the fraud doesn't come in a bad investment. Sometimes it comes in expensive information. The Bureau of Consumer Protection for the Federal Trade Commission explains that every year thousands of complaints are received about "business opportunity" programs advertised in infomercials, in newspapers, on the radio, and on the Internet. In virtually all instances, the spokespeople promise to train you in whatever they say made them rich: direct marketing, real estate investing, or some other high-stakes business. If you take the bait on the low-priced hook, they'll often try to sell you in with their expensive, advanced products or seminars.

Companies that sell investment strategies are one source of complaints. Wade Cook Financial Corporation (WCFC) is one of them. Wade Cook says he went from driving a cab to earning tens of thousands of dollars a day using the stock strategies that he teaches in his programs. Testimonials from students claim successes as high as $3,000 a day. At a free or low-cost introductory seminar, attendees are told that to make big bucks, they can attend a two-day $5,695 "Wall Street Workshop." When they get there, they are told that to make really big money, they should attend advanced seminars and purchase tapes and videos.

Is Cook's investment advice good? Authorities have yet to find a student who made any money. One student, a Florida businessman, says he lost $13,000 applying Cooks strategies. Prospective students might be more skeptical of Cooks guidance if they knew that in 1997, although his company had more than $60 million in net revenues from its seminar operations, it actually lost $806,000 on trading securities. A spokesman for WCFC responds that the company made $837,000 trading stocks in 1998. In other words, it took two years of trading in a bull market for the company to just about break even in an area where it boasts expertise.

Students might be even more wary if they knew that state and federal law enforcement agencies have a long record of dealing with Cook. In early 2000, Cook and several of his companies face a civil lawsuit in California for fraud, misrepresentation, false advertising, and other offenses. In Texas, Cook and his seminar subsidiary have been sued for violations of consumer-protection laws. They deny engaging in any unlawful activity. In spite of the legal problems, Cook continues to conduct his national seminars.

Classic scams

Many stock-market related scams that have appeared throughout the years are based on a few classic con games. We'll touch on some of those here.

Pump and dump classic

For those who are unaware of the classic pump and dump scam, we thought a quick primer would be in order. Don't be surprised if the following scam sounds like an experience you've had with a penny stock.

Phase 1: preconditions

For purposes of this scam, you need a worthless stock with a tight float and that is thinly traded. Small or microcap companies are needed as a precondition to this scam. "Tight float" means that most of the stocks are held by insiders and promoters, not by the general public. This is because it is much easier to manipulate the price of the stock when there are fewer stocks held by the general public because less buying of stock is needed to increase the price.

Phase 2: the front load

The manipulator buys stock of an otherwise worthless stock at low prices. This sets the stage for the manipulator to make money when the stock price elevates.

Phase 3: behind-the-scenes promotion

The manipulator will now start a promotional campaign to create interest in the stock. This is done in a number of ways. Promoters use advertising campaigns, cold calls, newsletters, newsgroups, message boards, chat rooms, e-mails, and any other method to promote the stock. The information they use is usually rumor, not fact. They try to entice the average investor with visions of making the big score, quickly and without much risk. The promoters will tour investor road shows to drum up excitement. Essentially, the promoter is playing on the investors' strings of greed to try to make the investors feel that she or he can't miss the next great investment play. With the advent of the Internet, today's promoter has a larger array of tools to mislead the public than in past years.

Phase 4: the pump

Promoters now will attempt to inflate the price of a stock. This is achieved in either one of two ways or a combination. Because the stock is thinly traded, promoters and insiders can quietly raise the price by buying up the stock. In other words, instead of putting bid offers at lower prices, they take the ask bids out and go up the price ladder. Because there is little public float, it doesn't take a lot of buying to get the price up.

The second method is to get the price up on promotion. With little public float, a little bit of buying will result in the price elevating.

Phase 5: the dump

When the price is at a sufficient level, the promoters sell their own stock during the promotion campaign to unsuspecting buyers.

Phase 6: the loss

When the promoters have sold their entire position, the promotional campaign stops. With no new buying coming in, the price of the stock starts to fall. With no new "positive news," there is no reason for new buyers to come into the market. At some point, the existing shareholders figure out that the stock is going nowhere and sell at whatever price necessary to recover any amount of their original investment. The stock price then spirals down or, in most cases, drifts down to oblivion with investors losing a great deal of money.

Some investors try to outsmart the promoter by trying to get in early enough to buy the target stock at low prices and make money, like the promoter, when the price rises. It is very difficult to time the market, however, because the investor will not know at what stage the promotion campaign has stopped.

Bottom line: If you are an unsophisticated investor, stick to the more senior, larger-cap securities that there is more credible information about.

To avoid being the victim of the pump and dump, keep the following in mind:

- Beware of unsolicited e-mail or telephone calls. Deal only with people you know. If you have any questions about a penny stock, call your broker, who can assist you in learning more about a stock.

- Don't make hasty decisions after speaking with an investment promoter or after hearing a tip.

- Don't believe any promise of great profits at no risk. No investment can deliver guaranteed profits at no risk.

- Don't believe in claims of inside information.

- Do your own research. Look at any of the company's recent press releases, and balance the company's views with those of analysts and SEC reports.

- Know what your tolerance to risk is and how much you are willing to invest and lose. If you invest in any penny stock or obscure company, be prepared to lose the entire investment amount.

- Be leery of what you see posted in newsgroups, in chat rooms, on message boards, and in your e-mail box. The promoter will try to use any method of communication to defraud investors.

Short and distort

"Short and distort" is the less familiar cousin to pump and dump. The classic pump and dump is a well known scam used by promoters to try to make unsuspecting investors part with their money. What the investor does not hear that much about is the stock scam of making money off the fall of a stock price.

Around the investment water cooler, this is sometimes referred to as the short and distort. The short refers to short selling—that is, the selling of stock by an investor who does not own the stock that he or she is selling.

These are the phases of the short and distort:

- **Phase 1: research**—The short and distort player will look for stocks that might be overvalued.

Bright Idea
If anyone contacts you about a great investment, tell them you're busy but would be happy to call them back. Get the company name and phone number. Legitimate firms have no problem with people contacting them. Scam operators will make excuses about why you won't be able to reach them.

- **Phase 2: the short sell**—When there is a bit of activity on a stock due to news, the short seller comes into the market and sells short (sells stock that he or she doesn't own).

- **Phase 3: the rumor mill**—Unlike the scamster in the pump and dump, the scamster will now engage in a campaign to undermine the worth of the stock by spreading rumor. This can be done by negative posts to message boards, chat rooms, newsgroups, issuance of newsletters recommending the sale of the stock, and so on. This plan of distortion is aimed at enticing investors to dump their stock with the prime objective of driving the price down. Instead of excitement, the distorted tries to stimulate fear.

- **Phase 4: the cover**—Now that the price is falling, the distorter must buy stock to cover his or her position. The distorter buys the stock at a discount, thereby making his profit. To create a selling frenzy, which the distorter must do to buy enough stock to cover his position and not drive the price up in the interim (thereby minimizing his profits), he will create the impression that there is a great deal of selling taking place. He will do this by having his friends and brokers cross stock to each other, giving the impression of large volume.

- **Phase 5: the loss**—The buyer who initially bought the stock at elevated prices sold it at lower prices on the mistaken belief that the stock was worthless based on the distortion campaign.

There are variations to the short and distort scam. A promoter of a worthless stock could artificially inflate a stock price of a thinly traded stock and then promote the stock and sell short. Then without news, the stock would drop back down to original levels, at which point the promoter covers his position at a profit.

The promoter could pump and dump and then short and distort and every year to continue the cycle. The underlying theme is stock manipulation by a person who is ultimately trying to make money off the backs of unsuspecting investors. What can you do?

If you purchase any stock and you see that it is falling, don't panic. Check the fundamentals of the stock; if nothing has changed, there might not be a reason to sell. Call your broker for more information as to why the stock might be falling.

Boiler room antics

With the recent bull market and the increase in the number of retail customers investing in stocks, boiler room operators are back at work trying to defraud investors.

Boiler room operators are salespeople who sit in one room making cold calls to potential investors trying to pressure them into purchasing worthless investments. They are usually armed with sophisticated sales scripts and high-pressure sales techniques used to convince their victims to purchase dubious investments. Their victims are usually individuals with money: businesspeople, professionals, and retirees.

Boiler room operators will try to sell penny or microcap stocks (addressed earlier in the chapter), foreign exchange investments, risky initial public offerings (IPOs), and house stocks.

Foreign exchange investments

Scam artists try to solicit money for investments in exchange instruments traded in foreign markets during periods of financial crisis in such markets. The promoter tries to convince its callers that certain foreign exchange instruments are good investments that are currently undervalued because of a crisis, which presents a tremendous buying opportunity. The investments are usually fictitious.

Risky initial public offerings (IPOs)

Companies that are initially becoming publicly traded companies usually do an initial public offering to raise money. Although many of such offerings are worthwhile investments, many are risky ventures. The boiler room operator will tend to downplay or neglect to tell the investor the negative aspects to ensure that the investor will invest. Many boiler room operators will try to sell IPOs that are underwritten by the investment firm they work for. "Underwritten" means that the investment firm either has been hired as an agent to find buyers for the initial offering or has purchased all or some of the initial offering itself and is trying to resell it to the public, usually at a profit. Accordingly, these boiler room operators are in a conflict of interest because they are looking out for the interest of their company, not of their clients.

House stocks

House stocks are stocks that an investment firm has purchased to resell at a profit. Brokers of these house stocks will try to manipulate the market by buying stock of thinly traded companies. They will pump these stock prices up to higher prices and then sell them to their clients at a profit. The clients will find that there are no other buyers to buy their stocks. Consequently, the stock price will fall, leaving many unsuspecting investors with worthless stock.

Other investment scams

There are signs you can always look out for before you invest in a company that is being improperly promoted:

- Be on the lookout for small-cap companies that pay a generous executive salary or compensation package. This is a telltale sign that any money that the company is raising is going into the pockets of insiders, not into the company itself.

- Be leery of small cap companies that are investing in projects unrelated to their businesses. Small-cap companies should not be changing their businesses when they have been created to pursue their original line of business.

- Beware of mining companies that change their focus, especially after another company has announced a large discovery. For example, you will have noticed that in the early 1990s, diamond stocks were very popular. Mining companies that were looking for gold suddenly started hinting in their news releases that they also had properties that could contain diamonds. This was an effort to fool investors into believing that their companies could be one that would make the next big diamond find.

- Beware of any stock that you learn about on in a chat room, in a newsgroup, or through e-mail. Unscrupulous operators may run scams in a chat room. A typical chat room conversation might run as follows:

Person A: "I just heard about a new company that a friend heard about. Had a name like Scamtech."

Person B: "Yeah I heard of that company. I think its name is Scamtech, and it is about to release new information on a purchase of a claim in Colombia. I called my broker to get more information for me."

Person C: "The company Scamtech, according to my broker, is a company that is about to explode. It will be announcing news tomorrow; according to my broker, the stock is going to fly."

This dialogue is a typical scam that tries to make people think that three unrelated people have heard about the same company.

Person C has tried to legitimize the company by referring to his broker. The aim of the dialogue is to create excitement relating to a worthless company so that insiders and promoters can sell their stock at inflated prices.

If you hear of any scams in respect of such promoters or companies and you want others to know about them, submit a complaint to the NASD at www.nasdr.com or contact appropriate agencies at the end of this chapter.

Where to turn for assistance

Finding information and assistance is not difficult. Get familiar with the main agencies that cover the world of investing. For investors, the top enforcement agency is the Securities and Exchange Commission (SEC).

The Securities and Exchange Commission (SEC)

The SEC has great resources available at its Web site for you to take advantage of. Some of the main services are these:

- **EDGAR filings**—Most public companies have reports that are available and easily searchable at the Web site. Do your homework here before you invest.

- **Reports on problem companies**—The SEC regularly reports on companies that have run afoul of securities laws.

- **Consumer and investor information**—Important information on investing and bulletins on the latest scams and industry developments are regularly presented.

- **Enforcement division**—The SEC's Division of Enforcement is charged with enforcing the federal securities laws.

To find out more, contact the SEC at:

SEC Division of Enforcement
Enforcement Complaint Center
450 Fifth St. NW
Washington, D.C. 20549-0710
Phone: 202-942-7040, 1-800-732-0330
Fax: 202-942-9570
E-mail: enforcement@sec.gov
Web site: www.sec.gov

The National Association of Securities Dealers

For help in carrying out its work, the SEC delegates significant regulatory authority to a number of private, member-owned and member-operated organizations. The National Association of Securities Dealers, Inc. (NASD) conducts its regulatory

Timesaver
Visit the NASD's regulatory Web site, www.nasdr.com, for help in looking up records to see if a particular broker has had problems such as disciplinary procedures or penalties.

activities through an independent subsidiary, NASD Regulation, Inc. The NASD also owns and operates the Nasdaq Stock Market.

The NASD's responsibilities include establishing rules governing its broker/dealer members' business conduct; setting qualification standards for securities industry professionals; examining members for their financial and operational condition, as well as their compliance with appropriate rules and regulations; investigating alleged violations of securities laws and the NASD's own rules; disciplining violations of securities laws; disciplining violations of applicable rules and regulations and NASD rules; and responding to inquiries and complaints from investors and members.

You can contact the NASD at:

National Association of Securities
Dealers, Inc.
The Nasdaq Stock Market
1735 K St. NW
Washington, D.C. 20006-1500
Phone: 301-590-6500
Web site: www.nasd.com

Investor protection resources

Fortunately, a wealth of information is just a few clicks away. Check out the following Web sites:

The Fraud Bureau
www.fraudbureau.com

Help 2 Go
www.help2go.com

Investors' Law Center, P.A.
www.investoraid.com

Investors' Protection
www.investorprotection.org

The National Consumer League's National Fraud Information Center and Internet Fraud Watch

www.fraud.org

Other agencies and organizations include these:

American Stock Exchange
86 Trinity Place
New York, NY 10006-1881
Phone: 212-306-1391

Boston Stock Exchange
One Boston Place
Boston, MA 02108
Phone: 617-723-9500

Chicago Board Options Exchange
400 S. LaSalle St.
Chicago, IL 60605
Phone: 312-786-7705

Chicago Stock Exchange
440 S. LaSalle St.
Chicago, IL 60605
Phone: 312-663-2222

Cincinnati Stock Exchange
36 E. Fourth St., Suite 906
Cincinnati, OH 45202
Phone: 312-786-8898

Federal Trade Commission
Division of Service Industry Practices
Washington, D.C. 20580
Phone: 202-326-2222

Municipal Securities Rulemaking Board
1818 N St. NW
Suite 800
Washington, D.C. 20036-2491
Phone: 202-223-9347

Moneysaver
A great source of information about investing and many other consumer topics is the 1998–1999 *Consumer's Resource Handbook* available for free by writing to CRH, Consumer Information Center, Pueblo, CO 81009. This resource is also available online at www.pueblo. gsa.gov/crh/ respref.htm.

National Association of Securities Arbitration Counselors
807 Tahoe Blvd.
Incline Village, NV 89451
Phone: 877-466-2722
Fax: 775-831-6732
E-mail: info@nasac.com
Web site: www.nasac.com
Comments: NASAC offers services for victimized investors who have lost money in the stock market resulting from fraud and other stockbroker abuses.

New York Stock Exchange
20 Broad St.
22nd Floor
New York, NY 10006
Phone: 212-656-3000

North American Securities Administrators Association, Inc.
One Massachusetts Ave., NW
Suite 310
Washington, DC 20001
Phone: 202-737-0900
Web site: www.nasaa.org
Comments: NASAA can provide you with the telephone number of your state securities regulator.

Pacific Stock Exchange
301 Pine St.
San Francisco, CA 94104
Phone: 415-393-4000

Philadelphia Stock Exchange
1900 Market St.
Philadelphia, PA 19103
Phone: 215-496-5000

Being a successful stockpicker takes time, effort, and your hard-earned money. You may not be able to keep your money away from relatives or the IRS, but fraud is avoidable. Before you invest your money, look at several sources of information and check it out with sources such as the SEC if you are uncertain.

Just the facts

- Stay away from obscure companies that have little public information available for investors.
- Stay informed about classic con games.
- Regularly visit the SEC and NASD Web sites to learn about new scams and about any companies or brokers that have been penalized or investigated.
- Whatever investment areas you get involved with, find out what agencies and organizations have legal and investigative power.
- Always go with what you know best. When you invest in areas in which you are a neophyte, there is greater risk either from fraud or from mistakes in judgment.

Stock Exchanges

To trade stock or to find more information on stocks and other securities, both in the United States and in international markets, check out the stock exchanges by visiting their Web sites. Many even offer tutorials, stock selection information, and much more.

Domestic stock exchanges

American Stock Exchange
www.amex.com/

Arizona Stock Exchange
www.azx.com

Boston Stock Exchange
www.bostonstock.com/

Chicago Stock Exchange
http://chicagostockex.com

Nasdaq
www.nasdaq.com/

New York Stock Exchange
www.nyse.com/

OTC Bulletin Board
www.otcbb.com/

Pacific Stock Exchange
www.pacificex.com/

Philadelphia Stock Exchange
www.phlx.com

Foreign stock exchanges

Amman Financial Market
http://accessme.com/AFM/

Argentina
(Argentine Stock Exchange System)
Bolsa de Comercio de Buenos Aires
www.bcba.sba.com.ar

Argentina
Bolsanet
www.bolsanet.sba.com.ar

Australian Stock Exchange
www.asx.com.au

Austria
Vienna Stock Exchange
http://apollo.wu-wien.ac.at

Bahrain Stock Exchange
www.bahrainstock.com

Belgium
Brussels Stock Exchange
www.tijd.be/tijd/beurs/

Bermuda Stock Exchange
www.bsx.com/

Bolivia
Bolsa Boliviana de Valores
http://bolsa-valores-bolivia.com/index.html

Brazil
Bolsa de Valores de Sao Paulo
www.bovespa.com.br

Brazil (Rio de Janeiro Stock Exchange)
Bolsa de Valores do Rio de Janeiro
www.bvrj.com.br

Bulgarian Stock Exchange
www.online.bg/bse

Canada
Alberta Stock Exchange
www.alberta.net/

Canada
Montreal Stock Exchange
www.me.org/

Canada
Toronto Stock Exchange
www.tse.com

Canada
Vancouver Stock Exchange
www.vse.com/

Canada
Winnipeg Stock Exchange
www.wse.ca

Cayman Islands Stock Exchange
www.csx.com.ky

Chile
Bolsa Electronica de Chile
www.bolchile.cl/

Chile
Bolsa de Comercio de Santiago
www.bolsantiago.cl/

Colombia
Bolsa de Bogota
www.bolsabogota.com.co/

Croatia
Zagreb Stock Exchange
www.zse.hr/

Cuba
Cuba Stock Exchange
www.cybercuba.com

Cyprus Stock Exchange
www.cse.com.cy/

Czechoslovakia
Prague Stock Exchange
www.pse.cz/

Denmark
Copenhagen Stock Exchange
www.xcse.dk

Ecuador
Bolsa de Valores de Guayaqui
www4.bvg.fin.ec/

Ecuador
Bolsa de Valores de Quito
www.ccbvq.com

Egypt
Egyptian Stock Exchanges
www.egyptse.com/

Estonia
Tallinn Stock Exchange
www.tse.ee

European Association of Securities Dealers
Automated Quotation
www.easdaq.be

Finland
Helsinki Stock Exchange
www.hse.fi

France
Bourse de Paris
www.bourse-de-paris.fr/

Germany
(Frankfurt Stock Exchange)
Gruppe Deutsche Brse
www.exchange.de

Ghana Stock Exchange
www.ghana.com/stockex/

Greece
Athens Stock Exchange
www.ase.gr/

Hong Kong Stock Exchange
www.sehk.com.hk

Hungary
Budapest Stock Exchange
www.fornax.hu/fmon/

India
Bangalore Stock Exchange Limited
http://206.252.12.4/bgse/

National Stock Exchange of India
www.nseindia.com./

India
Bombay Stock Exchange
www.bseindia.com/

Indonesia
Jakarta Stock Exchange
www.jsx.co.id/

Iran
Tehran Stock Exchange
www.neda.net/tse/

Italy
(Italian Stock Exchange)
La Borsa Valori Italiana
www.borsaitalia.it

Israel
Tel Aviv Stock Exchange
www.tase.co.il/

Jamaica Stock Exchange
www.jamstockex.com/

Japan
Tokyo Stock Exchange
www.tse.or.jp/

Karachi Stock Exchange
www.kse.org/

Kuala Lumpur Stock Exchange
www.klse.com.my/

Latvia
Riga Stock Exchange
www.rfb.lv/

Lebanon
Beirut Stock Exchange
www.bse.com.lb

Lithuania
National Stock Exchange of Lithuania
www.nse.lt

Luxembourg Stock Exchange
www.bourse.lu/

Le Nouveau March
www.nouveau-marche.fr/bourse

Macedonian Stock Exchange
www.mse.org.mk

Mauritius
Stock Exchange of Mauritius
http://lynx.intnet.mu/semdex/

Mexico
Bolsa Mexicana de Valores
www.bmv.com.mx

Moldova Stock Exchange
www.moldse.com

Nagoya Stock Exchange
www.iijnet.or.jp/nse-jp

Namibian Stock Exchange
www.nse.com.na/

Netherlands
Amsterdam Stock Exchange
www.aex.nl

New Zealand Stock Exchange
www.nzse.co.nz

Nicaragua
Bolsa de Valores de Nicaragua
http://bolsanic.com

Norway
Oslo Stock Exchange
www.nettvik.no/finansen/

Panama
Bolsa de Valores de Panama
www.urraca.com/bvp

Peru
Bolsa de Valores de Lima
www.bvl.com.pe/

Poland
Warsaw Stock Exchange
www.atm.com.pl

Portugal
Lisbon Stock Exchange
www.bvl.pt/

Romania
Bucharest Stock Exchange
www.delos.ro/bse/

Russia
International Stock Exchange
Russian Exchange
www.re.ru

Russia
South Urals Stock Exchange
http://195.54.24.1

Russia
St. Petersburg Stock Exchange
http://bsd.lse.spb.su/

Singapore Stock Exchange
www.ses.com.sg/

Slovenia
Ljubljana Stock Exchange
www.ljse.si/

South Africa
Johannesburg Stock Exchange
www.jse.co.za

South Korea
Korea Stock Exchange
www.kse.or.kr/

Spain (Barcelona Stock Exchange)
Bolsa de Barcelona
www.borsabcn.es/

Spain (Madrid Stock Exchange)
Bolsa de Madrid
www.bolsamadrid.es/

Sri Lanka
Colombo Stock Exchange
www.lanka.net/

Sweden
Stockholm Stock Exchange
www.xsse.se/

Switzerland
Geneva Stock Exchange
www.bourse.ch/

Taiwan Stock Exchange
www.tse.com.tw/

Thailand
Stock Exchange of Thailand
www.set.or.th/

Turkey
Istanbul Stock Exchange
www.ise.org

Ukraine
The Baltic Exchange
www.balticexchange.co.uk

Ukraine Stock Exchange
www.ifs.kiev.ua/

United Kingdom
London Stock Exchange
www.londonstockex.co.uk/

Venezuela
Venezuela Electronic Stock Exchange
www.venezuelastock.com

Venezuela
Bolsa de Valores de Caracas
www.caracasstock.com/

Yugoslavia
(see Croatia, Slovenia)

Zambia
Lusaka Stock Exchange
www.luse.co.zm/

Zambia Stock Exchange
http://mbendi.co.za/exza.htm

Investing Information Resources

Internet stock investing Web sites

The following is a comprehensive list of stock-market related Web sites. Be aware of some precautions with these Web sites and resources: There are no guarantees, expressly or implied, regarding the integrity and accuracy of these Web sites. Don't take as gospel information or views from any single source in this list (or from any place in this book). Instead, use these resources as starting points for your own research to make an informed judgment.

Value investing

Active Investment Research
www.stockresearch.com/

Ben Graham Stockpiles
www.erols.com/rjshome/stockpiles/

Global Penny Stocks
www.pennystock.com/

Graham and Doddsville Revisited
http://web.idirect.com

Investorama
www.investorama.com/

Today's Value Investor
www.tvinvestor.com/

Value Investing Forum
http://worthnet.com

Technical analysis

Analysts Online
www.analystsonline.com

Applied Derivatives Trading
www.adtrading.com

Ask Research
www.askresearch.com

BarChart.com
www.Barchart.com

Big Charts
www.bigcharts.com

ClearStation
www.clearstation.com

Elliott Wave Theorist
www.elliottwave.com

InvestorTech
www.easystock.com

The Nasdaq Web page
www.nasdaq.com

Pattern Traders
www.patterntrader.com

Quote.com
www.quote.com/

Standard and Poor's Index Services
www.spglobal.com/ssindexmain500.html

StockTables.com
www.stocktables.com

IPOs

IPO Central
www.ipocentral.com

IPO Maven
www.ipomaven.com/

IPO Monitor
www.ipomonitor.com/

International stock investing

4StockMarket
www.4stockmarket.com

Wall Street City
www.wallstreetcity.com/international/

World Flash
www.worldflash.com

General stock market information

Active Traders Net
http://activetraders.net

Bear Tracker
www.beartracker.com

Bloomberg
www.bloomberg.com

Briefing.com
www.briefing.com/index.htm

Business Week
www.businessweek.com/

CBS Market Watch
http://cbs.marketwatch.com

CNNfn
www.cnnfn.com

The Daily Rocket
www.dailyrocket.com/index.stm

SEC and EDGAR sites

Disclosure Corporate Snapshot
www.disclosure-investor.com

Disclosure Filings
www.disclosure-investor.com/

EDGAR Online
www.edgar-online.com/

FreeEDGAR Summary & Filings
www.freeedgar.com/

Securities & Exchange Commission
www.sec.gov

Company research and news

ABC News.com Business Profile
http://webapp.abcnews.com

Hoovers Capsule
www.hoovers.com/

INVESTools Research and Newsletters
www.investools.com/

Investors Research Network
www.irn.net/company/

Motley Fool
http://quote.fool.com/

NASDAQ Company Report
www.nasdaq.com/

News.com Investor Report
www.news.com/Investor/

Insider holdings

Insider Trader
www.insidertrader.com/

10 K Wizard
www.10kwizard.com

Company news

Companies Online
www.companiesonline.com

DLJ Direct News
www.dljdirect.com

News Alert Quotes & News
www.newsalert.com/free/

Quote.Com News
http://fast.quote.com

Reuters MoneyNet News
www.moneynet.com

The Street.com Profile
www.thestreet.com

Ticker Symbol
www.secapl.com

Wright Investors Service Company Analysis
http://profiles.wisi.com

Yahoo! Company Profile
http://biz.yahoo.com

Stock quotes

bullsession.com
www.bullsession.com/

CNNfn Quote Search
http://cnnfn.com/markets/quotes.html

DBC Online
www2.dbc.com

free realtime.com
www.freerealtime.com/

Quote Central
www.quotecentral.com/

Newsletters

The following is a list of some of the popular newsletters that have given quality information on stock investing and related topics. Most are happy to give you a no-risk trial subscription. Contact the individual publications for updated information on rates, services, and so on.

Blue Chip Growth Letter
Publisher: Phillips International, Inc.
Phone: 1-800-211-8565, 301-340-2100
Web site: www.navellier.com
Comments: Covers all the top 600–700 stocks (by market size), including the S&P 500, and selects the top 5 percent that Wall Street will buy next.
Issue frequency: Monthly
Subscription price: Individual $249; foreign $250

Bob Nurock's Advisory/Private Elves Report
Publisher: Investor's Analysis, Inc.
Phone: 505-820-2737
Comments: Provides comprehensive stock market strategy and specific investment ideas.
Issue frequency: Semiweekly
Subscription price: Individual $497

Dessauer's Journal of Financial Markets
Publisher: Limmat Pubs, Inc.
Phone: 508-255-1651

Web site: www.dessauersfinancialworld.com
Comments: Covers U.S. stock market, international markets, and the gold market.
Issue frequency: Semimonthly
Subscription price: Individual $195

Doug Casey's International Speculator
Publisher: Agora, Inc.
Phone: 410-234-0691
Web site: www.dougcasey.com
Comments: Casey has a long record of successful stock investing. He is especially keen on how international politics can affect investments. His specialty is precious metals mining stocks.
Issue frequency: Monthly
Subscription price: Individual $199

Dow Theory Letters
Publisher: Dow Theory Letters, Inc.
Phone: 619-454-0481
Fax: 619-454-1265
Comments: Contains analyses of market trends under the Dow Theory, plus numerous technical studies.
Issue frequency: Biweekly
Subscription price: Individual and Canadian $250; foreign $276

Elliott Wave Theorist
Publisher: Elliott Wave International
Phone: 1-800-336-1618, 770-536-0309
Web site: www.elliottwave.com
Comments: Analyzes Elliott Wave patterns, mathematical relationships, cycles of stocks and bonds, interest rates, and precious metals.

Issue frequency: Monthly
Subscription price: Individual $233; foreign
$250

Fleet Street Letter

Publisher: Agora, Inc.
Phone: 1-800-433-1528
Web site: www.fleetstreetletter.com
Comments: Covers investing in stocks using a
value-oriented approach.
Issue frequency: Monthly
Subscription price: Individual $109

Jack Adamo's Inside Track

Publisher: Phillips Publishing, Inc.
Phone: 301-340-2100
Web site: http://adamoinsidetrack.com
Comments: Specializes in investing in stocks
by analyzing insider trading.
Issue frequency: Monthly
Subscription price: Individual $295

Mark Skousen's Forecasts and Strategies

Publisher: Phillips International, Inc.
Phone: 1-800-211-7662
Web site: www.forecasts-strategies.com
Comments: Mark Skousen, a former CIA
economist with a Ph.D., in economics, uses
his knowledge of the Austrian school of eco-
nomics for profitable stock investing.
Issue frequency: Monthly
Subscription price: Individual $99.95

Personal Finance

Publisher: KCI Communications, Inc.
Web site: www.pfnewsletter.com
Comments: Is a highly rated financial newslet-
ter that gives specific recommendations in

stocks and other investment vehicles.
Issue frequency: Monthly
Subscription price: $69

The Prudent Speculator
Publisher: Al Frank Asset Management, Inc.
Phone: 1-800-258-7786, 714-497-7657
Fax: 714-497-7658
Comments: Gives a market commentary and investment strategies, with fundamental stock selections. Reports trades in Al Frank's actual portfolio; lists current recommendations.
Issue frequency: Monthly
Subscription price: Individual and Canadian $175; foreign $199

Safe Money Report
Publisher: Weiss Research, Inc.
Phone: 1-800-236-0407
Web site: www.martinweiss.com
Comments: Rates stocks based on risk and financial strength of individual companies. Also provides financial safety ratings for insurance companies, HMOs, and banks.
Issue frequency: Monthly
Subscription price: Individual $148

This above list is by no means comprehensive because there are many excellent publications. To find more financial newsletters, visit the following Web sites:

Newsletter Access
www.newsletteraccess.com

Oxbridge Communication's Media Finder
www.mediafinder.com

Super Money Links
www.supermoneylinks.com

Books

Achelis, Steven B. *Technical Analysis from A to Z*. Chicago: Probus Publishing, 1995.

Arms, Richard W. *Volume Cycles in the Stock Market: Market Timing Through Equivolume Charting*. Homewood, IL: Dow Jones Irwin, 1983.

Colby, Robert W., and Thomas A. Meyers. *The Encyclopedia of Technical Market Indicators*. Homewood, IL: Down Jones-Irwin, 1988.

Edwards, Robert D., and John Magee. *Technical Analysis of Stock Trends*, 6th ed. New York: Institute of Finance, 1992.

Fosback, Norman G. *Stock Market Logic*. Chicago: Dearborn Financial Publishing, Inc., 1992.

Frost, Robert J., and Robert R. Prechter. *Elliott Wave Principle: Key to Stock Market Behavior*, 7th ed. Gainesville, GA: New Classics Library, 1995.

Granville, Joseph. *New Strategy of Daily Stock Market Timing for Maximum Profits*. Chicago: Dearborn Financial Publishing, Inc., 1992.

Hurst, J.M. *The Profit Magic of Stock Transaction Timing*. Englewood Cliffs, NJ: Prentice Hall, 1970.

Pring, Martin J. *Technical Analysis Explained*, 3rd ed. New York: McGraw Hill, 1991.

Stock Brokers

Accutrade
Phone: 1-800-494-8939
Web site: www.Accutrade.com

Online trades: $29.95 for up to 1,000 shares, and then add 2 cents per share
Broker-assisted trades: $39 and up
Online account minimum: $5,000

Ameritrade
Phone: 1-800-669-3900
Web site: www.Ameritrade.com
Online trades: $8 for trades, $13 for limit and stop orders; touch-tone and broker assisted trades cost more
Online account minimum: $2,000

Datek
Phone: 1-888-463-2835
Web site: www.datek.com
Online trades: $9.99
Broker-assisted trades: $25 and up
Online account minimum: $2,000

Discover Direct (Lombard)
Phone: 1-800-584-6837
Web site: www.lombard.com
Online trades: Market orders $14.95; limit orders $19.95
Broker-assisted trades: $34
Online account minimum: $2,000

DLJ Direct (formerly PCFN)
Phone: 1-800-825-5723
Web site: www.DLJdirect.com
Online trades: $20 for up to 1,000 shares, and then add 2 cents per share
Online account minimum: No account minimum

ETrade
Phone: 1-800-786-2575
Web site: www.etrade.com

Online trades: $14.95 for listed market orders; $19.95 for limit and unlisted orders
Broker-assisted trades: Additional $15
Online account minimum: $1,000

Fidelity Web Xpress
Phone: 1-800-544-3063
Web site: www.fidelity.com
Online trades: Market orders $19.95 for up to 1,000 shares, and then 3 cents per share up to 5,000 shares; for orders over 5,000 shares, add 2 cents for each share above 1,000. A $3 premium is charged for limit and stop orders. Rates are $5 lower for $20,000 accounts with more than 36 trades per year.
Online account minimum: $5,000

NDB Online—National Discount Brokers
Phone: 1-800-888-3999
Web site: www.ndb.com
Online trades: Market orders $14.75; limit orders $19.75
Online account minimum: None

Quick and Reilly
Phone: 1-800-453-2517
Web site: www.quickreilly.com
Online trades: Market orders $14.95 and limit orders $19.95 for up to 5,000 shares, plus 2 cents for each share above 5,000
Online account minimum: None

Schwab
Phone: 1-800-435-4000
Web site: www.schwab.com
Online trades: $29.95 for up to 1,000 shares, and then add 3 cents per share
Broker-assisted trades: $39 and up
Online account minimum: $2,500

Scottrade

Phone: 1-800-619-7283

Web site: www.scottrade.com

Online trades: $7 online trades; $12 touch-tone trades

Broker-assisted trades: $17 and up.

Online account minimum: $2,000

Suretrade

Phone: 1-401-642-6900

Web site: www.suretrade.com

Online trades: $7.95 for online market orders, $9.95 for limit orders up to 5,000 shares; then add 1 cent per share

Online account minimum: No minimum for cash accounts, $2,000 for margin

Waterhouse

Phone: 1-800-934-4410

Web site: www.waterhouse.com

Online trades: $12 trades for up to 5,000 shares; $35 for touch-tone trades

Broker-assisted trades: $45

Online account minimum: $2,000

A

K

Keogh plans, 367

L

Labor Department, 251, 252–253
Lagging indicators, 259–260
Leading Economic Indicators
(LEI), 257–258
Liabilities
book value and, 6
debt-to-assets ratio (DAR),
225, 234–235, 245
debt-to-equity ratio (DER),
235, 245–246
in personal balance sheet, 76, 78
Library resources
books, 139–144
for company comparisons,
242–245
references and periodicals,
130–139
Life cycle of a stock, 10–12
LIFO (last-in, first-out)
accounting, 176–177
Limit order
day order, 42, 329
defined, 42, 327
stop limit order, 328
trading process, 43–45
Liquid assets, 172–173
Liquidity ratios
current ratio, 230–231
quick ratio, 231–232
Living expenses, 79–82
Long-term capital gains, 355–356
Long-term contracts revenue,
179–180
Long-term financial goals, 92–93
Losses. *See also* Failure,
reasons for
capital losses, 354–356
limiting, 300–301
on stagnant stocks, 121–122,
299
Lynch, Peter, 103, 209

M

M1, M2, and M3 money supply
measures, 250
Magazines. *See* Periodicals
Management effectiveness
measures
return on assets (ROA),
233–234, 240
return on equity (ROE),
238–239, 245
return on investment (ROI),
239–240

Managerial excellence, 111–112
Margin accounts, 325, 333–337,
347, 349–351
Market cycles. *See* Bear market;
Bull market
Market makers, 46
Market order, 42, 326–327
Market presence
high barriers to entry,
106–108
of Microsoft, 104–106
Market risk, 33–34
Market value, 6–7
MarketWatch.com, 64–65
Maturity phase of stock life
cycle, 12
Media
monitoring news and events,
382–389
mood as "reverse" indicator,
281–283, 293, 295
stock decline and, 302–303
stock rise and, 297
Web sites, 383–385
Megatrends, 108–110
Message boards and chat rooms,
153–154, 411, 429–430
Microcap stocks, 116, 403,
404–412
Microsoft, 26, 53, 54, 65,
104–106, 112, 216, 269,
373
Momentum investing, 119, 206
Money Magazine, 150, 281
Money market accounts, 91
Money market funds, 73,
90–91
Money-making secrets, buying,
404, 420–422
Monitoring investments
diversification, 16–17,
371–378
following news and events,
382–389
reading the stock pages,
389–401
Value Line analysis service,
378–382
Monopolies
private, 267–269
regulated, 269–271
*Moody's Handbook of Common
Stocks,* 134, 244
Moving average (MA), 287–289
MSIs (most successful
investors), 93–94, 301
Mutual Fund Education
Alliance, 29

The *Unofficial Guide*™ Reader Questionnaire

If you would like to express your opinion about picking stocks or this guide, please complete this questionnaire and mail it to:

The *Unofficial Guide*™ Reader Questionnaire
Business Guides
IDG Books Worldwide, Inc.
645 N. Michigan Ave.
Suite 800
Chicago, IL 60611

Gender: ___ M ___ F

Age: ___ Under 30 ___ 31–40
___ 41–50 ___ Over 50

Education: ___ High school ___ College
___ Graduate/Professional

What is your occupation?

_____

How did you hear about this guide?
___ Friend or relative
___ Newspaper, magazine, or Internet
___ Radio or TV
___ Recommended at bookstore
___ Recommended by librarian
___ Picked it up on my own
___ Familiar with the *Unofficial Guide*™ travel series

Did you go to the bookstore specifically for a book on picking stocks? Yes ___ No ___

Have you used any other *Unofficial Guides*™?
Yes ___ No ___

If "Yes," which ones?

_____

_____

_____

What other book(s) on picking stocks have you purchased?

_____

_____

_____

Was this book:
____ more helpful than other(s)
____ less helpful than other(s)

Do you think this book was worth its price?
Yes ____ No ____

Did this book cover all topics related to picking stocks adequately? Yes ____ No ____

Please explain your answer:

_____

_____

_____

Were there any specific sections in this book that were of particular help to you? Yes ____ No ____

Please explain your answer:

_____

_____

_____

On a scale of 1 to 10, with 10 being the best rating, how would you rate this guide? ____

What other titles would you like to see published in the _Unofficial Guide_™ series?

_____

_____

_____

Are _Unofficial Guides_™ readily available in your area? Yes ____ No ____

Other comments:

_____

_____

_____

Get the inside scoop...
with the *Unofficial Guides*™!

Health and Fitness

The Unofficial Guide to Alternative Medicine
ISBN: 0-02-862526-9

The Unofficial Guide to Coping with Menopause
ISBN: 0-02-862694-X

The Unofficial Guide to Dieting Safely
ISBN: 0-02-862521-8

The Unofficial Guide to Having a Baby
ISBN: 0-02-862695-8

The Unofficial Guide to Living with Diabetes
ISBN: 0-02-862919-1

The Unofficial Guide to Smart Nutrition
ISBN: 0-02-863589-2

The Unofficial Guide to Surviving Breast Cancer
ISBN: 0-02-863491-8

Career Planning

The Unofficial Guide to Acing the Interview
ISBN: 0-02-862924-8

The Unofficial Guide to Earning What You Deserve
ISBN: 0-02-862716-4

The Unofficial Guide to Hiring and Firing People
ISBN: 0-02-862523-4

Business and Personal Finance

The Unofficial Guide to Beating Debt
ISBN: 0-02-863337-7

The Unofficial Guide to Investing
ISBN: 0-02-862458-0

The Unofficial Guide to Investing in Mutual Funds
ISBN: 0-02-862920-5

The Unofficial Guide to Managing Your Personal Finances
ISBN: 0-02-862921-3

The Unofficial Guide to Marketing Your Business Online
ISBN: 0-7645-6268-1

The Unofficial Guide to Picking Stocks
ISBN: 0-7645-6202-9

The Unofficial Guide to Starting a Business Online
ISBN: 0-02-863340-7

The Unofficial Guide to Starting a Home-Based Business
ISBN: 0-7645-6151-0

The Unofficial Guide to Starting a Small Business
ISBN: 0-02-862525-0

Home

The Unofficial Guide to Buying a Home
ISBN: 0-02-862461-0

The Unofficial Guide to Buying a Home Online
ISBN: 0-02-863751-8

Family and Relationships

The Unofficial Guide to Childcare
0-02-862457-2

The Unofficial Guide to Divorce
0-02-862455-6

The Unofficial Guide to Eldercare
0-02-862456-4

The Unofficial Guide to Online Genealogy
0-02-863867-0

The Unofficial Guide to Planning Your Wedding
0-02-862459-9

Hobbies and Recreation

The Unofficial Guide to Casino Gambling
ISBN: 0-02-862917-5

The Unofficial Guide to eBay® and Online Auctions
ISBN: 0-02-863866-2

The Unofficial Guide to Finding Rare Antiques
0-02-862922-1

The Unofficial Guide to Selecting Wine
0-02-863668-6

All books in the *Unofficial Guide*™ series are available at your local bookseller.